Gal Gohan

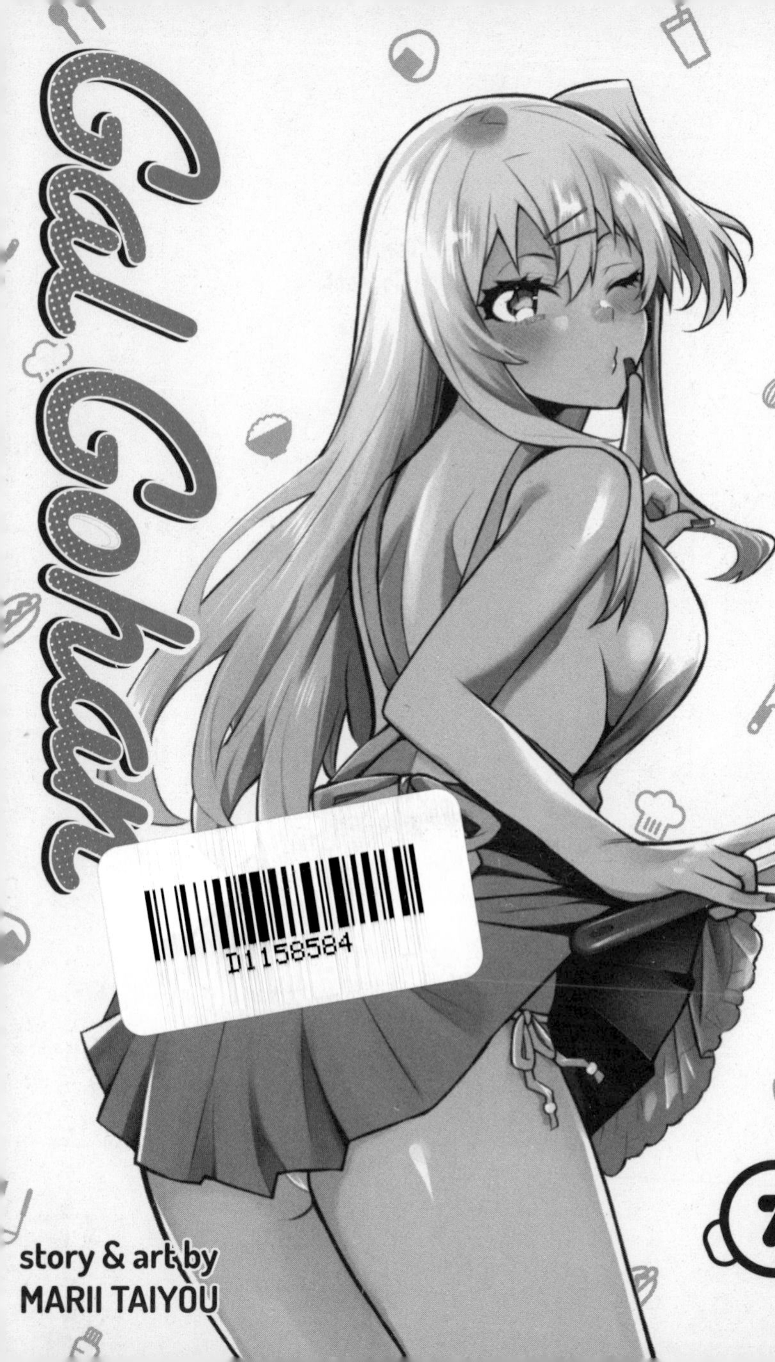

7

story & art by
MARII TAIYOU

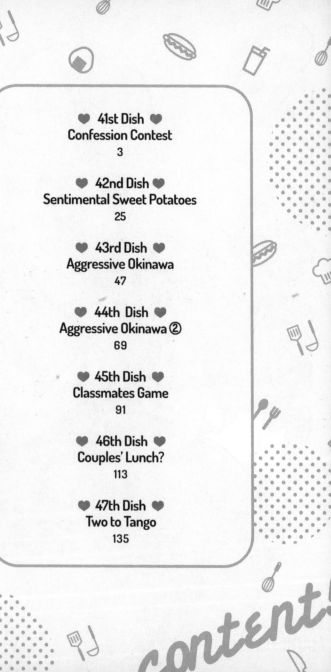

content!

Double Trouble

What will Yabe Shinji do when the school president and a Gal both propose to him at the school festival beauty contest? A secret sleepover and a school trip lead to all the sexy times a guy could want!

MIKU♡

No. 1

Seven Seas Entertainment
sevenseasentertainment.com

$12.99 USA
($16.99 CAN)   OLDER TEEN
ISBN 978-1-64827-096-3
51299>

9 781648 270963

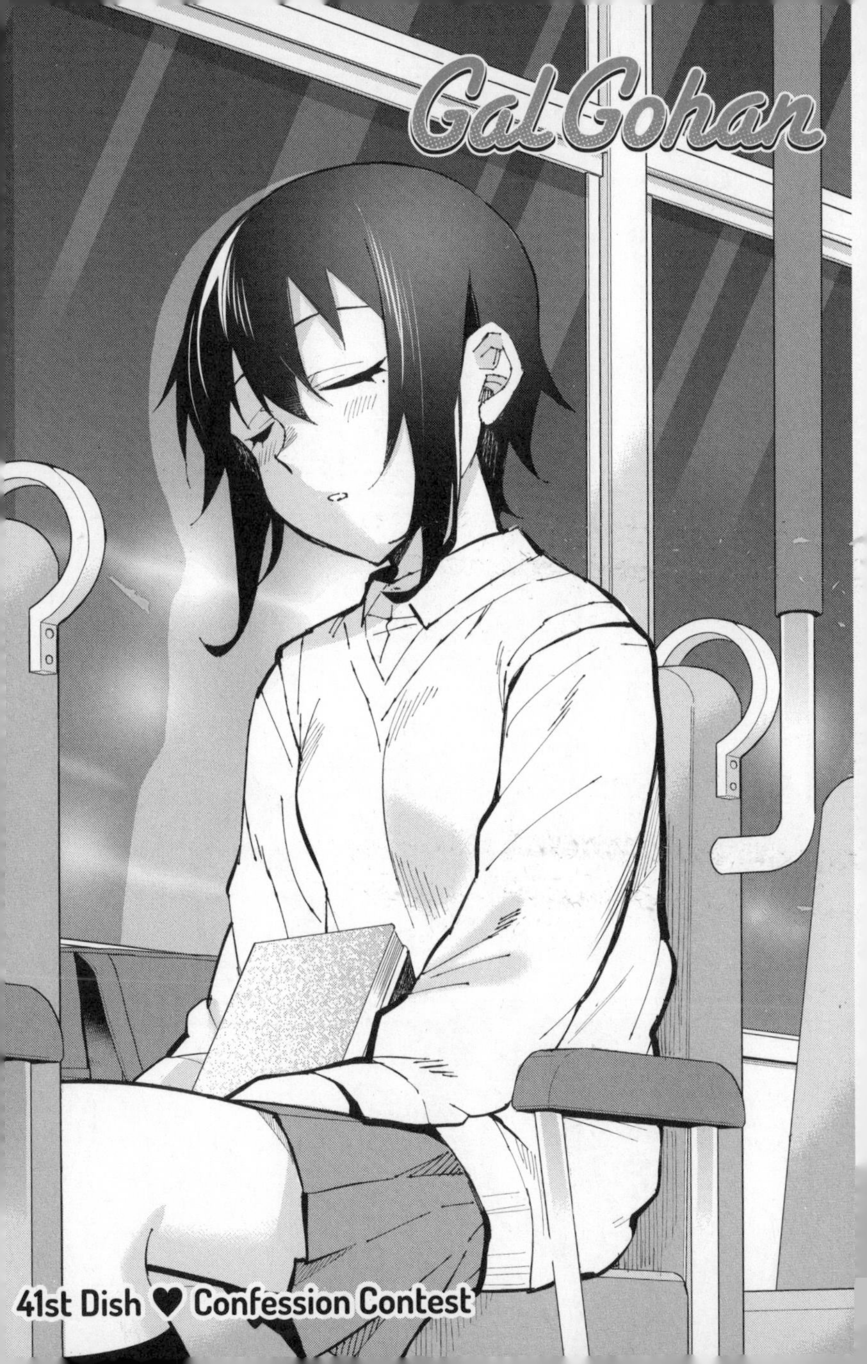
Gal Gohan
41st Dish ♥ Confession Contest

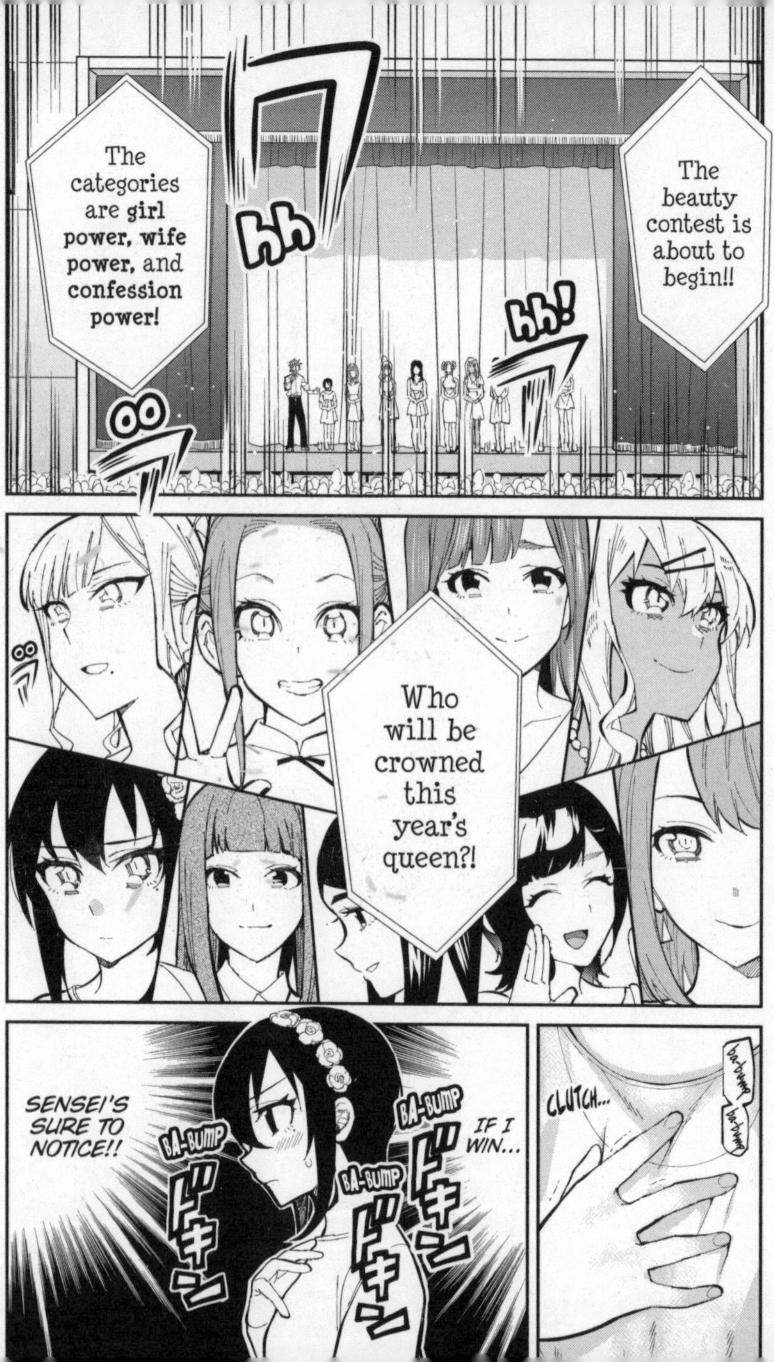
The beauty contest is about to begin!!
hh!
hh
The categories are girl power, wife power, and confession power!
oo
Who will be crowned this year's queen?!
CLUTCH...
ba-bump ba-bump
IF I WIN...
BA-BUMP
BA-BUMP
BA-BUMP
SENSEI'S SURE TO NOTICE!!

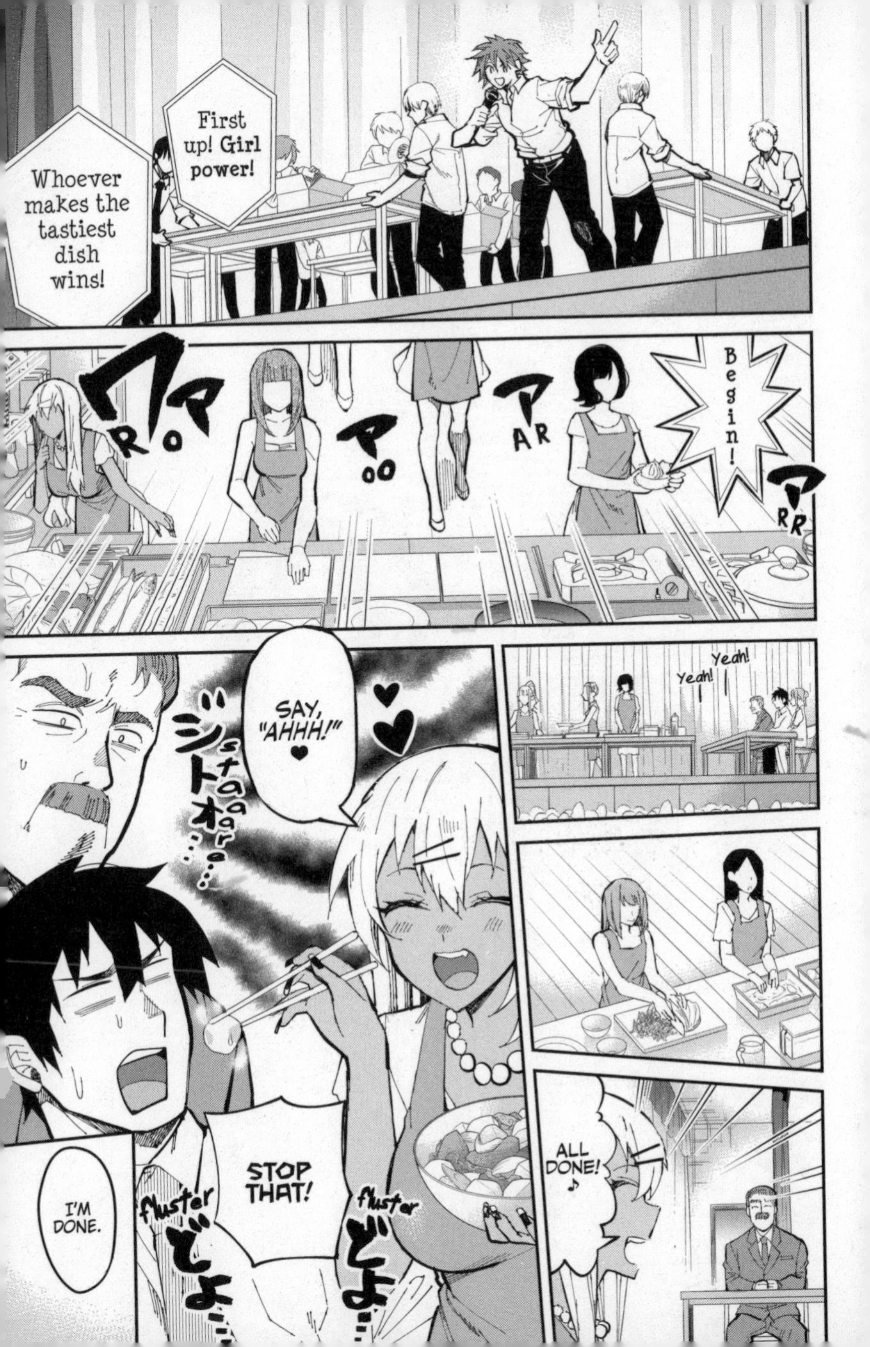
First up! Girl power!
Whoever makes the tastiest dish wins!
Begin!
RR
AR
oo
o
R
Yeah!
Yeah!
ALL DONE! ♪
SAY, "AHHH!" ♥
ジトォ staaare...
flustér どよ...
STOP THAT!
flustér どよ...
I'M DONE.

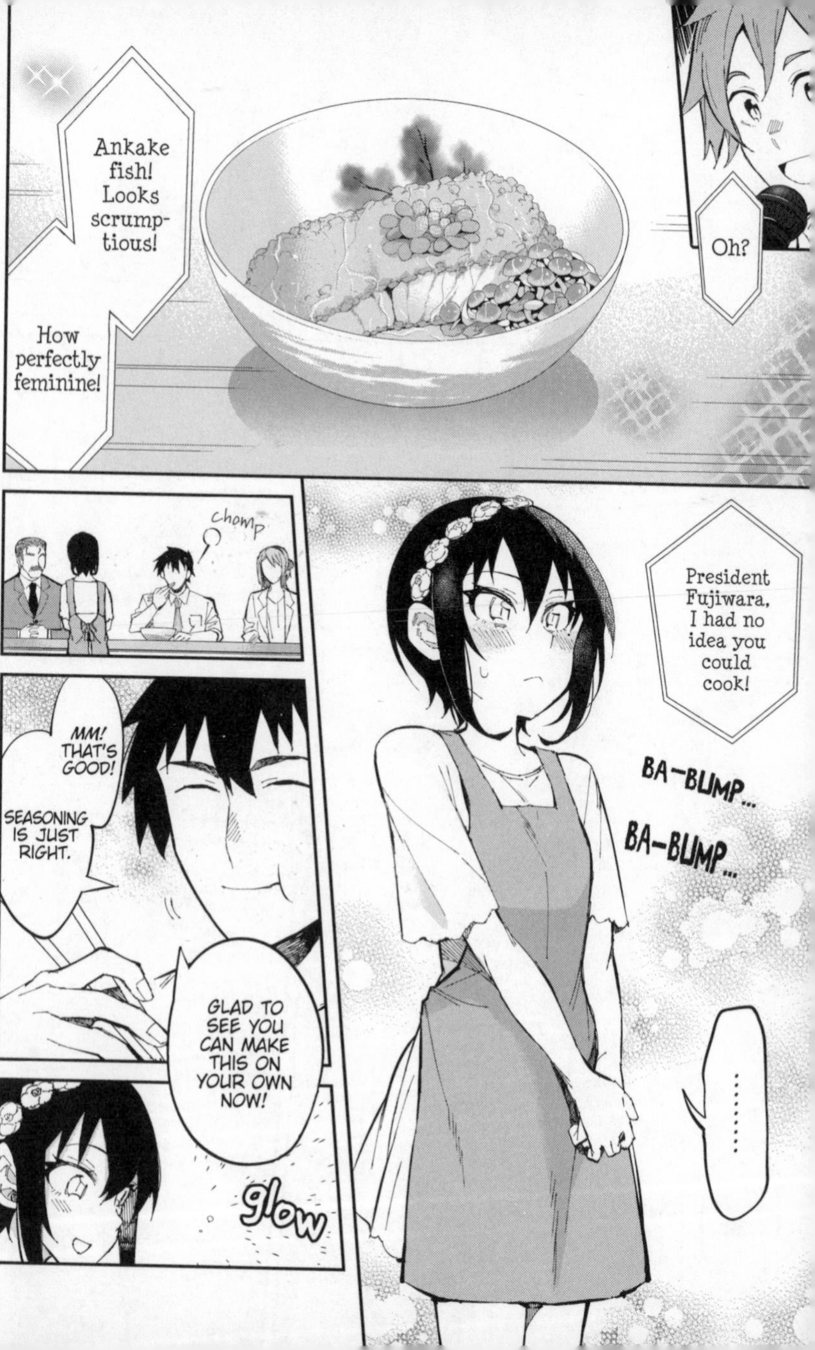
Oh?
Ankake fish! Looks scrump-tious!
How perfectly feminine!
President Fujiwara, I had no idea you could cook!
BA-BUMP...
BA-BUMP...
....
chomp
MM! THAT'S GOOD!
SEASONING IS JUST RIGHT.
GLAD TO SEE YOU CAN MAKE THIS ON YOUR OWN NOW!
glow

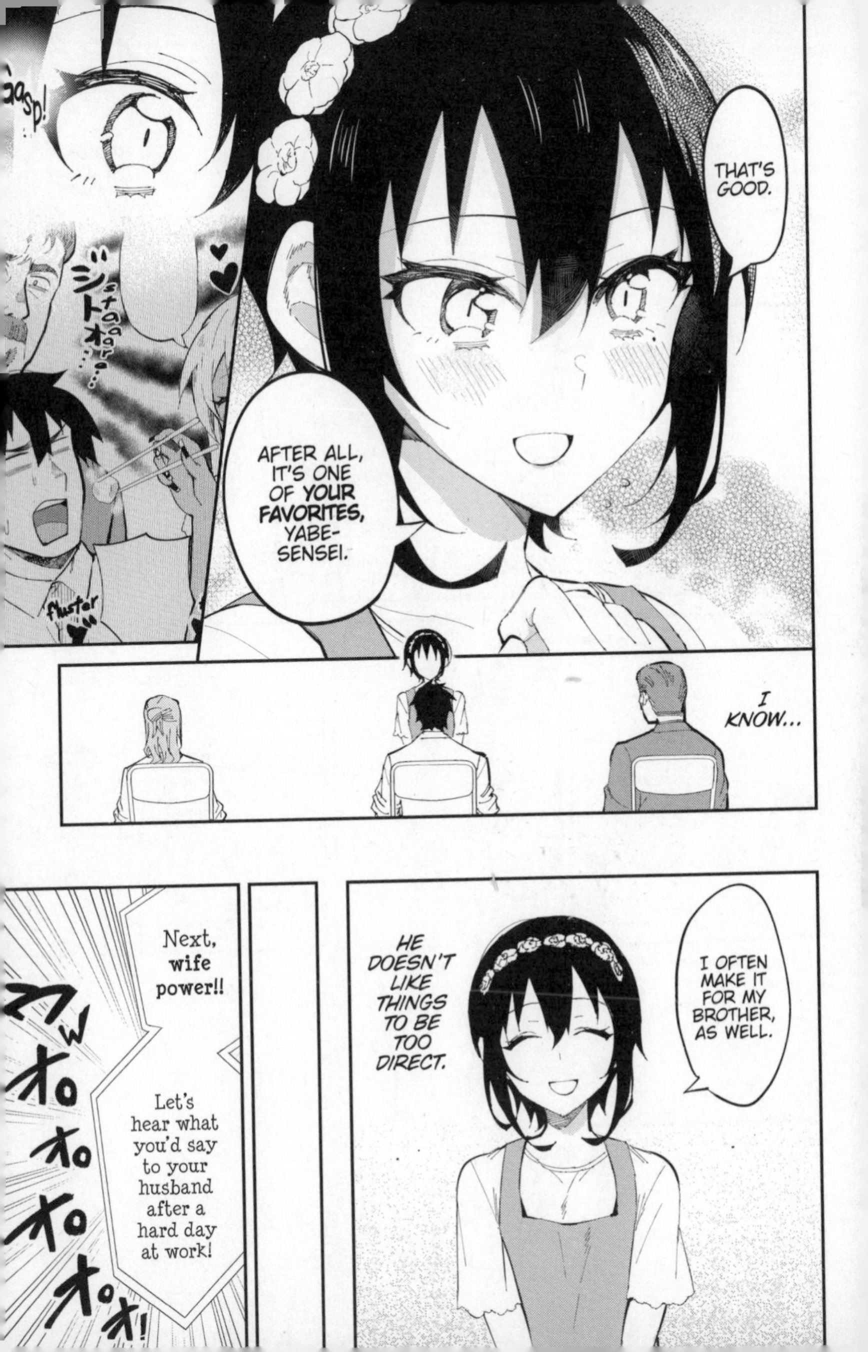
THAT'S GOOD.
AFTER ALL, IT'S ONE OF YOUR FAVORITES, YABE-SENSEI.
gasp!
fluster
I KNOW...
I OFTEN MAKE IT FOR MY BROTHER, AS WELL.
HE DOESN'T LIKE THINGS TO BE TOO DIRECT.
Next, wife power!!
Let's hear what you'd say to your husband after a hard day at work!

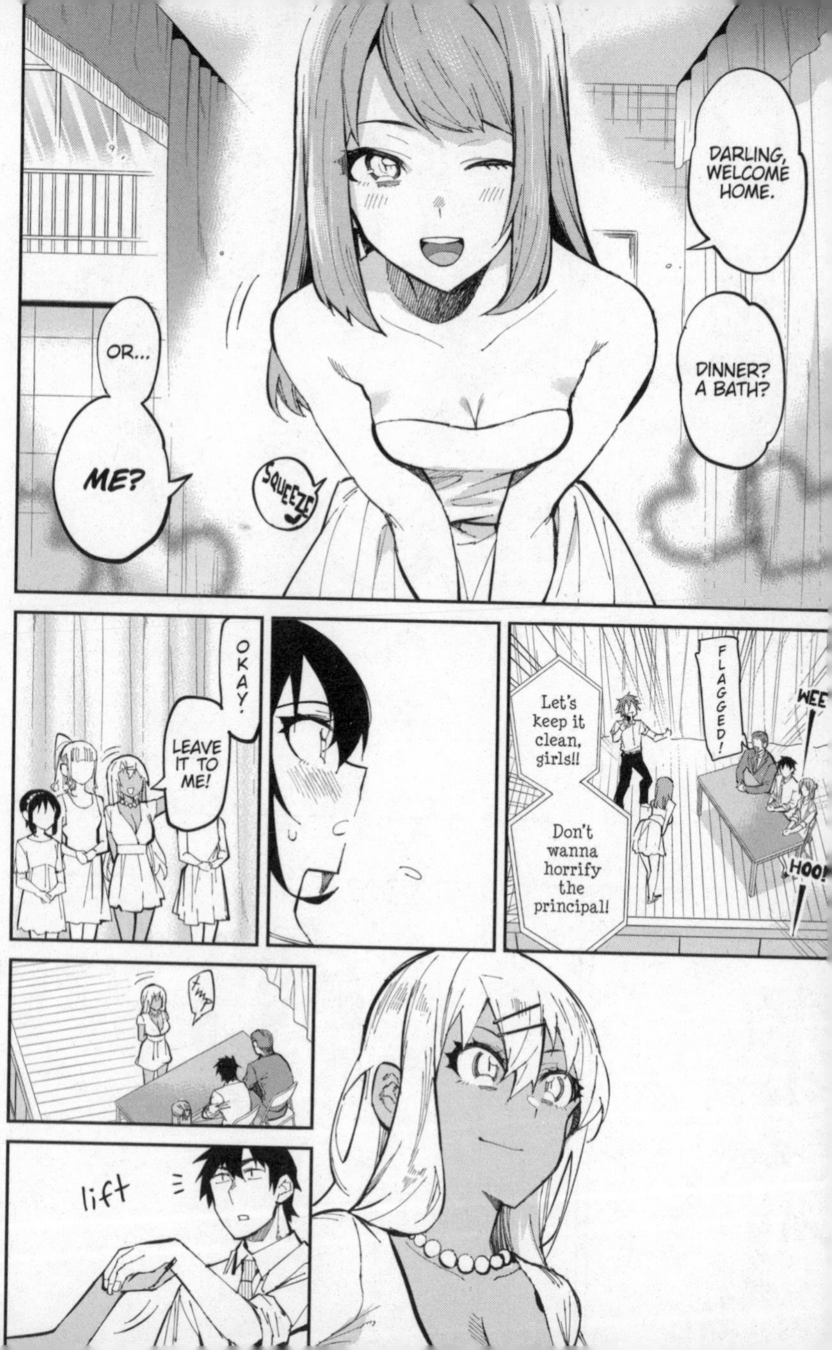
DARLING, WELCOME HOME.
DINNER? A BATH?
OR...
ME?
SQUEEZE
FLAGGED!
WEE
Let's keep it clean, girls!!
HOO!
Don't wanna horrify the principal!
OKAY.
LEAVE IT TO ME!
lift

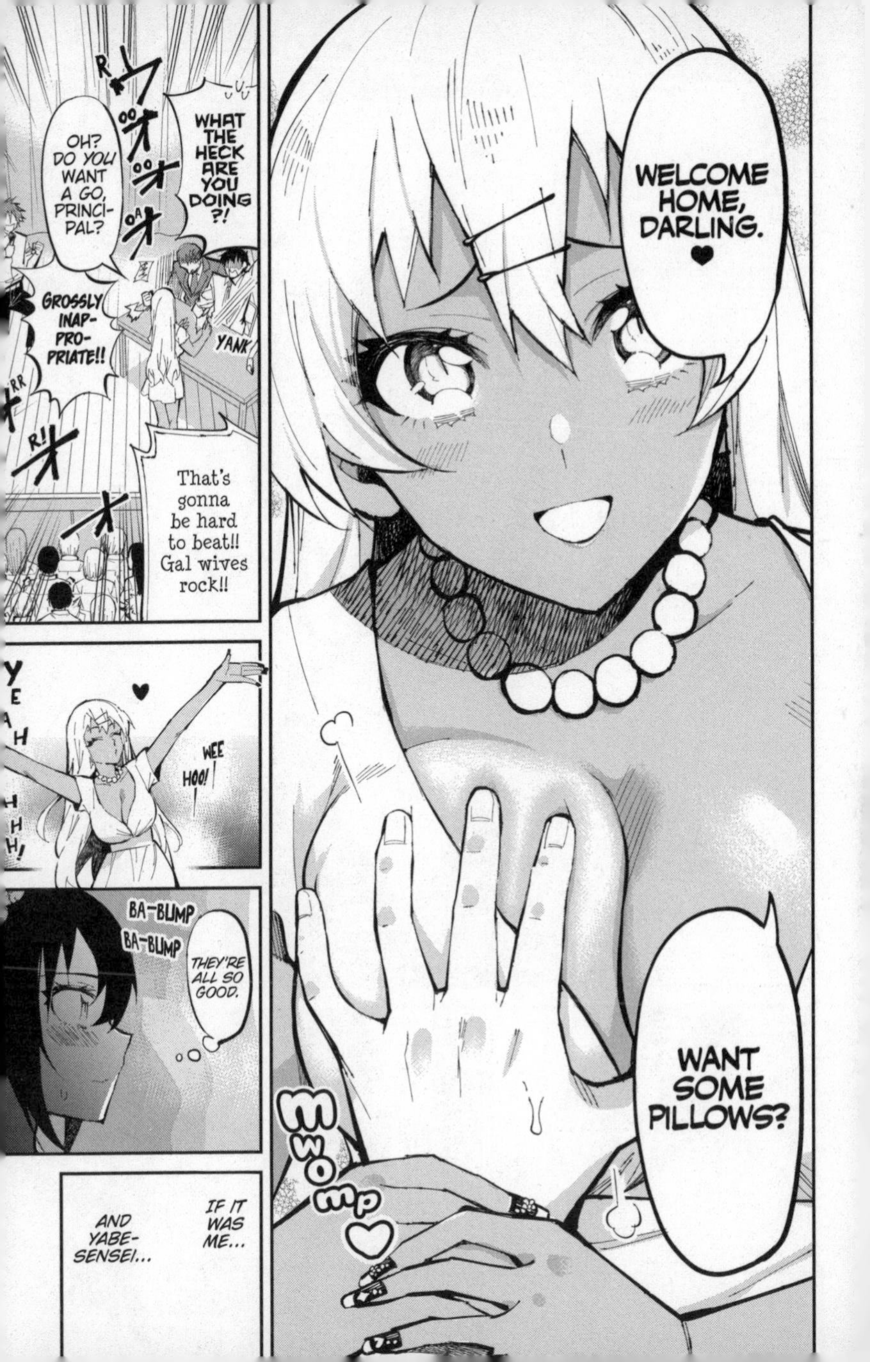
WELCOME HOME, DARLING. ♥
WANT SOME PILLOWS?
mwomp ♥
WHAT THE HECK ARE YOU DOING?!
OH? DO YOU WANT A GO, PRINCI-PAL?
GROSSLY INAP-PRO-PRIATE!!
YANK
That's gonna be hard to beat!! Gal wives rock!!
WEE HOO!
YEAHHHH!
BA-BUMP
BA-BUMP
THEY'RE ALL SO GOOD.
IF IT WAS ME...
AND YABE-SENSEI...

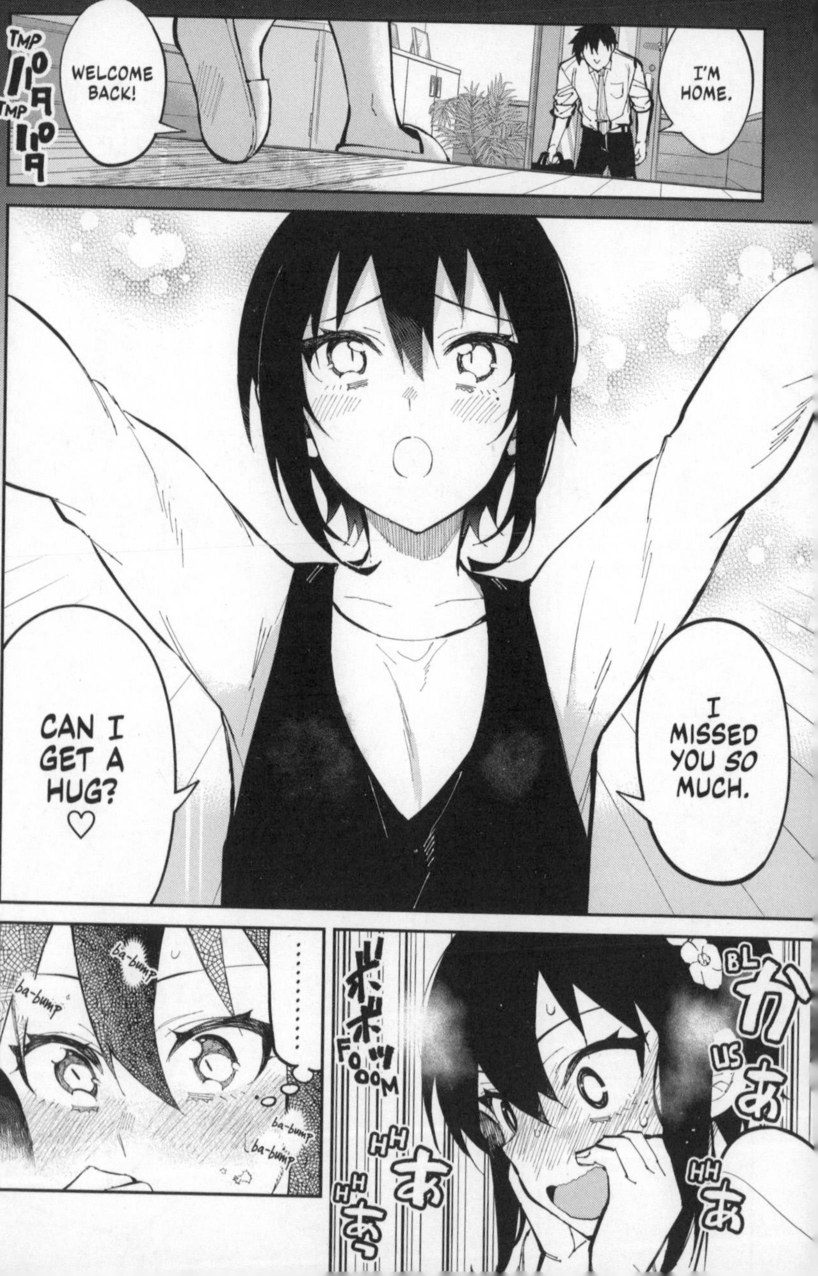
I'M HOME.
WELCOME BACK!
TMP
TMP
I MISSED YOU SO MUCH.
CAN I GET A HUG? ♡
BL
US
HH
FOOOOM
HH
HH
ba-bump
ba-bump
ba-bump
ba-bump
......

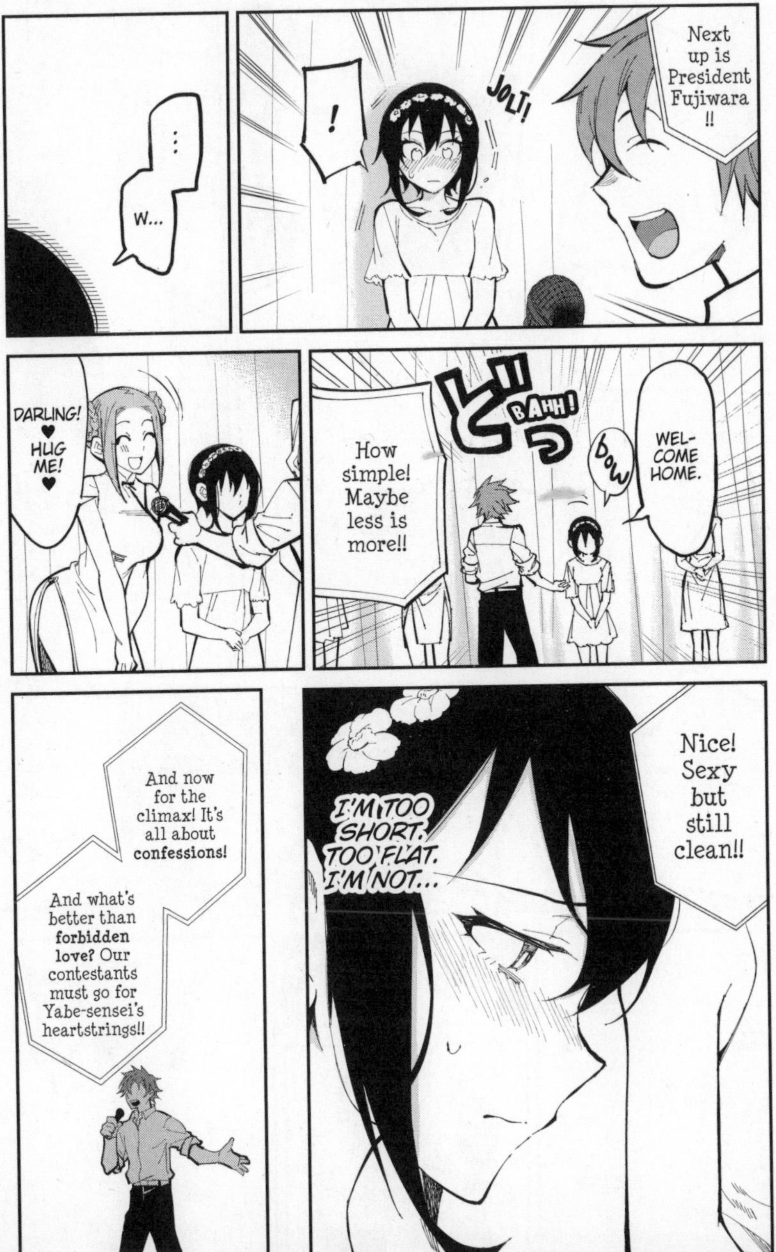
Next up is President Fujiwara !!
JOLT!
!
...
W...
WEL-COME HOME.
BOW
BAHH!
どっ
How simple! Maybe less is more!!
DARLING! ♥ HUG ME! ♥
Nice! Sexy but still clean!!
I'M TOO SHORT. TOO FLAT. I'M NOT...
And now for the climax! It's all about **confessions**!
And what's better than **forbidden love**? Our contestants must go for Yabe-sensei's heartstrings!!

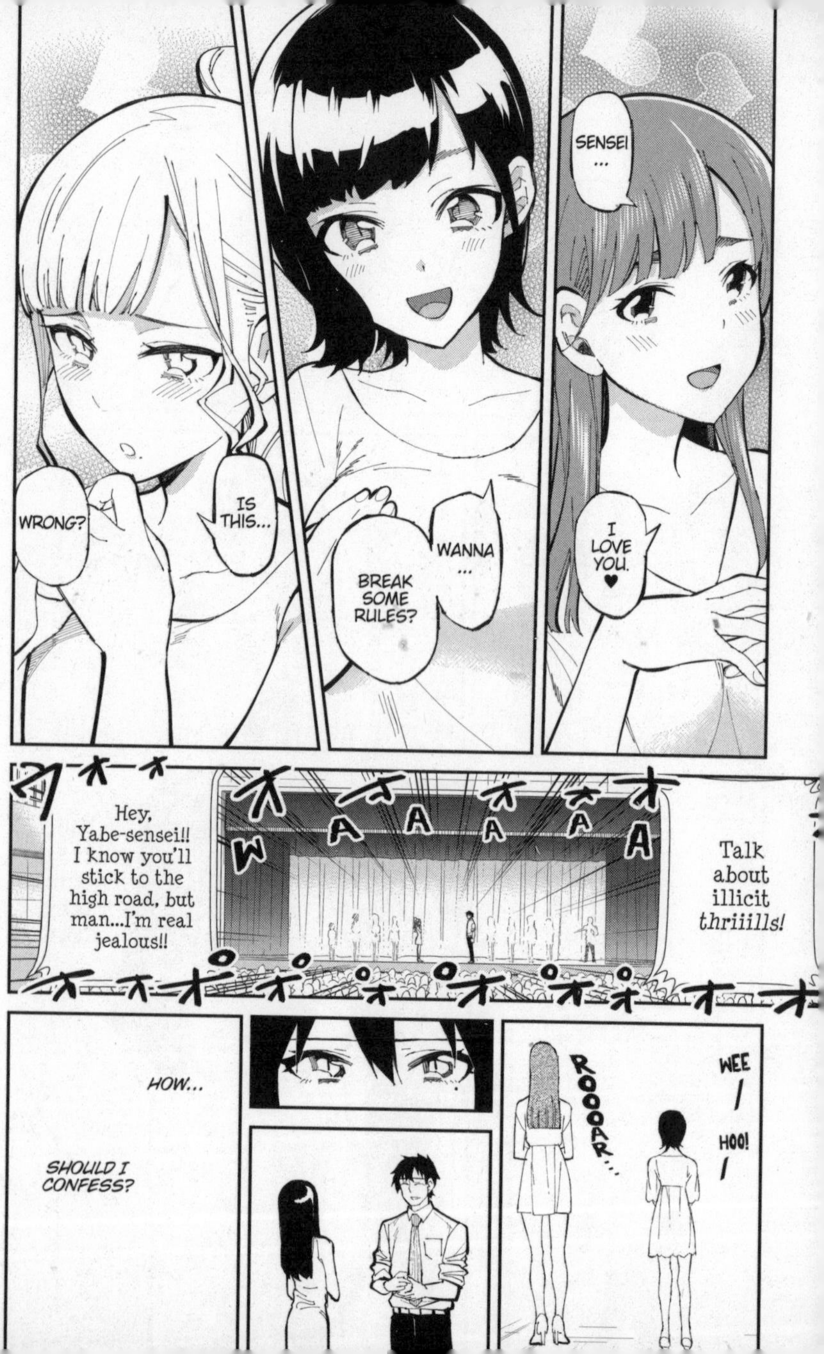
SENSEI ...
I LOVE YOU. ♥
WANNA ...
BREAK SOME RULES?
IS THIS...
WRONG?
WAAAAAA
Talk about illicit *thriiiills!*
Hey, Yabe-sensei!! I know you'll stick to the high road, but man...I'm real jealous!!
ROOOAR...
WEE-HOO!
HOW...
SHOULD I CONFESS?

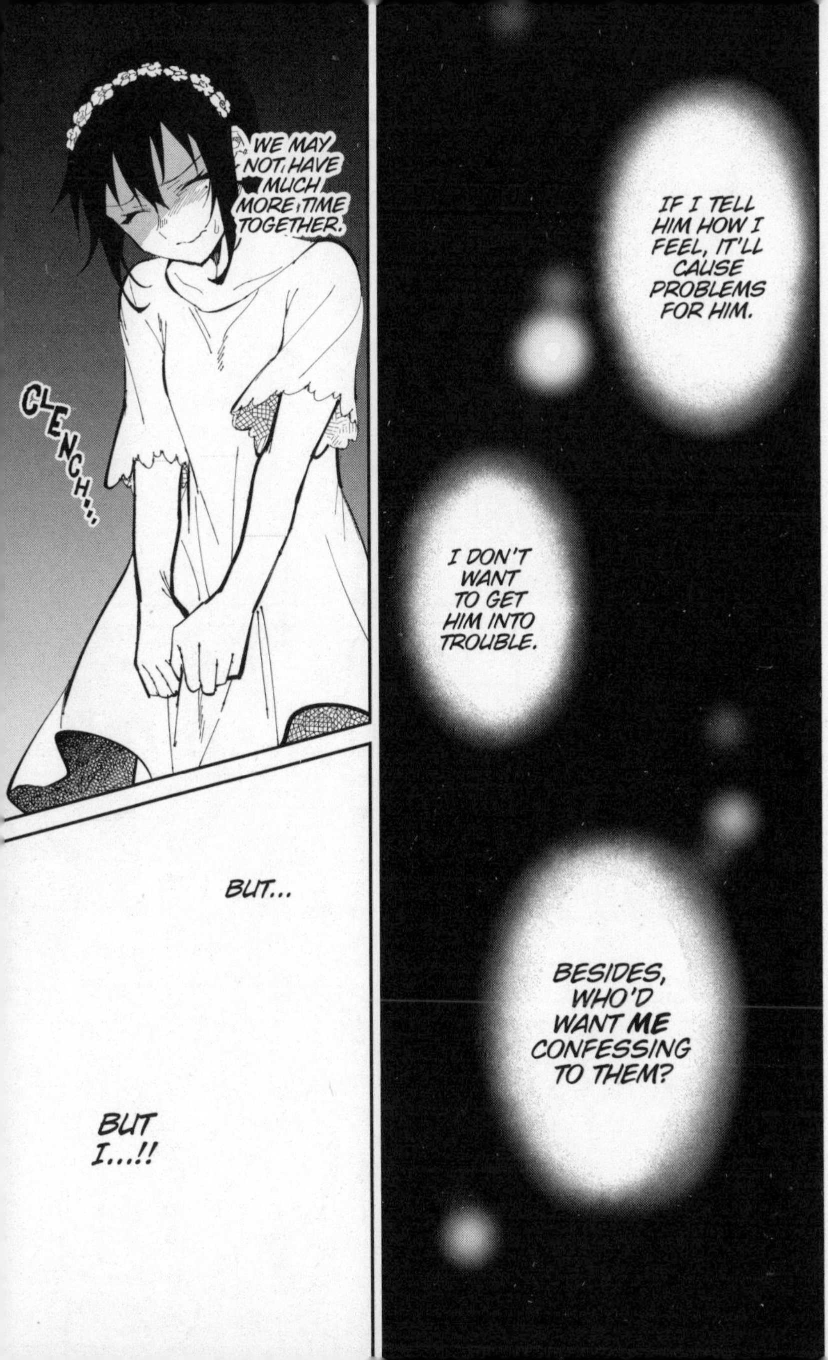
IF I TELL HIM HOW I FEEL, IT'LL CAUSE PROBLEMS FOR HIM.
I DON'T WANT TO GET HIM INTO TROUBLE.
BESIDES, WHO'D WANT **ME** CONFESSING TO THEM?
WE MAY NOT HAVE MUCH MORE TIME TOGETHER.
CLENCH...
BUT...
BUT I...!!

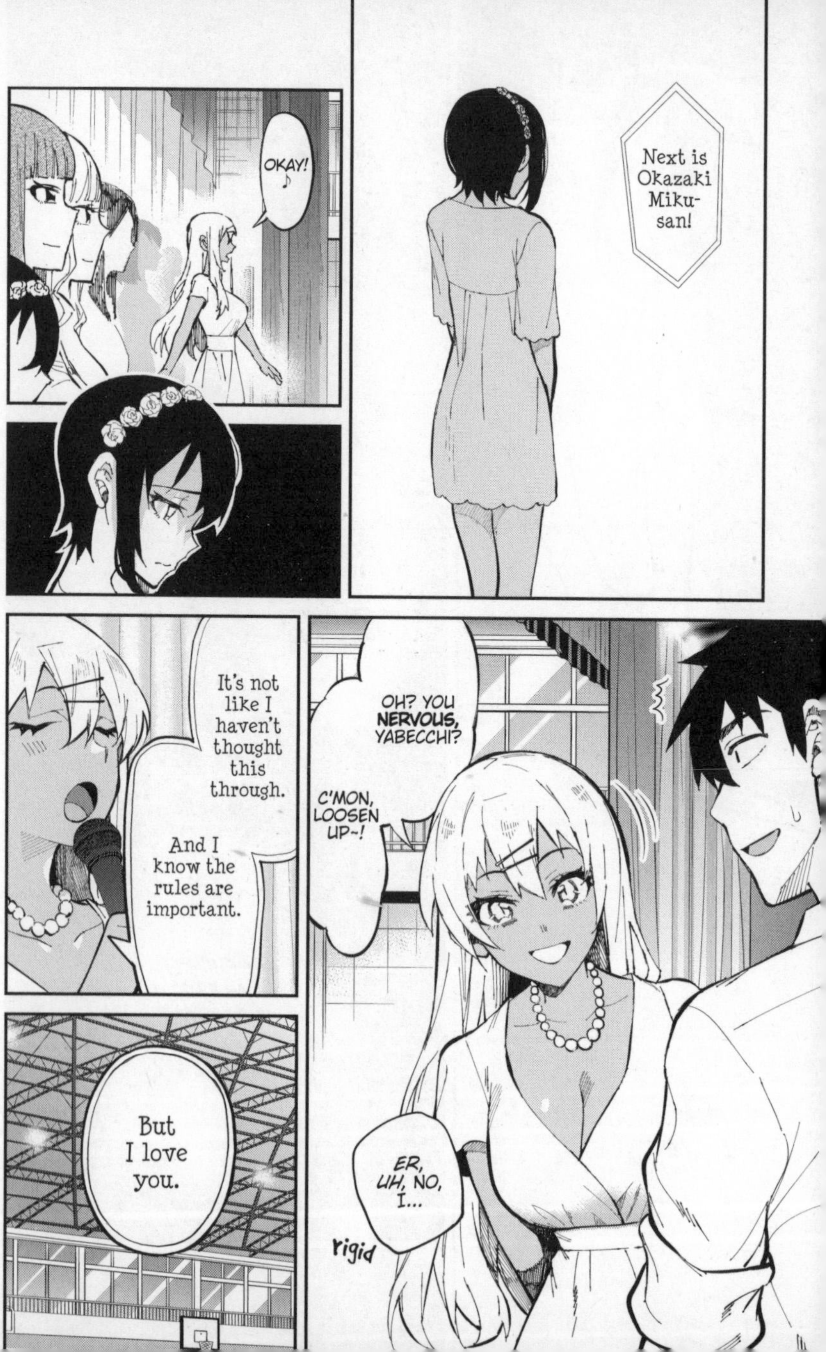
Next is Okazaki Miku-san!
OKAY! ♪
OH? YOU NERVOUS, YABECCHI?
C'MON, LOOSEN UP~!
ER, UH, NO, I...
rigid
It's not like I haven't thought this through.
And I know the rules are important.
But I love you.

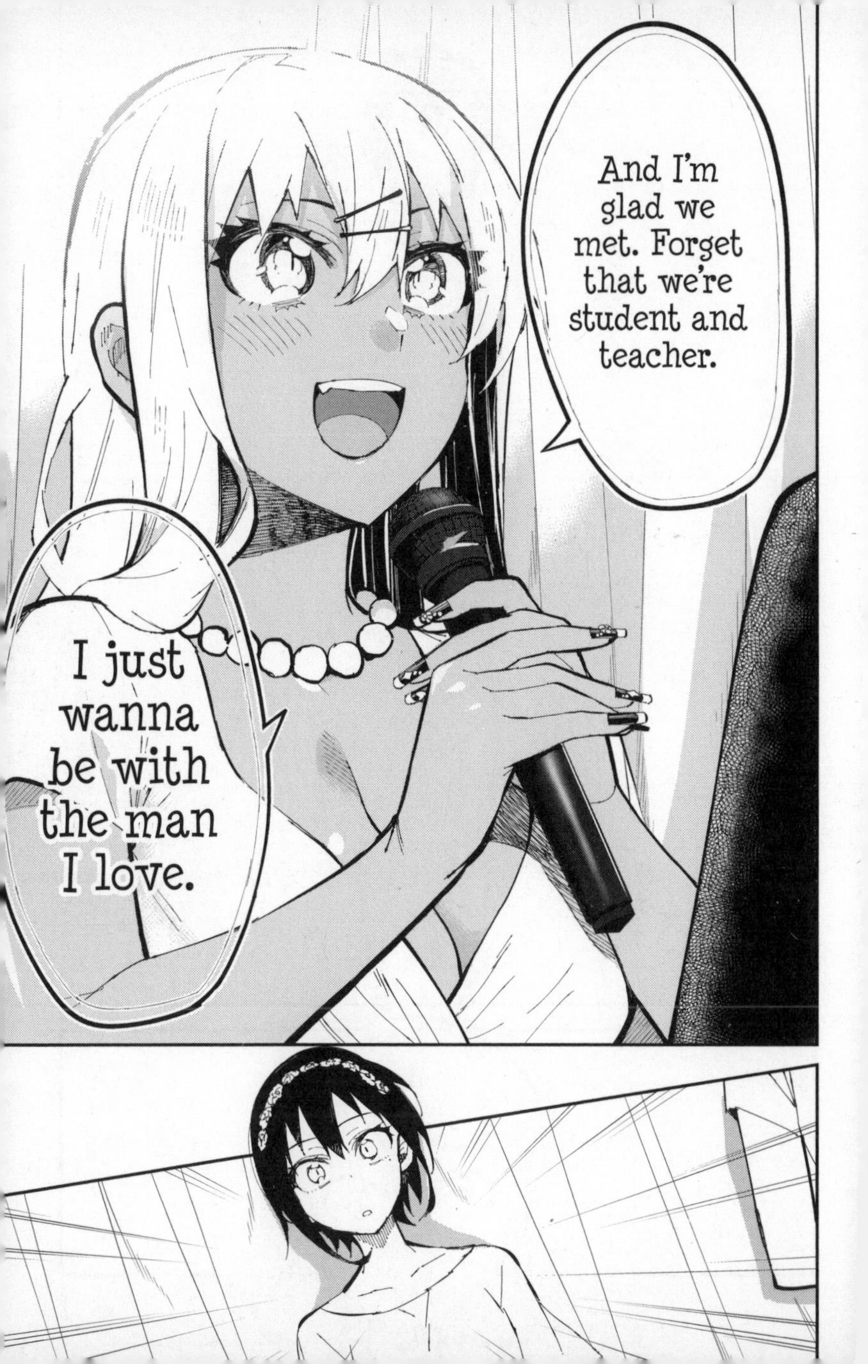
And I'm glad we met. Forget that we're student and teacher.
I just wanna be with the man I love.

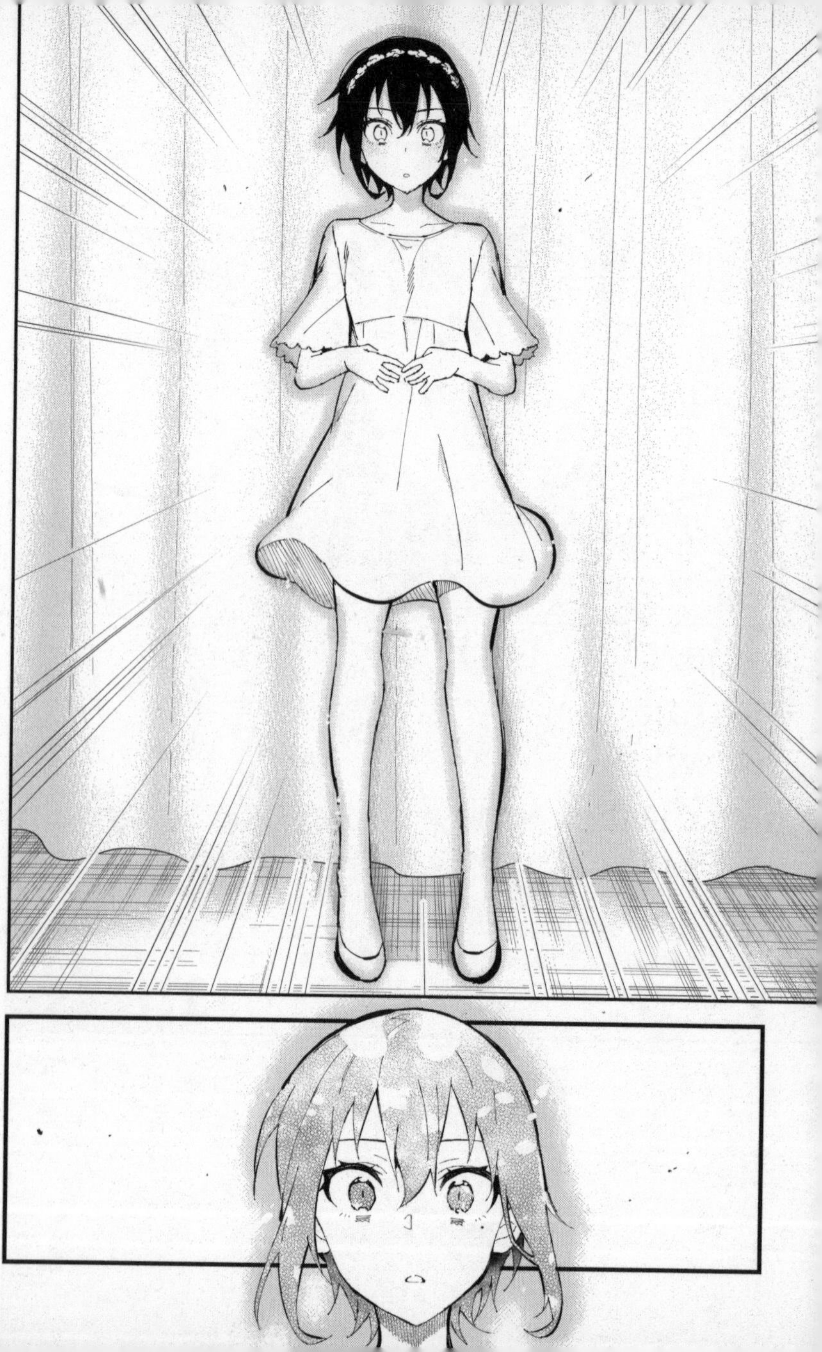

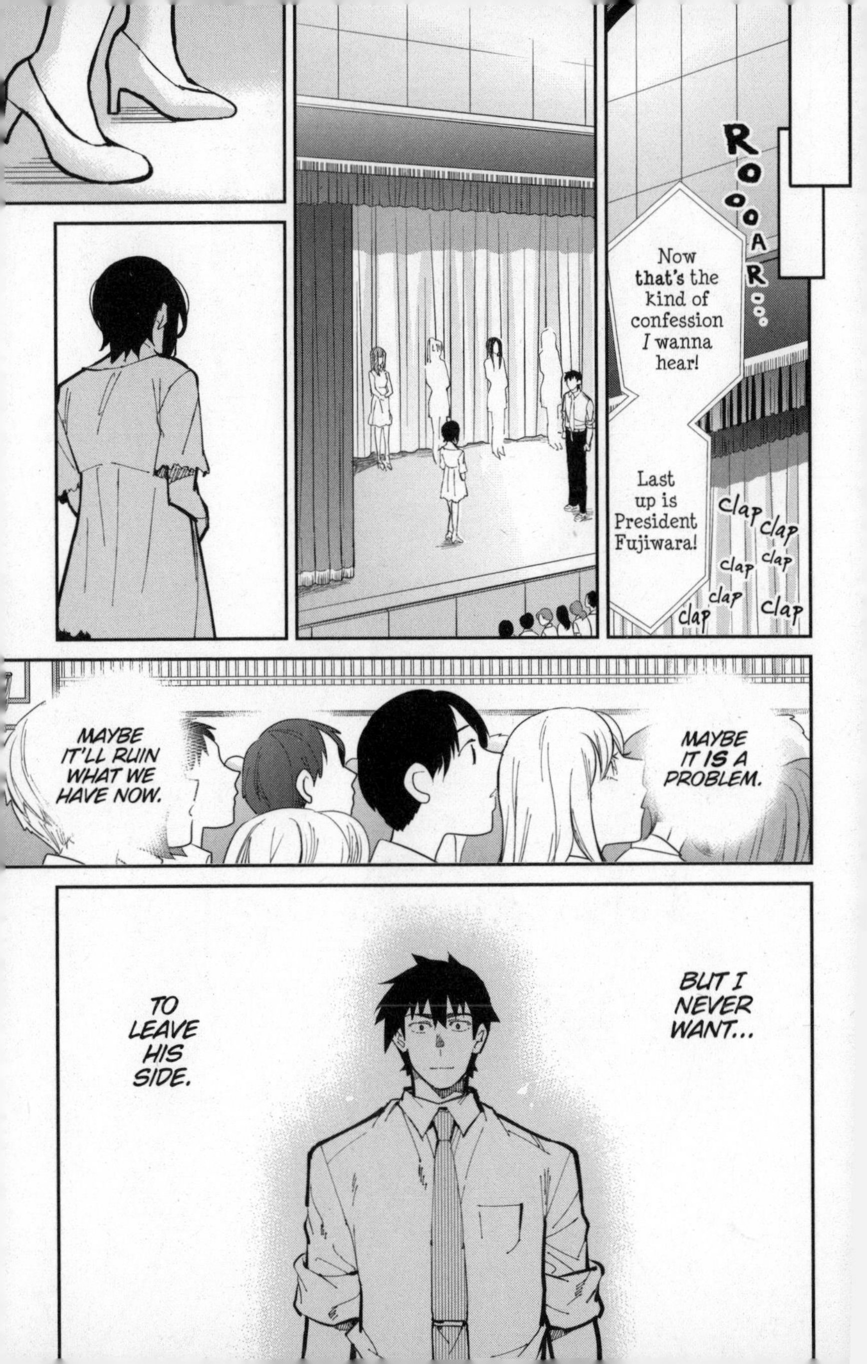
ROOOAR...
Now that's the kind of confession I wanna hear!
Last up is President Fujiwara!
clap clap clap clap clap clap clap
MAYBE IT IS A PROBLEM.
MAYBE IT'LL RUIN WHAT WE HAVE NOW.
BUT I NEVER WANT...
TO LEAVE HIS SIDE.

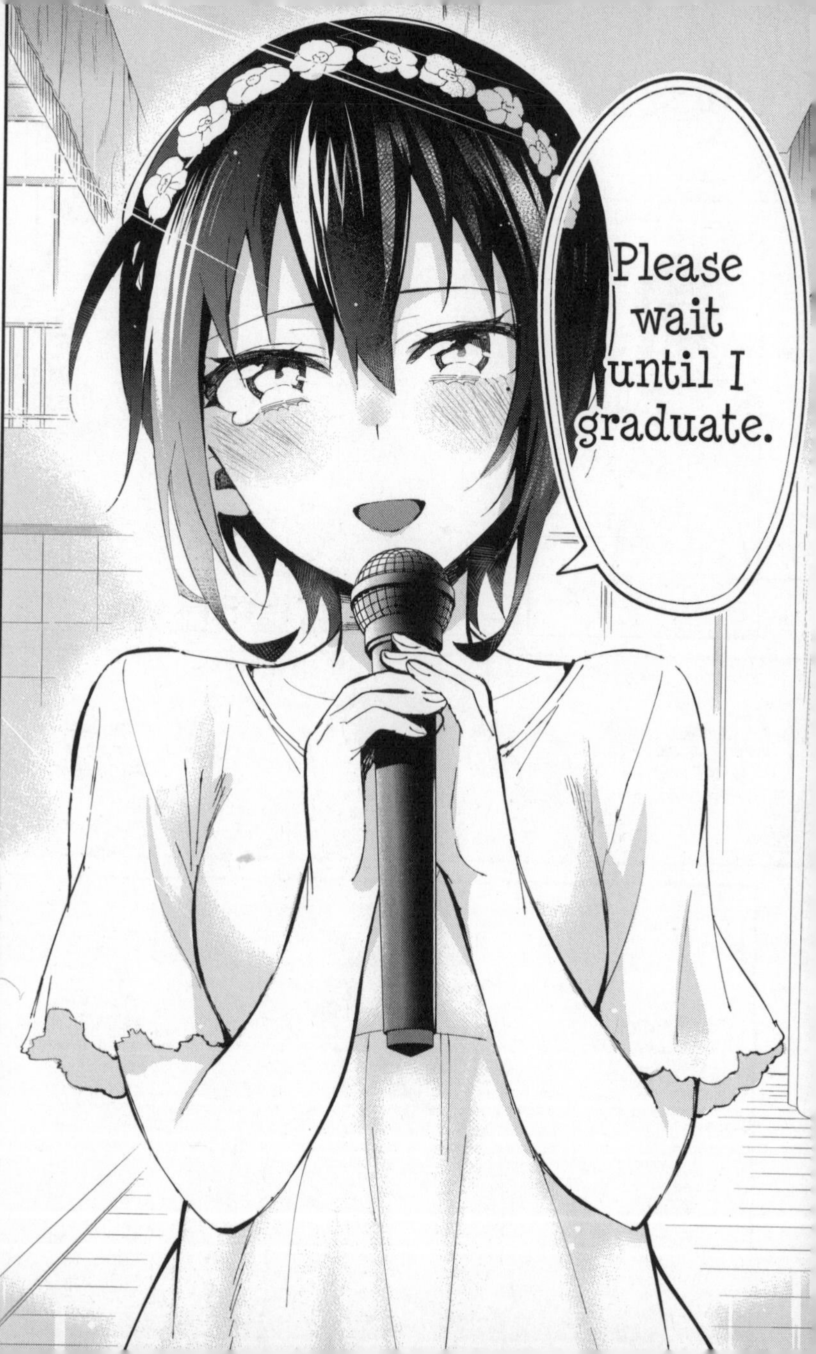
Please wait until I graduate.

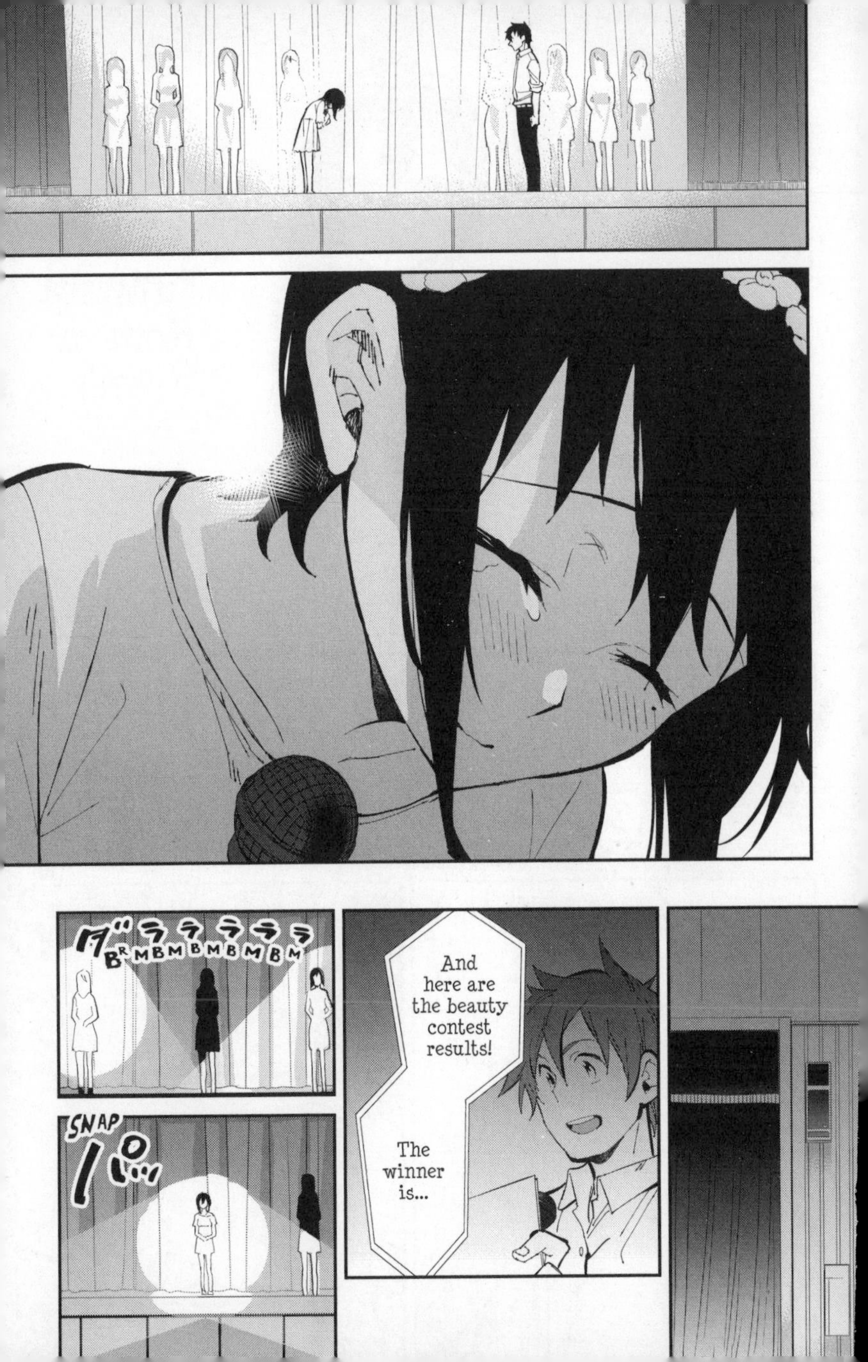
And here are the beauty contest results!
The winner is...
BRMBMBMBMBM
SNAP

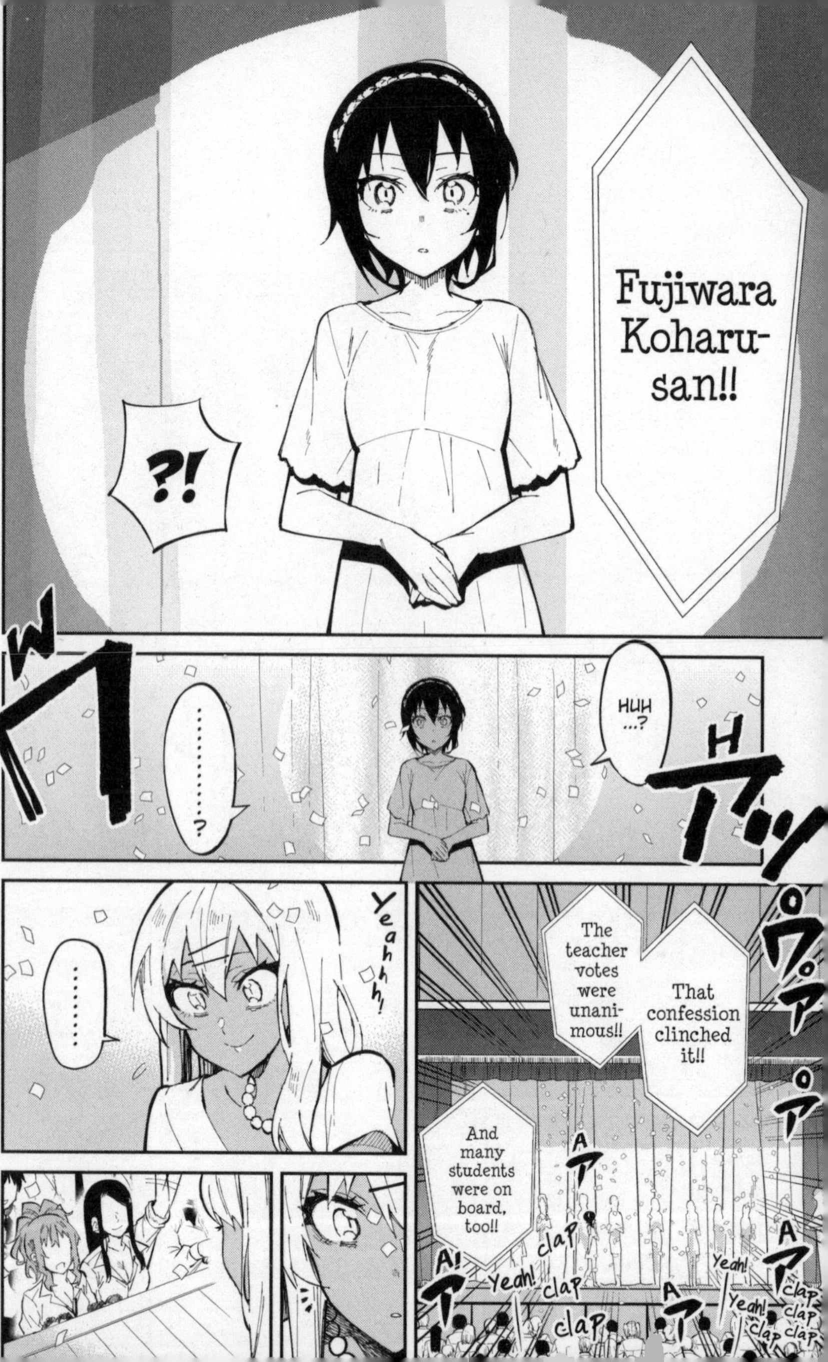

Fujiwara Koharu-san!!
?!
HUH ...?
H
......?
W
That confession clinched it!!
The teacher votes were unanimous!!
And many students were on board, too!!
A
A
A!
A
clap
clap
clap
Yeah!
Yeah!
Yeah!
clap
clap
clap
clap
Yeahhhh!
......

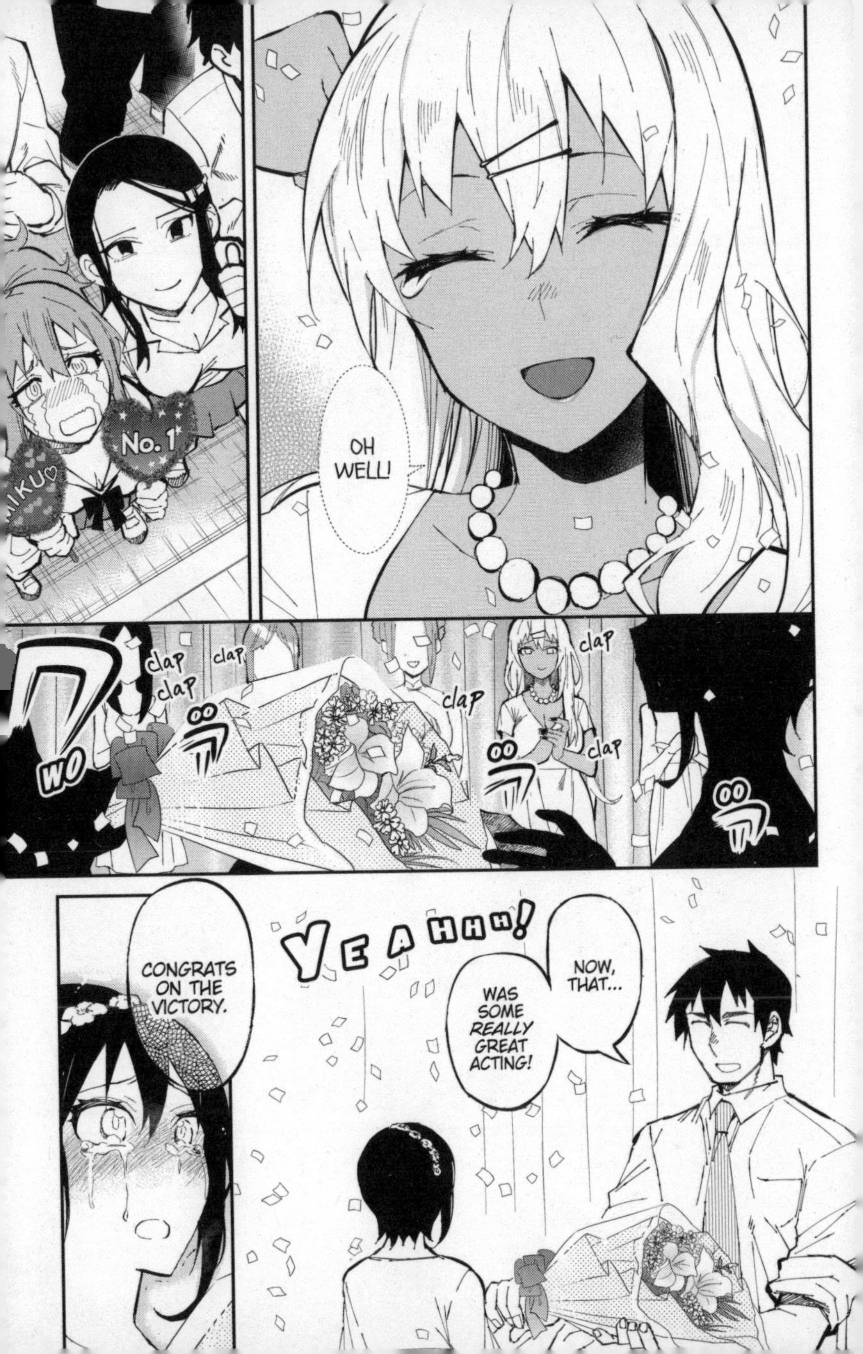
OH WELL!
No. 1
MIKU♡
clap
clap
clap
clap
clap
clap
WO
YEAHHH!
NOW, THAT...
WAS SOME REALLY GREAT ACTING!
CONGRATS ON THE VICTORY.

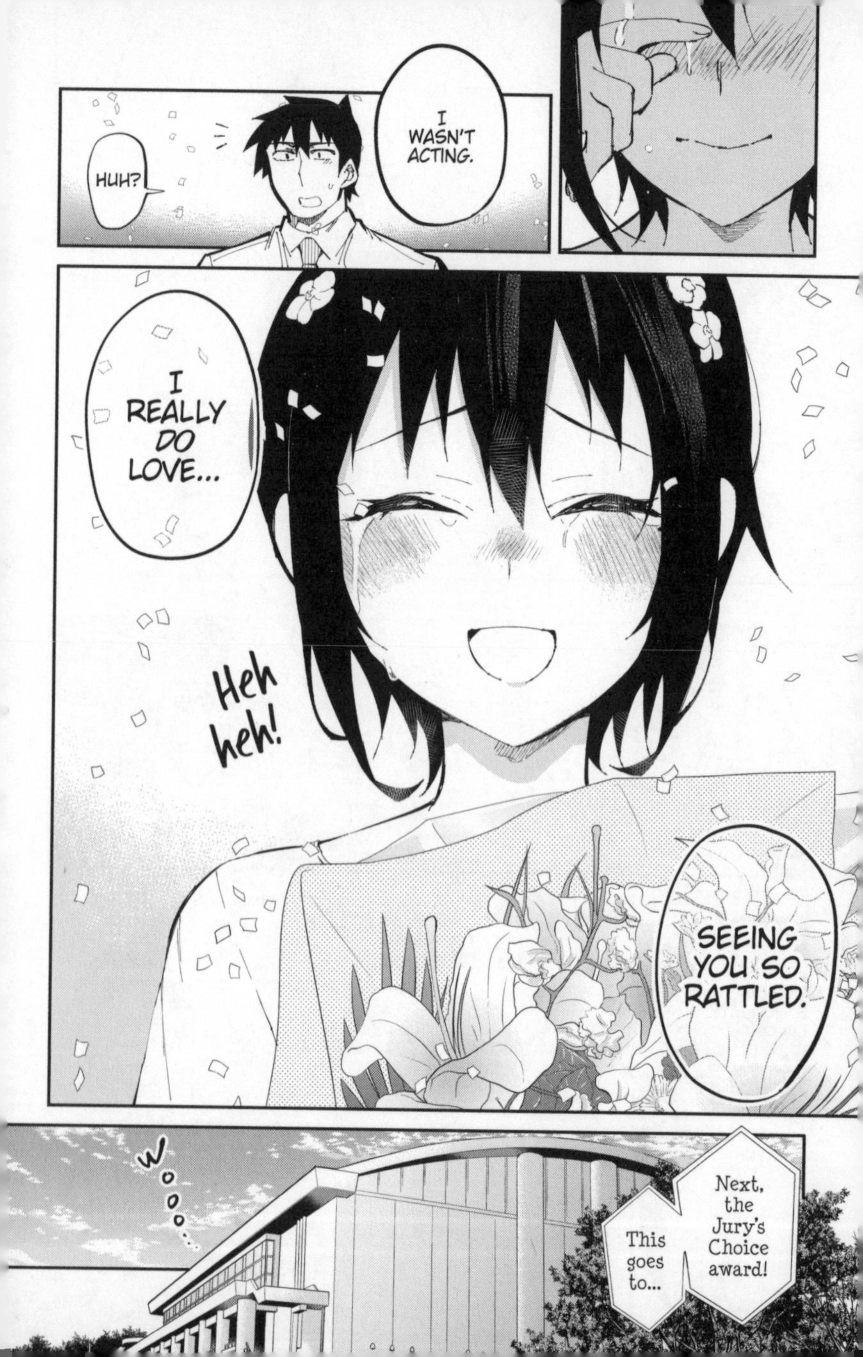
I WASN'T ACTING.
HUH?
I REALLY DO LOVE...
Heh heh!
SEEING YOU SO RATTLED.
Next, the Jury's Choice award!
This goes to...
Wooo...

Gal
Gohan

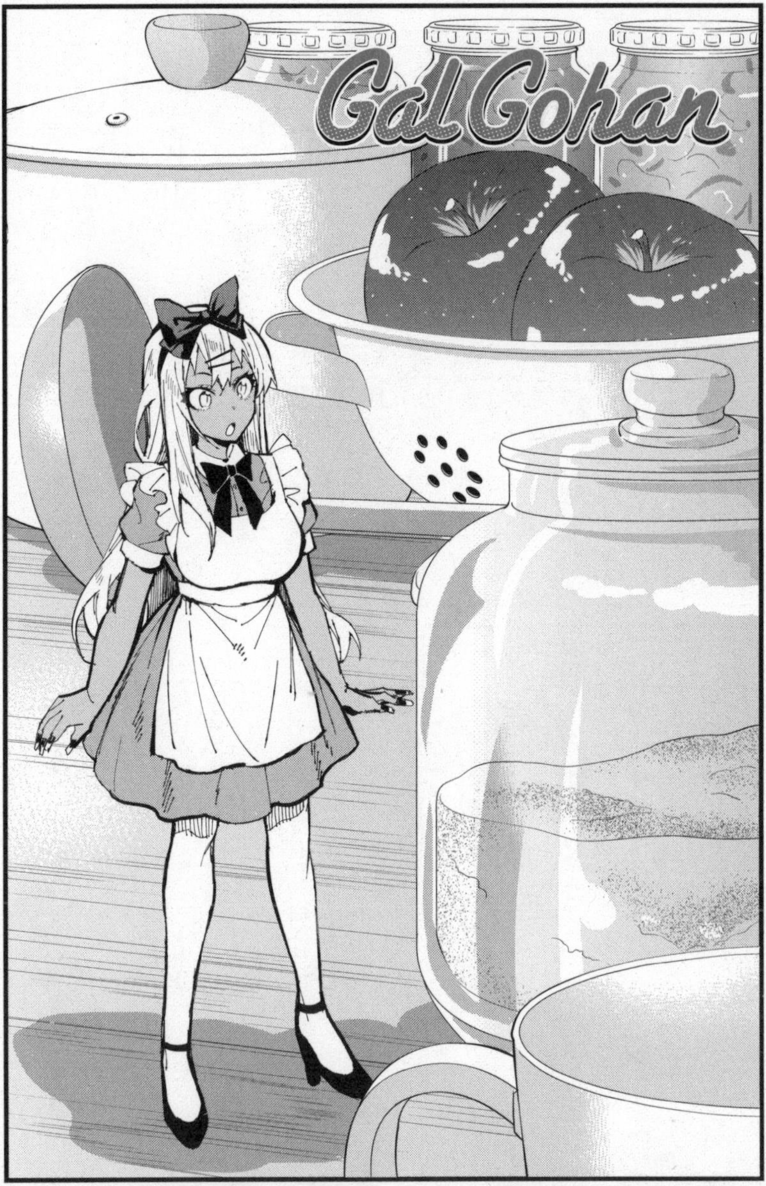
Gal Gohan

42nd Dish ♥ Sentimental Sweet Potatoes

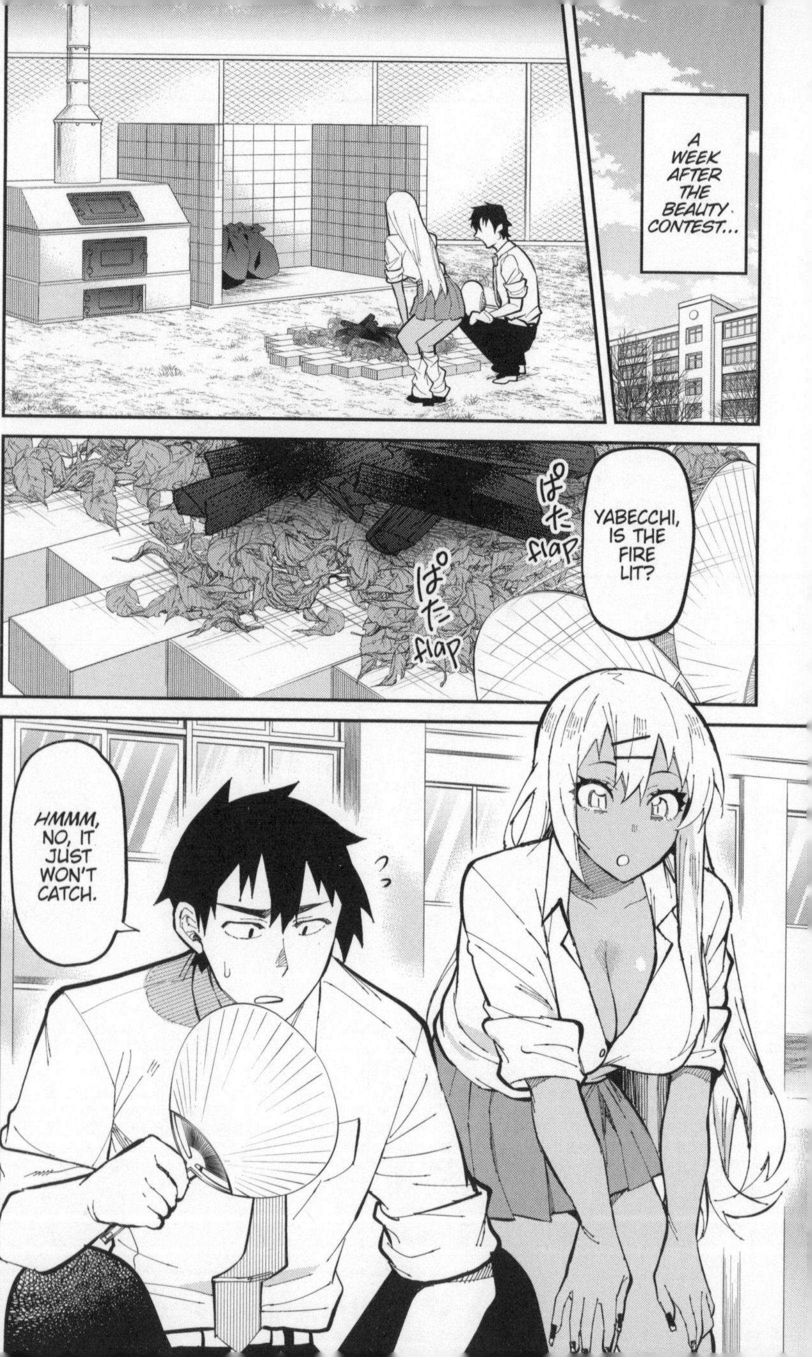
A WEEK AFTER THE BEAUTY CONTEST...
YABECCHI, IS THE FIRE LIT?
ぱた flap
ぱた flap
HMMM, NO, IT JUST WON'T CATCH.

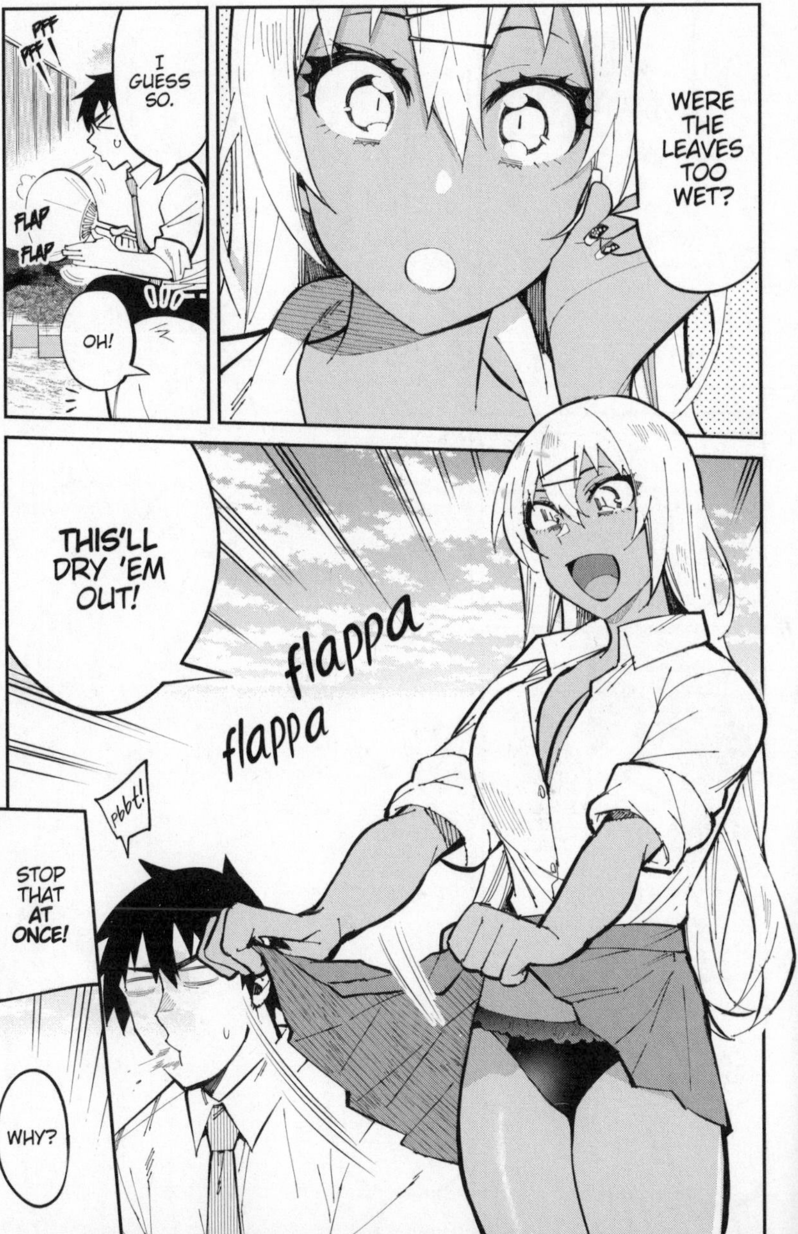
WERE THE LEAVES TOO WET?
PFF PFF
I GUESS SO.
FLAP FLAP
OH!
THIS'LL DRY 'EM OUT!
flappa flappa
pbbt!
STOP THAT AT ONCE!
WHY?

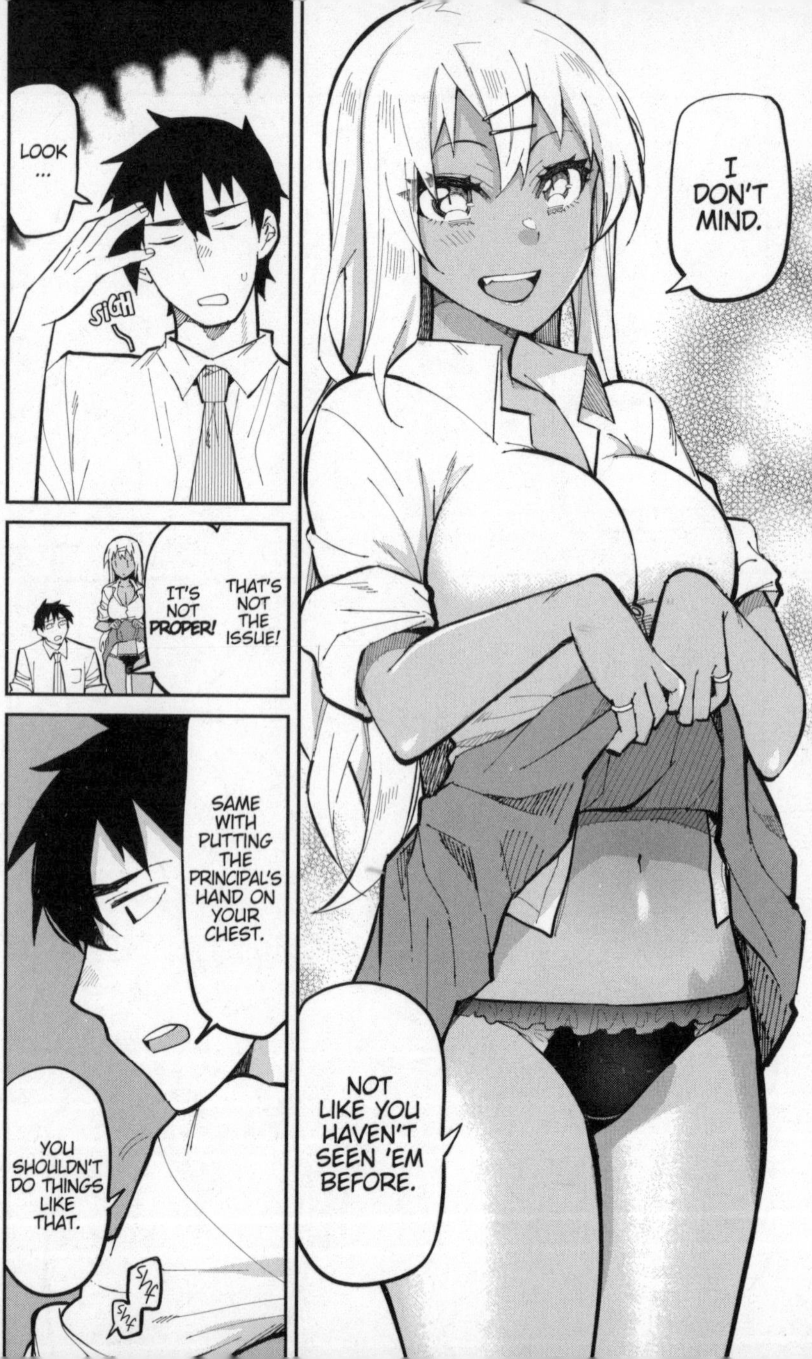
I DON'T MIND.
NOT LIKE YOU HAVEN'T SEEN 'EM BEFORE.
LOOK ...
SIGH
THAT'S NOT THE ISSUE!
IT'S NOT PROPER!
SAME WITH PUTTING THE PRINCIPAL'S HAND ON YOUR CHEST.
YOU SHOULDN'T DO THINGS LIKE THAT.
SHF
SHF

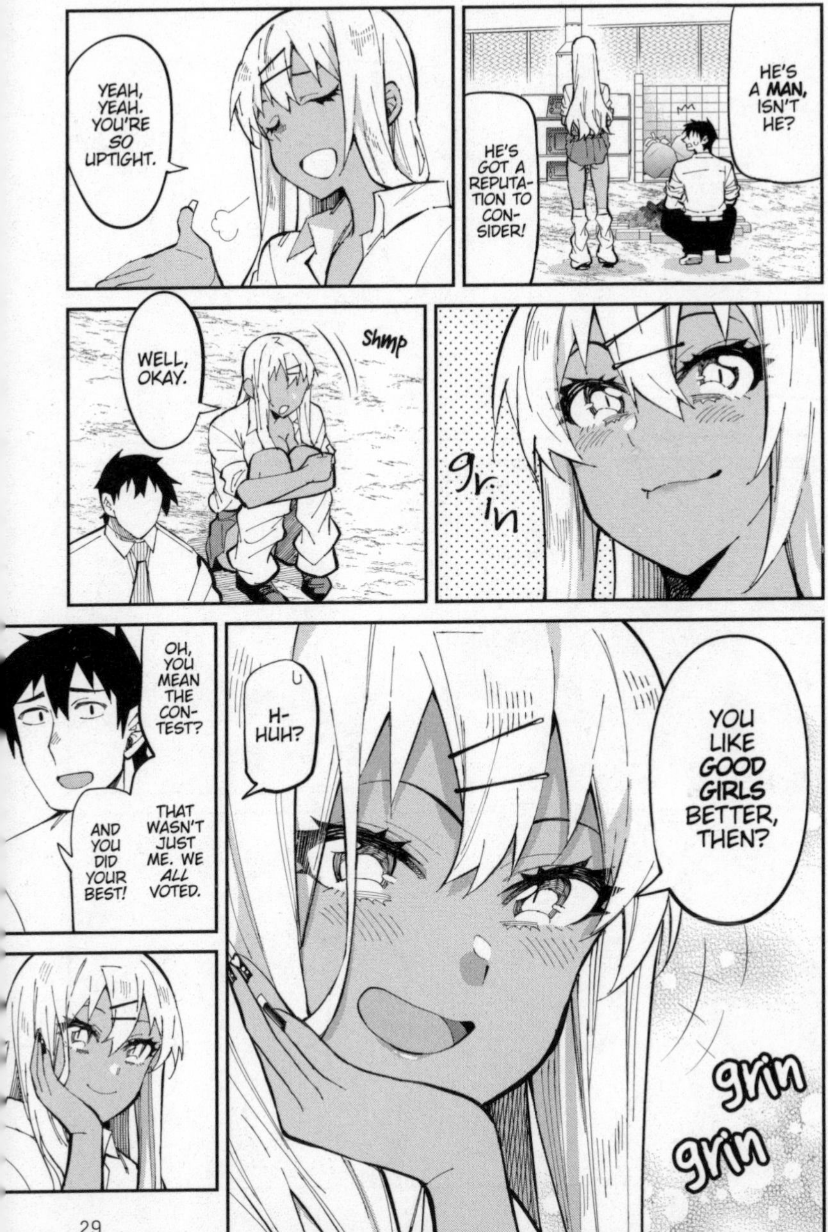
HE'S A MAN, ISN'T HE?
HE'S GOT A REPUTATION TO CONSIDER!
YEAH, YEAH. YOU'RE SO UPTIGHT.
grin
shmp
WELL, OKAY.
YOU LIKE GOOD GIRLS BETTER, THEN?
H-HUH?
grin grin
OH, YOU MEAN THE CONTEST?
THAT WASN'T JUST ME. WE ALL VOTED.
AND YOU DID YOUR BEST!

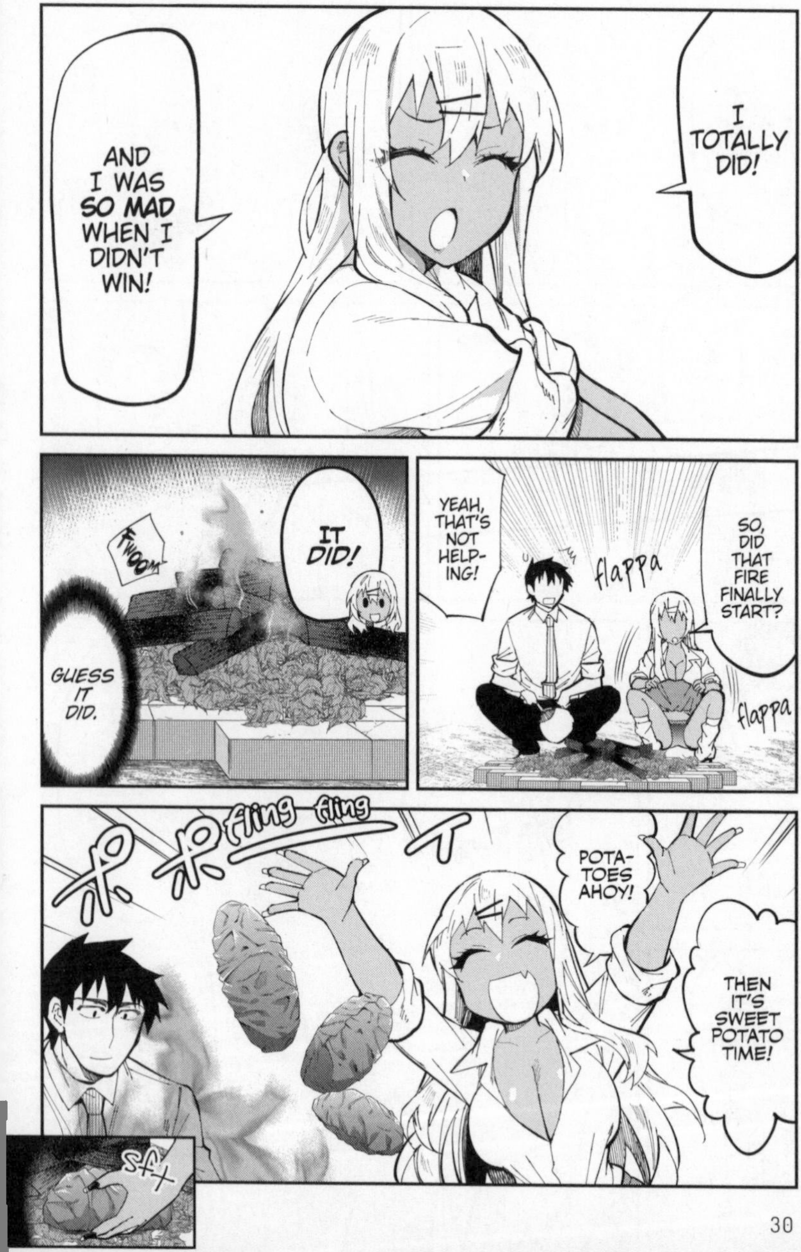
I TOTALLY DID!
AND I WAS SO MAD WHEN I DIDN'T WIN!
SO, DID THAT FIRE FINALLY START?
flappa
flappa
YEAH, THAT'S NOT HELPING!
FWOOM
IT DID!
GUESS IT DID.
fling fling
POTA-TOES AHOY!
THEN IT'S SWEET POTATO TIME!
sfx

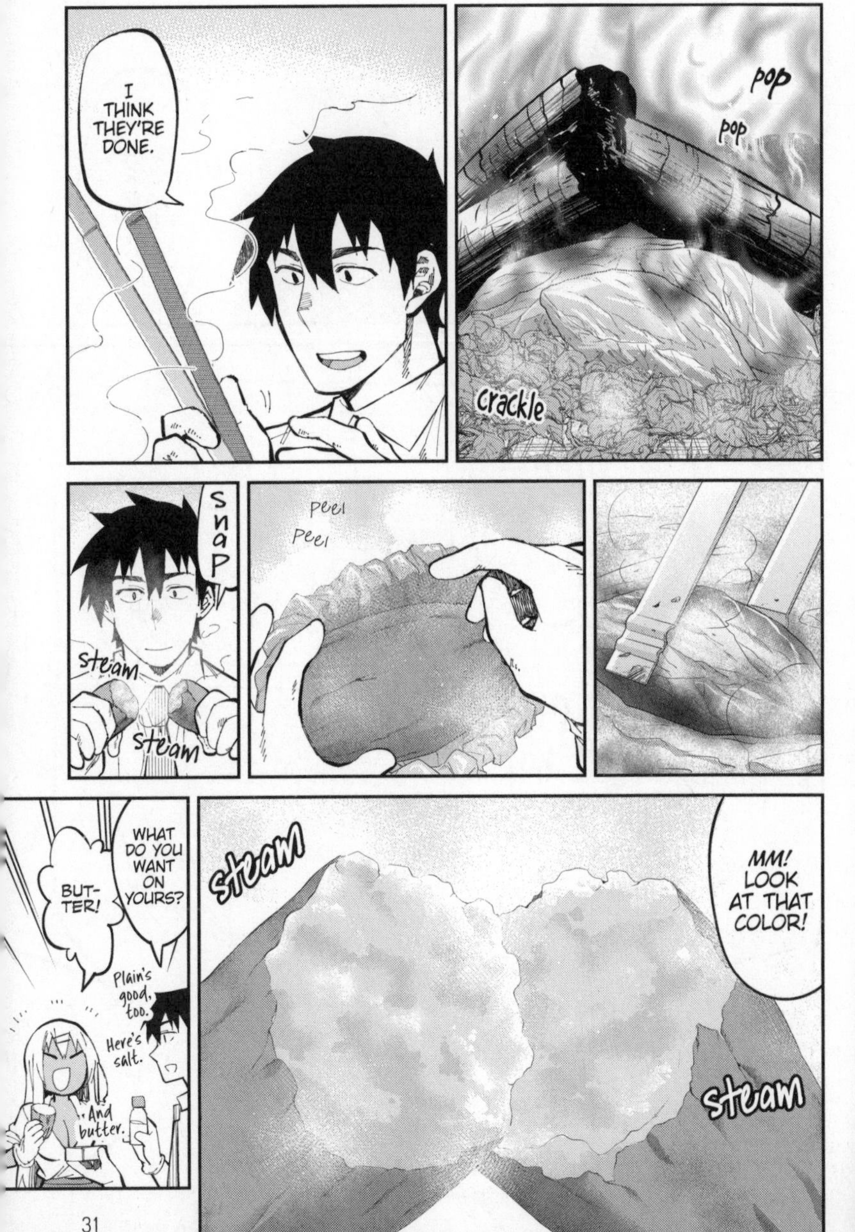
pop
pop
crackle
I THINK THEY'RE DONE.
peel
peel
SNAP
steam
steam
steam
MM! LOOK AT THAT COLOR!
steam
WHAT DO YOU WANT ON YOURS?
BUT-TER!
Plain's good, too.
Here's salt.
And butter.

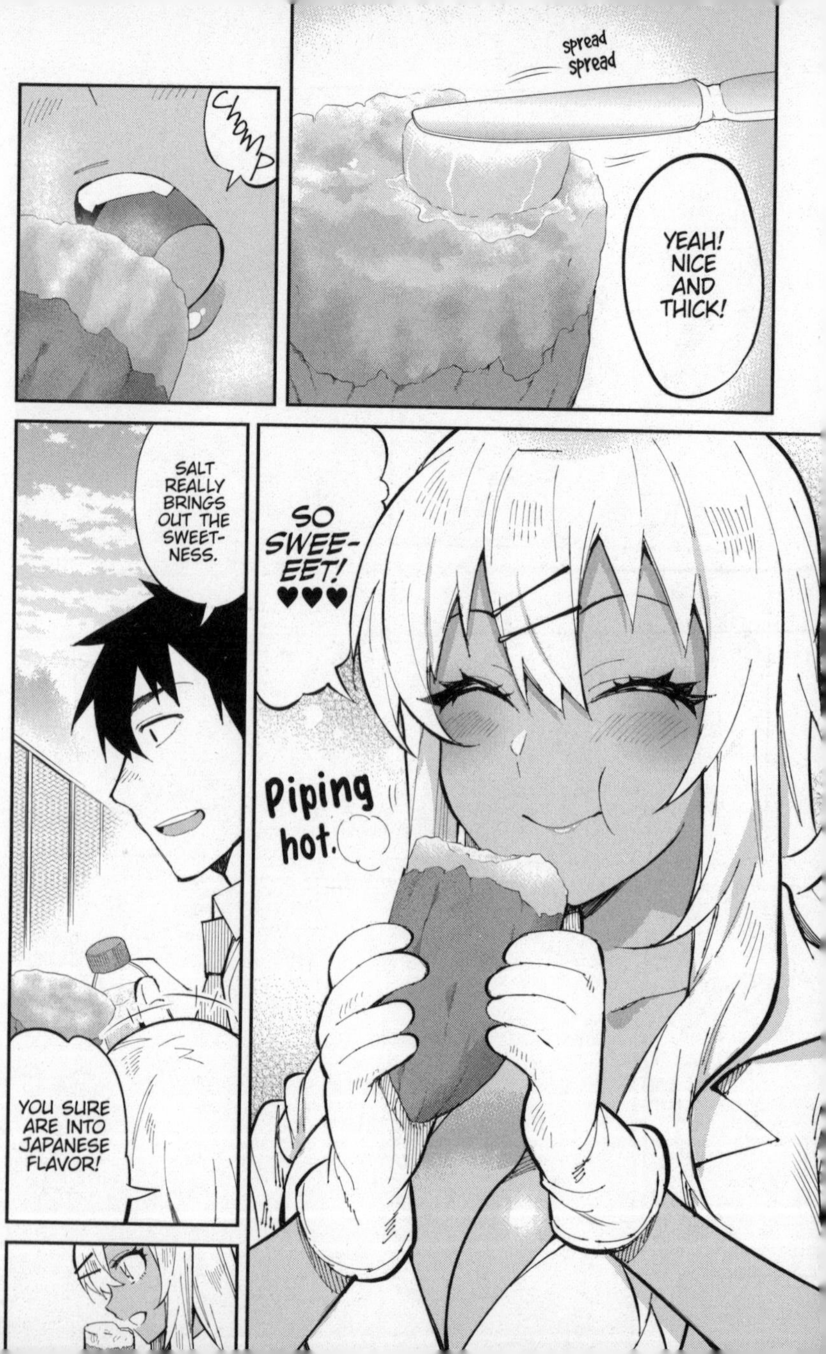
spread
spread
YEAH! NICE AND THICK!
CHOMP
SO SWEEE-EET! ♥♥♥
Piping hot.
SALT REALLY BRINGS OUT THE SWEET-NESS.
YOU SURE ARE INTO JAPANESE FLAVOR!

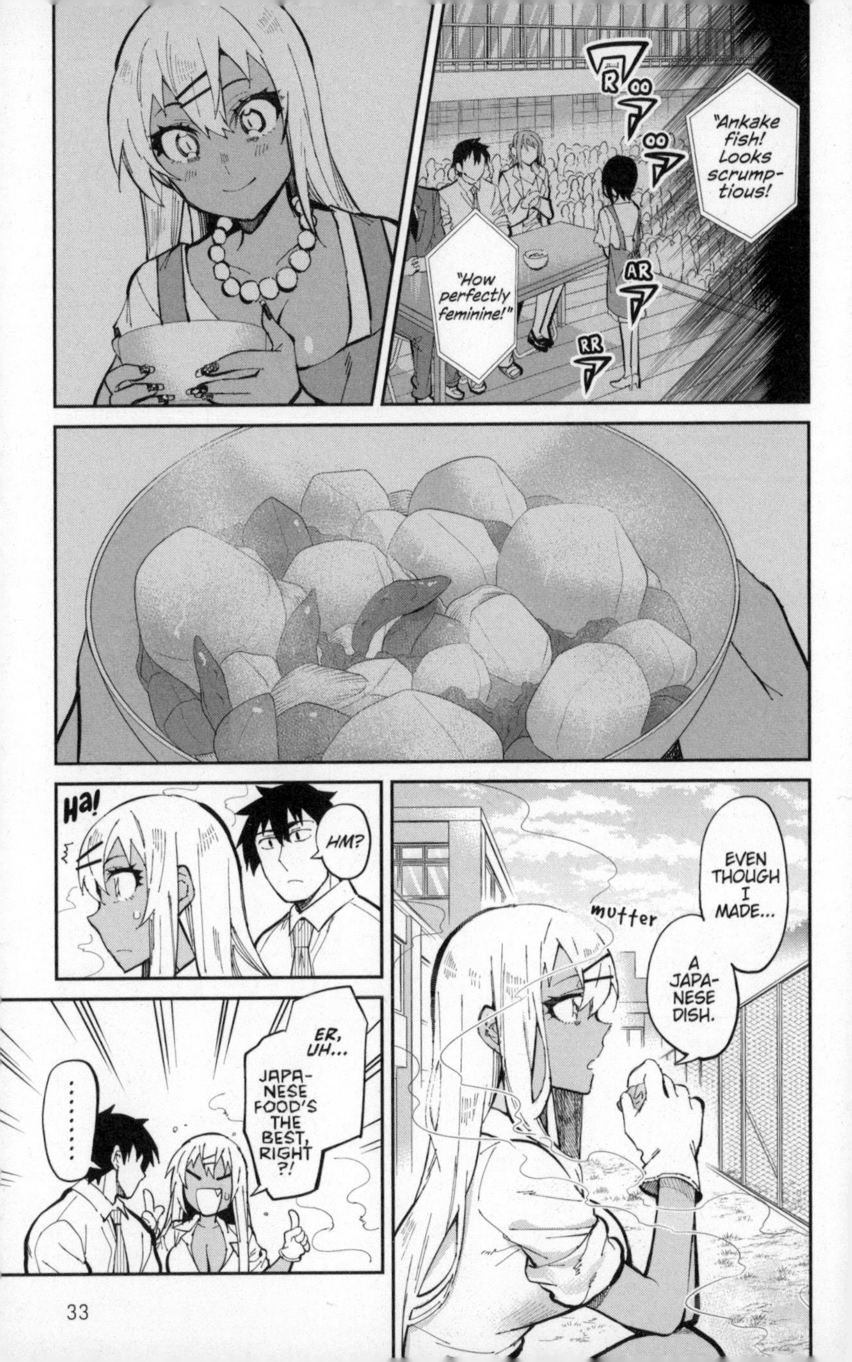
R oo
oo
"Ankake fish! Looks scrumptious!
"How perfectly feminine!"
AR
RR
EVEN THOUGH I MADE...
mutter
A JAPANESE DISH.
Ha!
HM?
ER, UH...
JAPANESE FOOD'S THE BEST, RIGHT?!
......

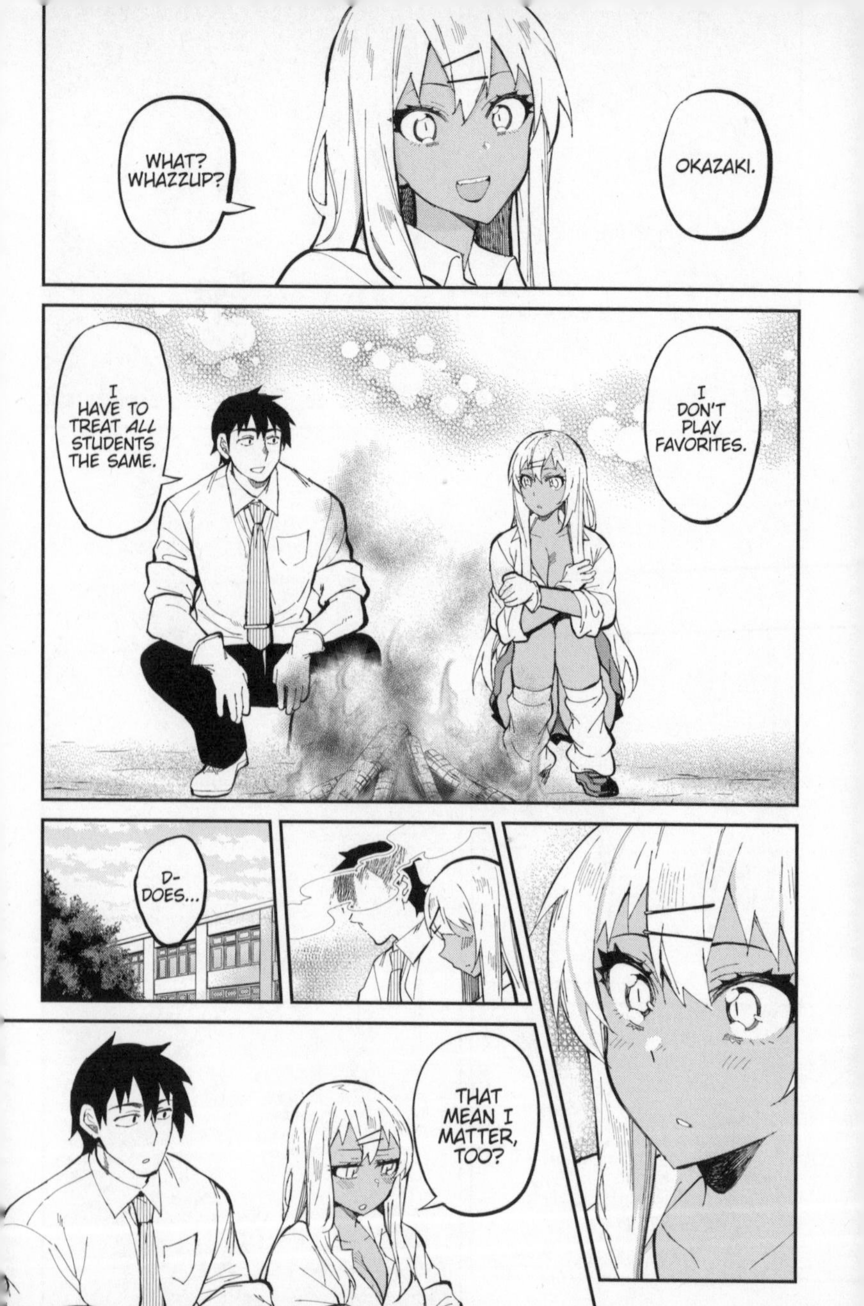
OKAZAKI.
WHAT? WHAZZUP?
I DON'T PLAY FAVORITES.
I HAVE TO TREAT *ALL* STUDENTS THE SAME.
D- DOES...
THAT MEAN I MATTER, TOO?

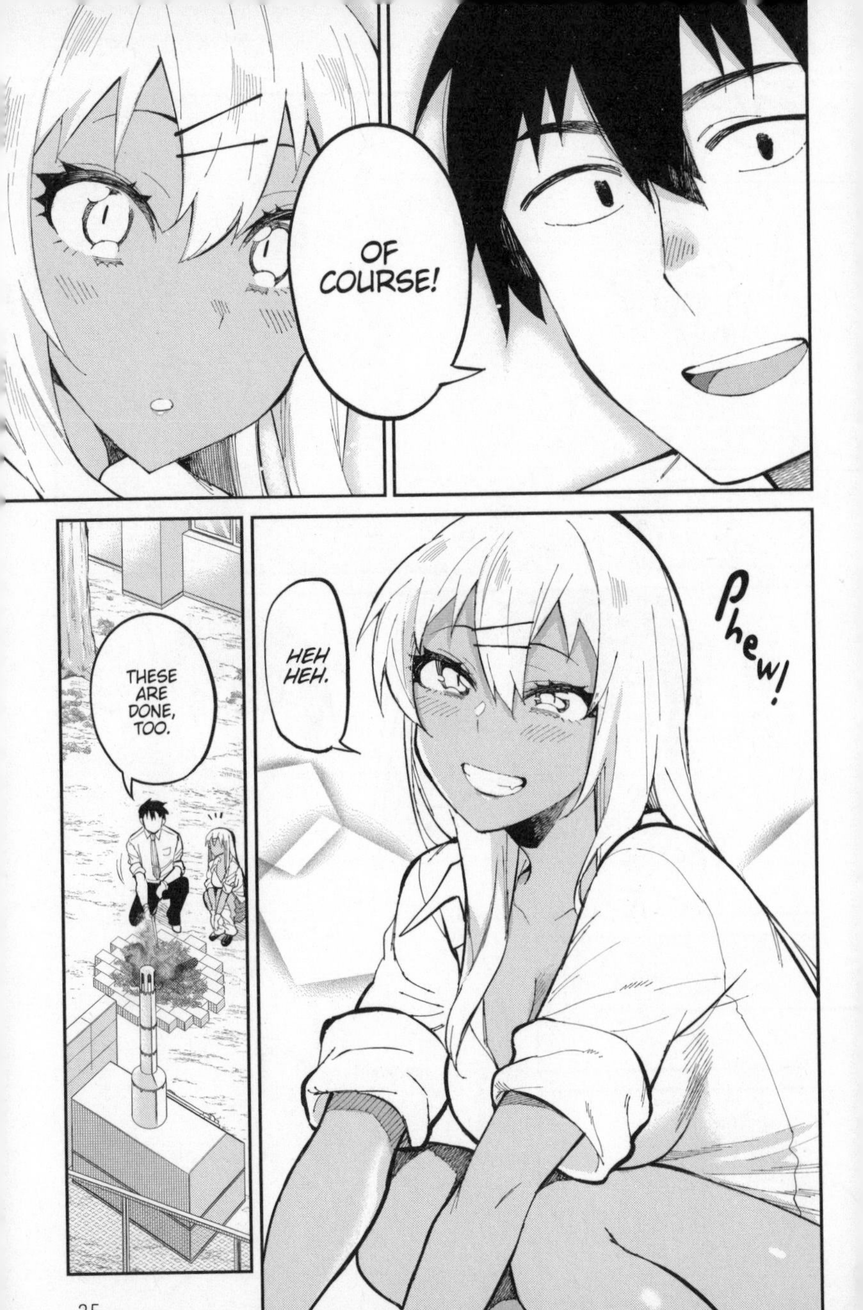
OF COURSE!
Phew!
HEH HEH.
THESE ARE DONE, TOO.

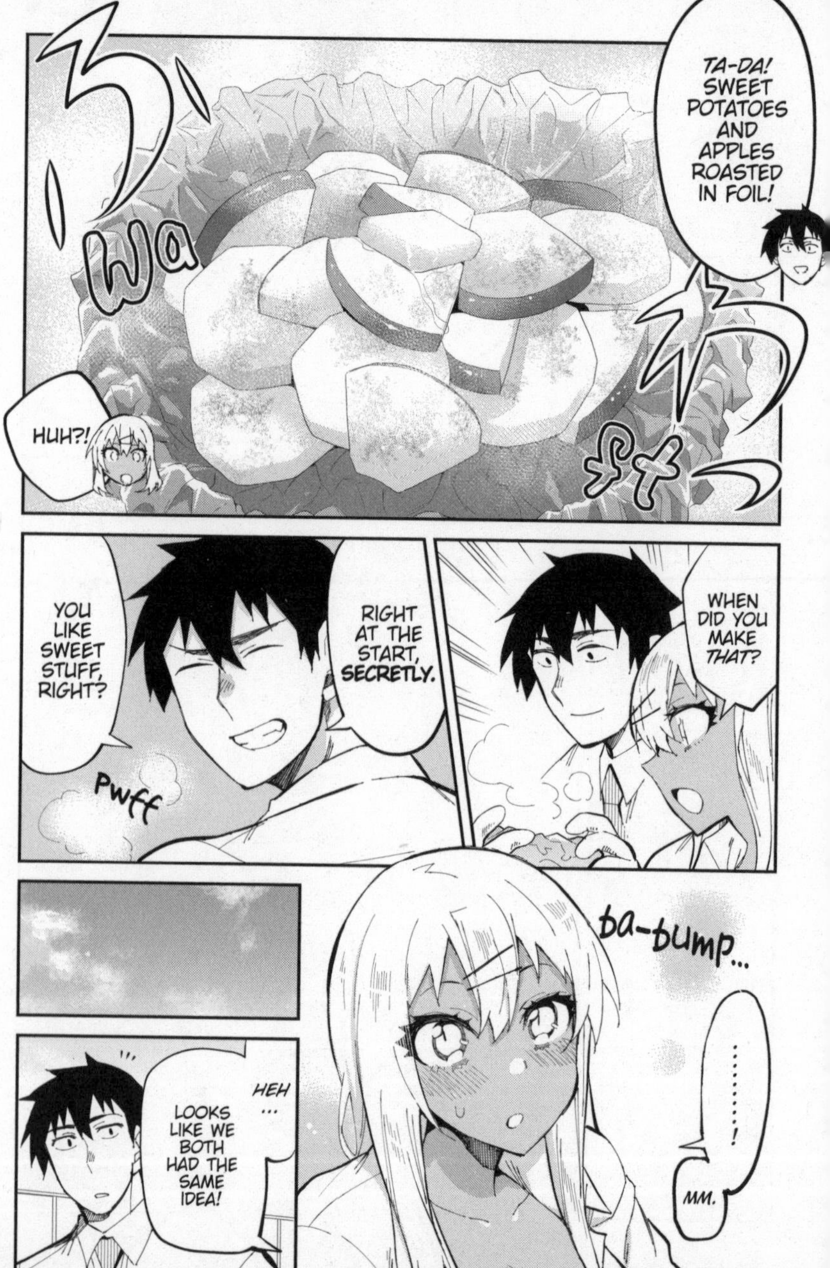
TA-DA! SWEET POTATOES AND APPLES ROASTED IN FOIL!
Wa
ft
HUH?!
WHEN DID YOU MAKE *THAT*?
RIGHT AT THE START, **SECRETLY**.
YOU LIKE SWEET STUFF, RIGHT?
Pwff
ba-bump...
......!
MM.
HEH...
LOOKS LIKE WE BOTH HAD THE SAME IDEA!

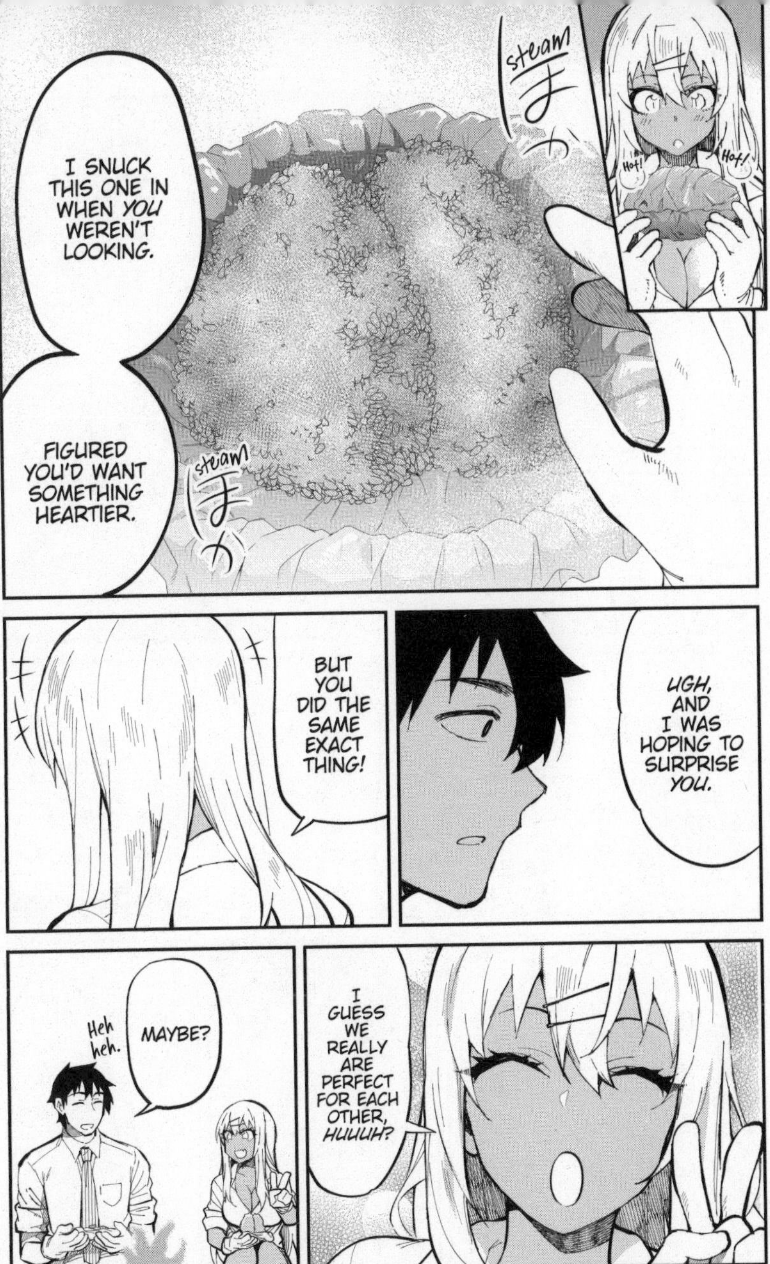
steam
Hot!
Hot!
I SNUCK THIS ONE IN WHEN *YOU* WEREN'T LOOKING.
FIGURED YOU'D WANT SOMETHING HEARTIER.
steam
UGH, AND I WAS HOPING TO SURPRISE YOU.
BUT YOU DID THE SAME EXACT THING!
I GUESS WE REALLY ARE PERFECT FOR EACH OTHER, *HUUUH?*
MAYBE?
Heh heh.

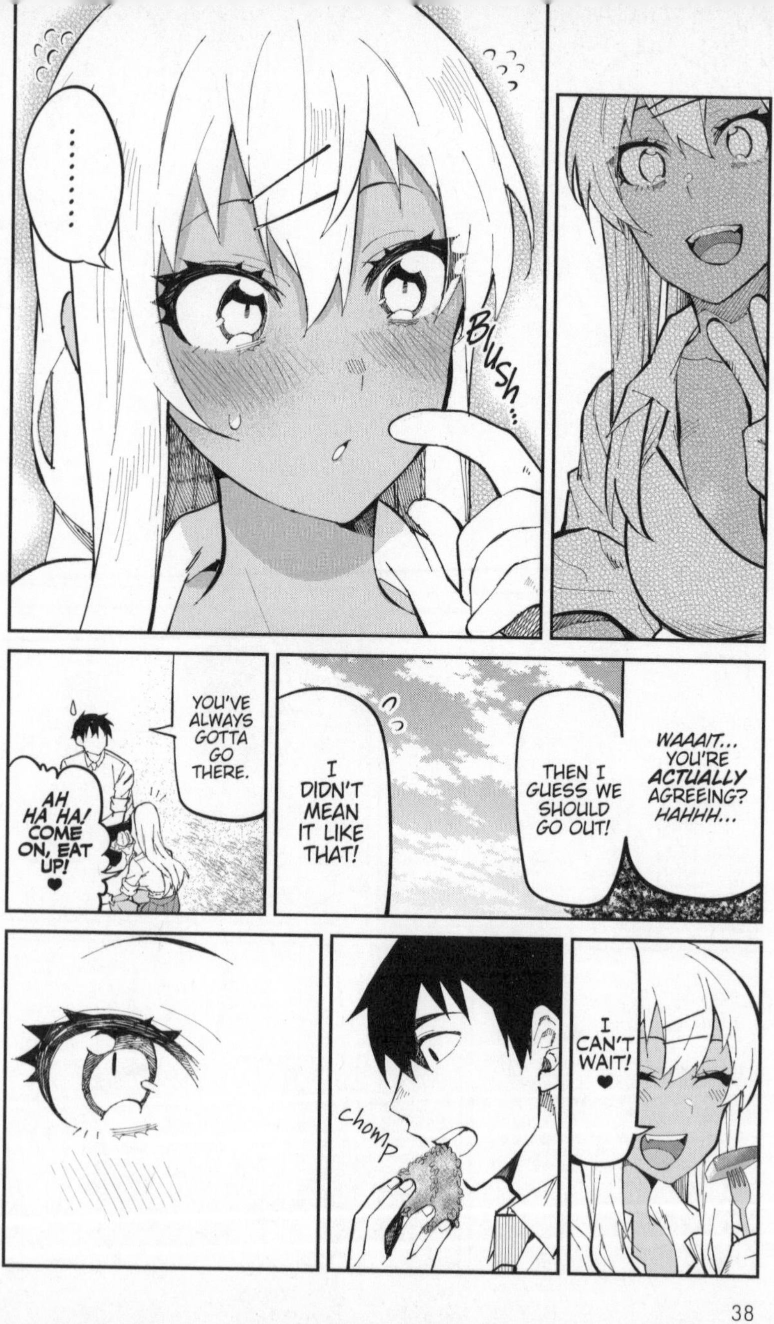
......
BLUSH...
WAAAIT... YOU'RE *ACTUALLY* AGREEING? HAHHH...
THEN I GUESS WE SHOULD GO OUT!
I DIDN'T MEAN IT LIKE THAT!
YOU'VE ALWAYS GOTTA GO THERE.
AH HA HA! COME ON, EAT UP! ♥
I CAN'T WAIT! ♥
CHOMP

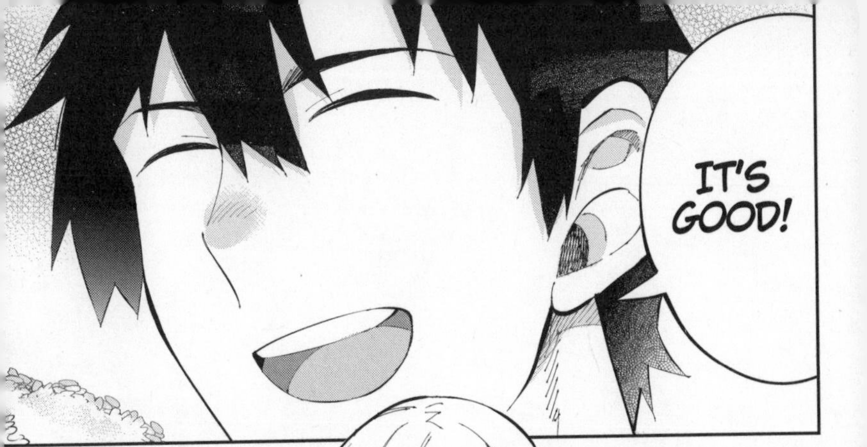
IT'S GOOD!
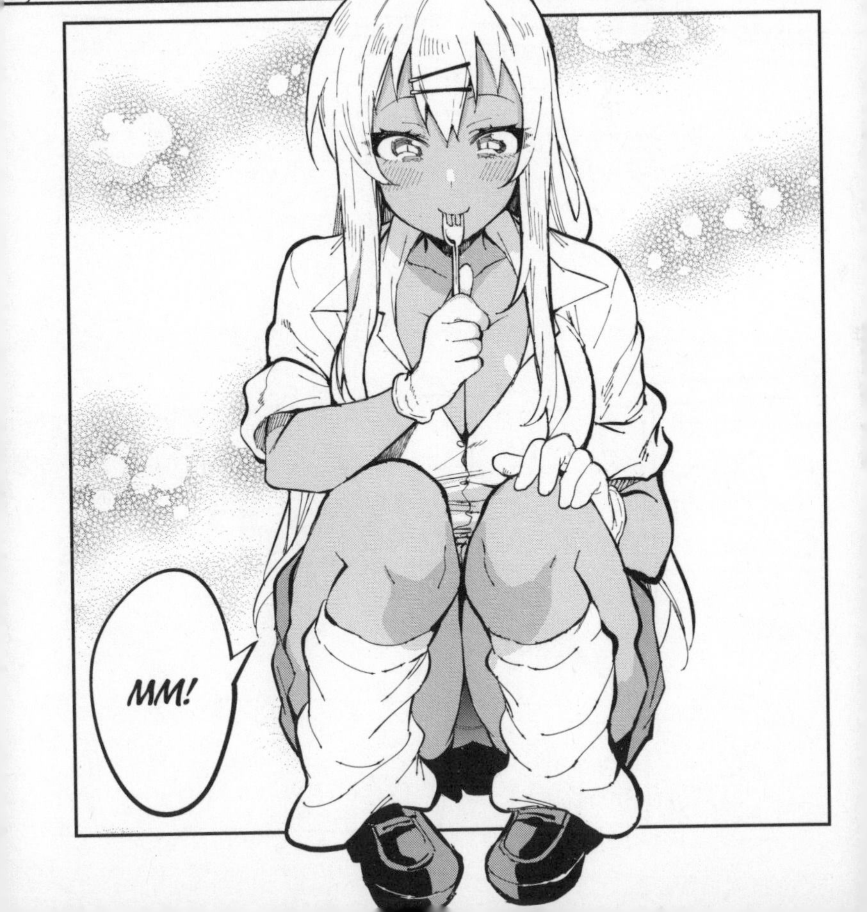
MM!

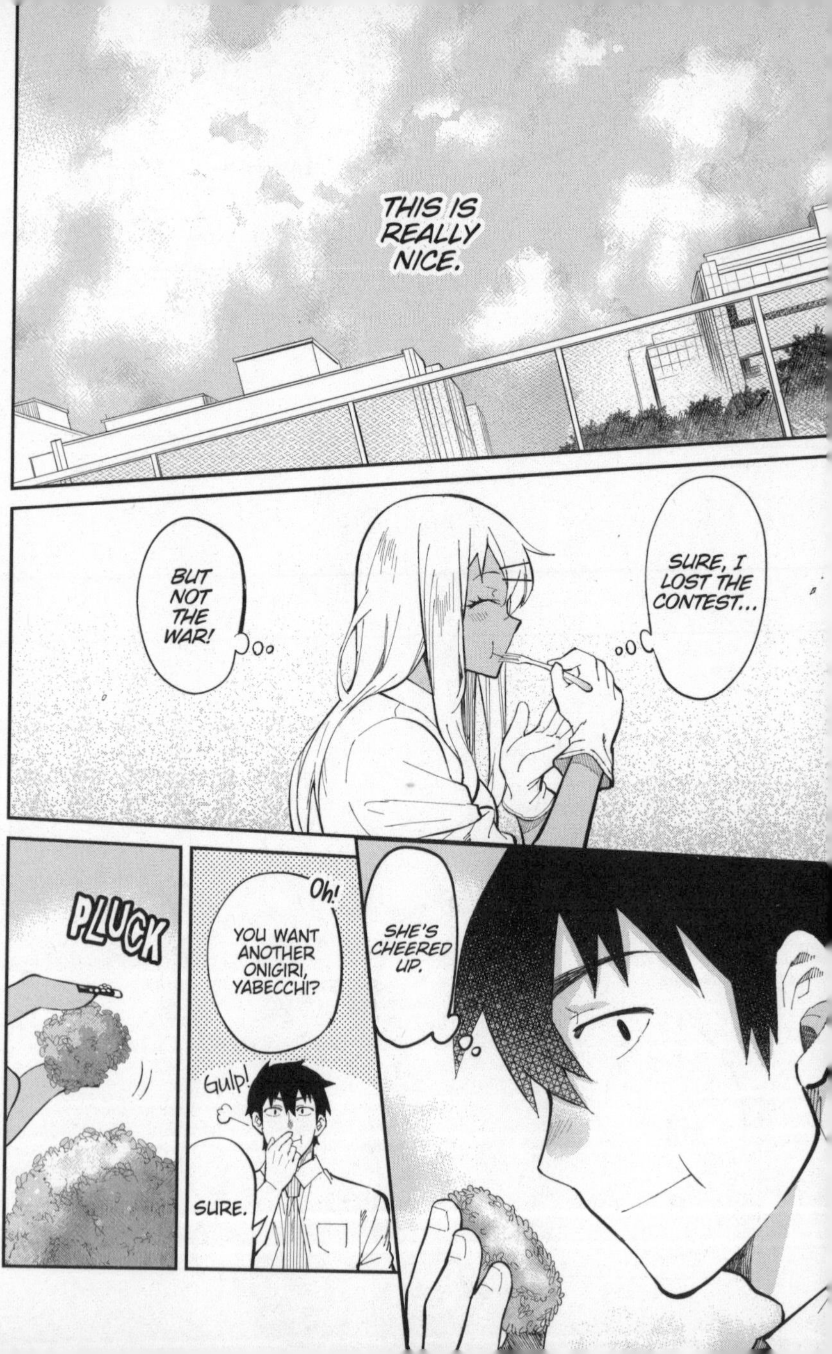
THIS IS REALLY NICE.
SURE, I LOST THE CONTEST...
BUT NOT THE WAR!
SHE'S CHEERED UP.
Oh!
YOU WANT ANOTHER ONIGIRI, YABECCHI?
Gulp!
SURE.
PLUCK

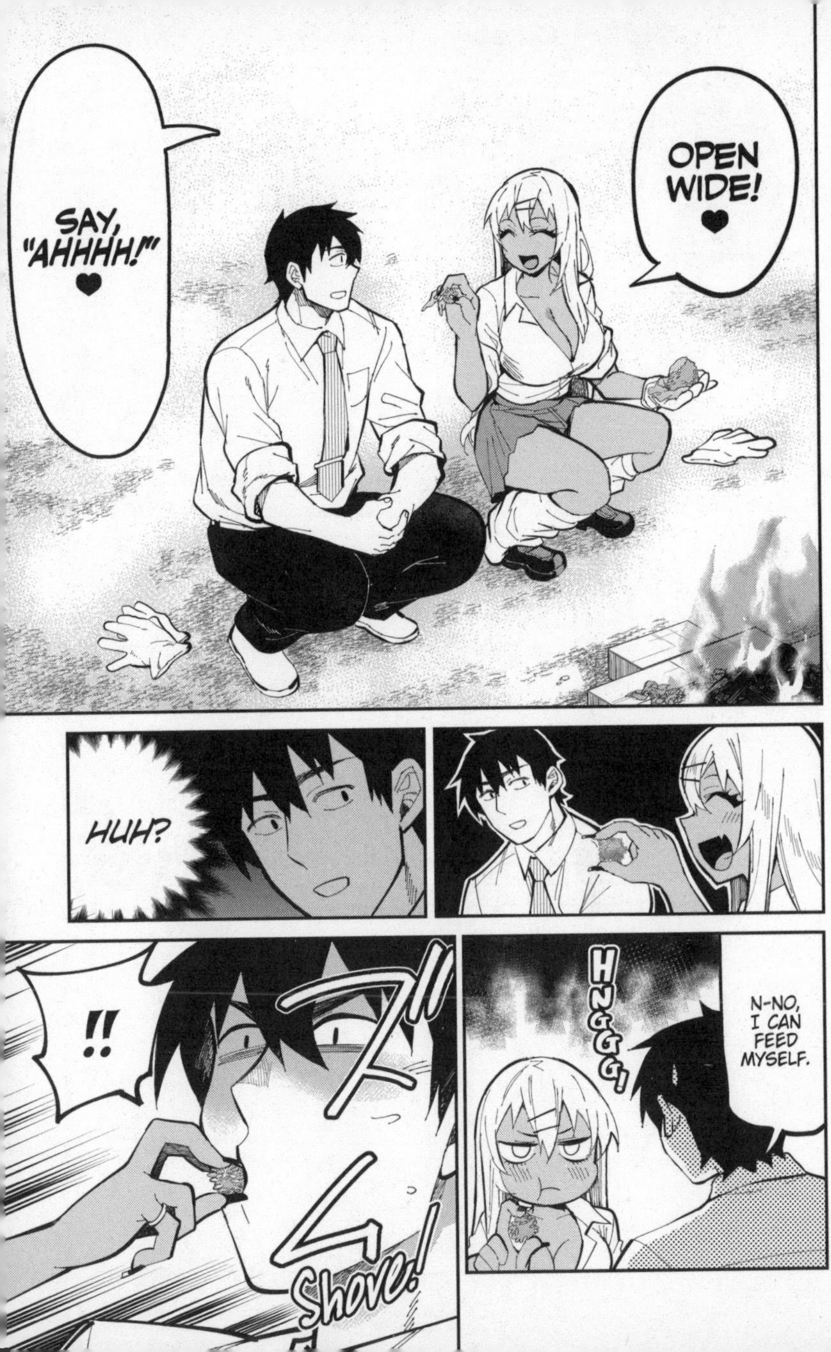
OPEN WIDE! ♥
SAY, "AHHHH!" ♥
HUH?
N-NO, I CAN FEED MYSELF.
HNGGG!
!!
Shove!

WELL?
YOU
LIKE
IT?

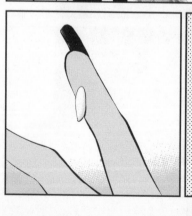

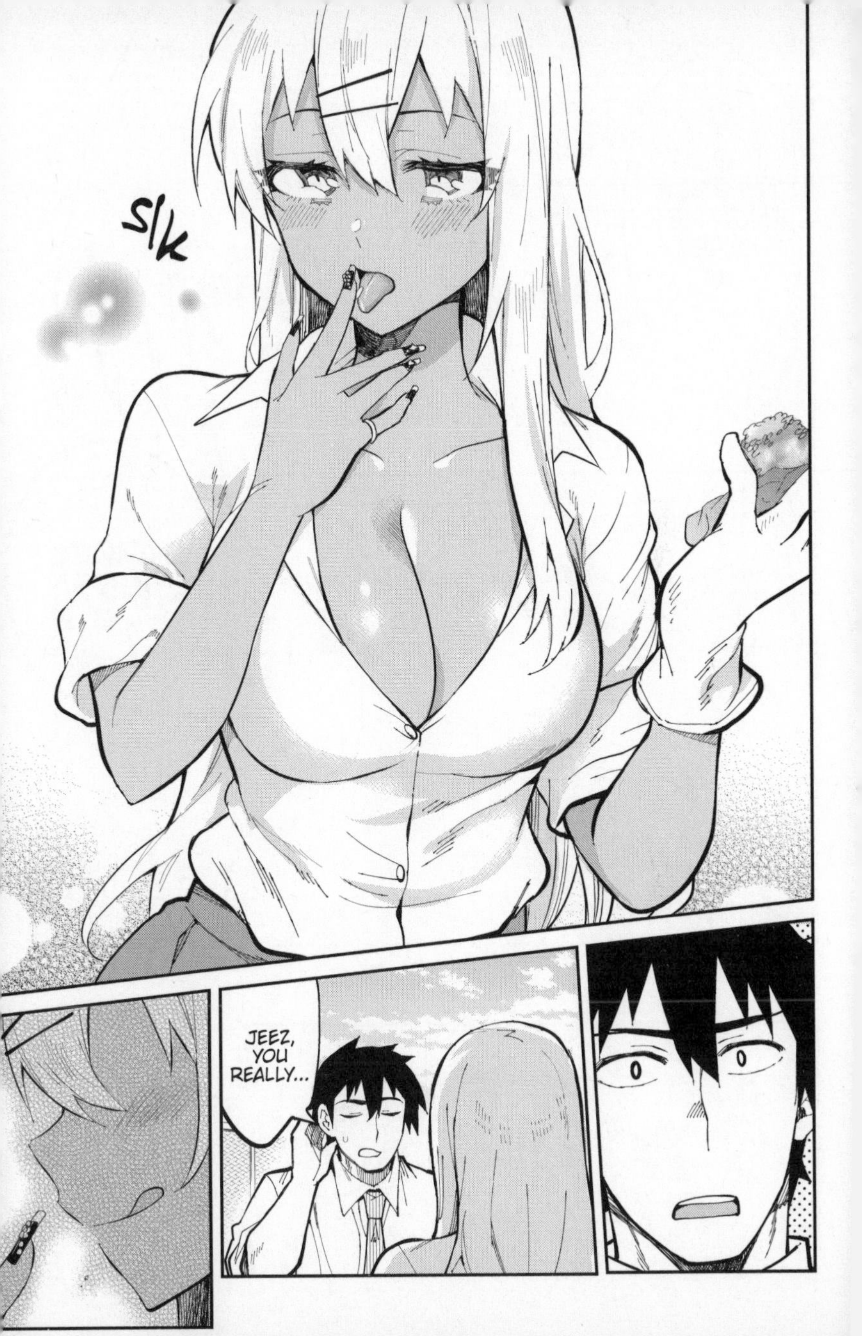
SLK
JEEZ, YOU REALLY...

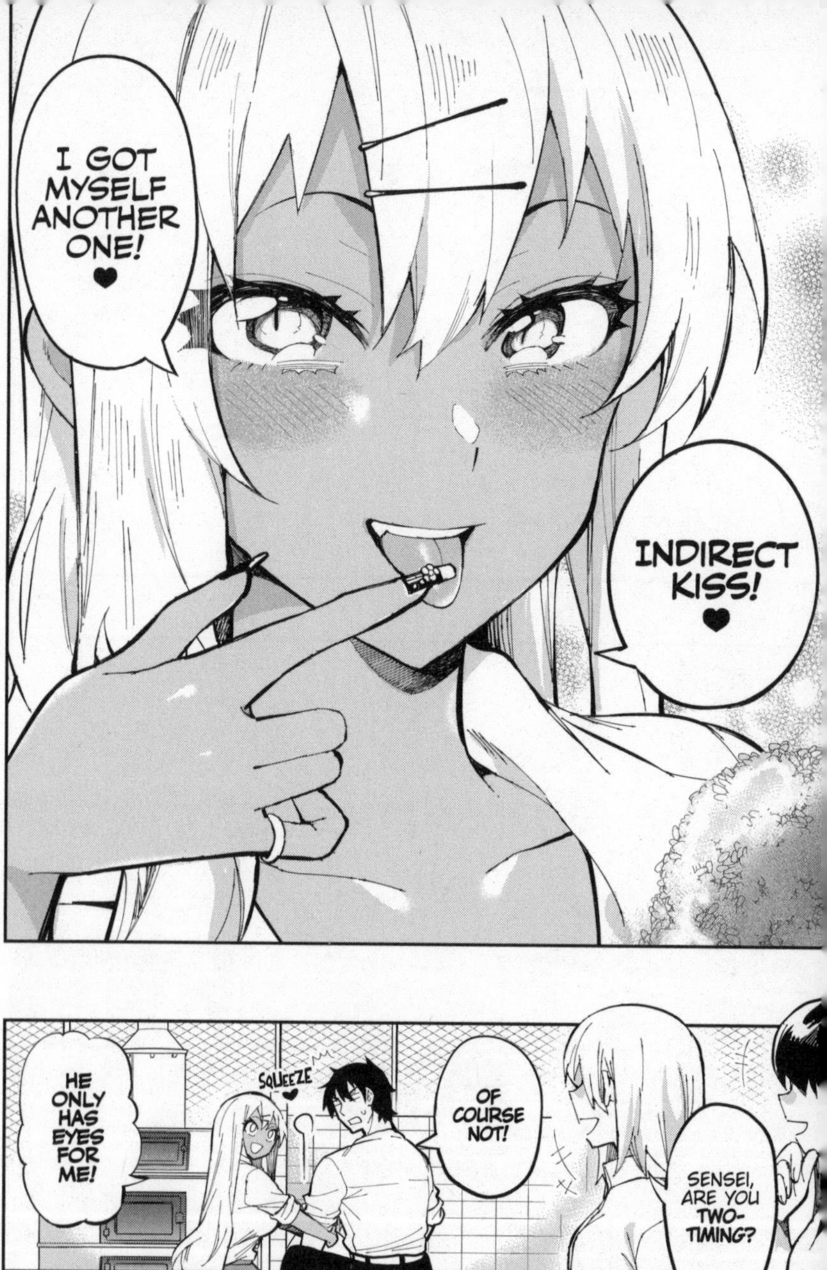
I GOT MYSELF ANOTHER ONE! ♥
INDIRECT KISS! ♥
SENSEI, ARE YOU TWO-TIMING?
OF COURSE NOT!
SQUEEZE ♥
HE ONLY HAS EYES FOR ME!

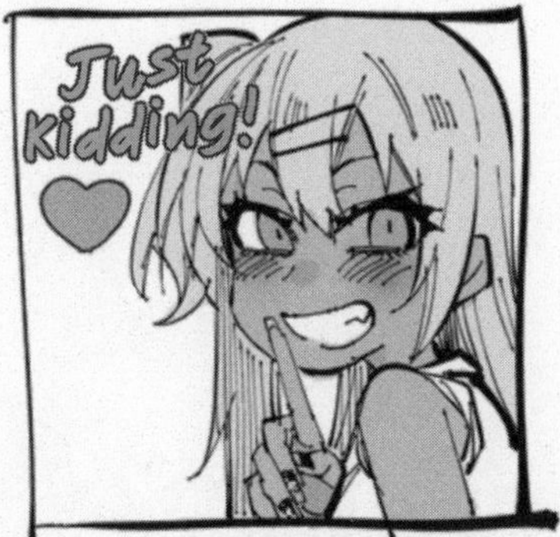
Just kidding!

Gal
Gohan

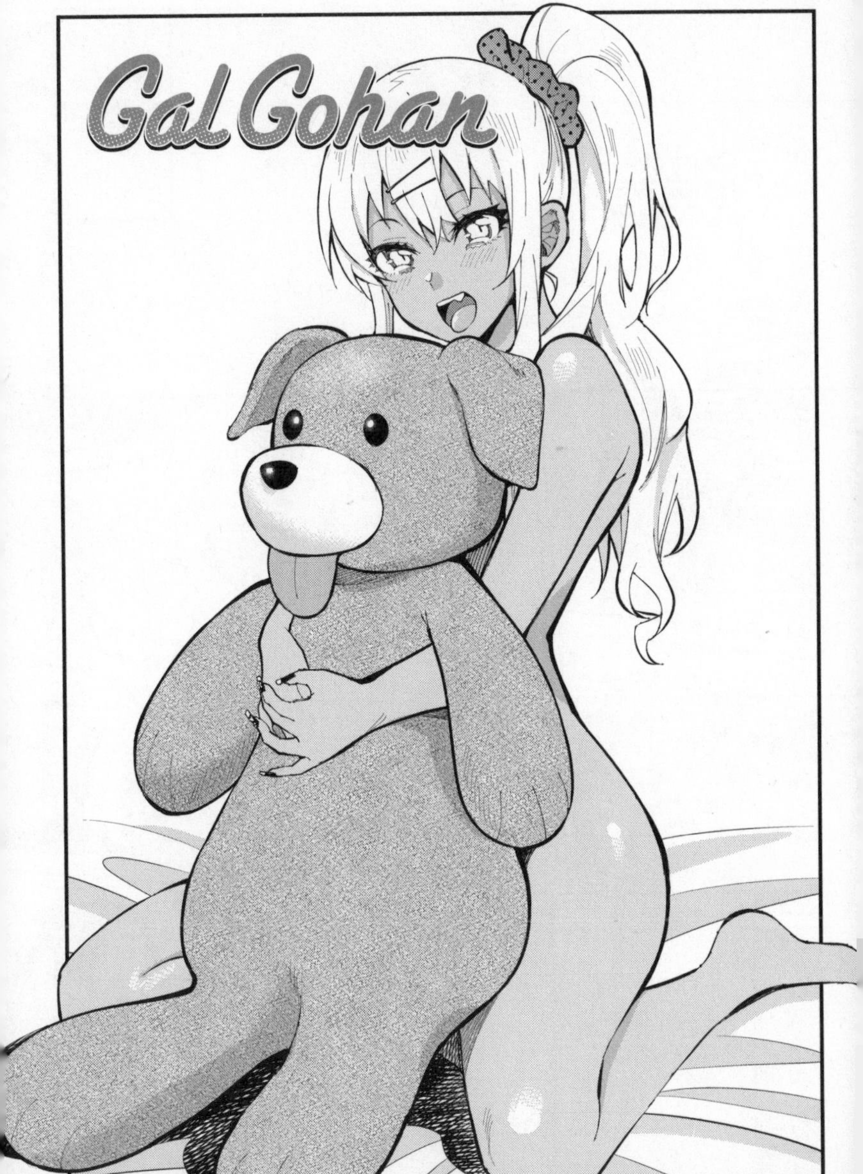
Gal Gohan

43rd Dish ♥ Aggressive Okinawa

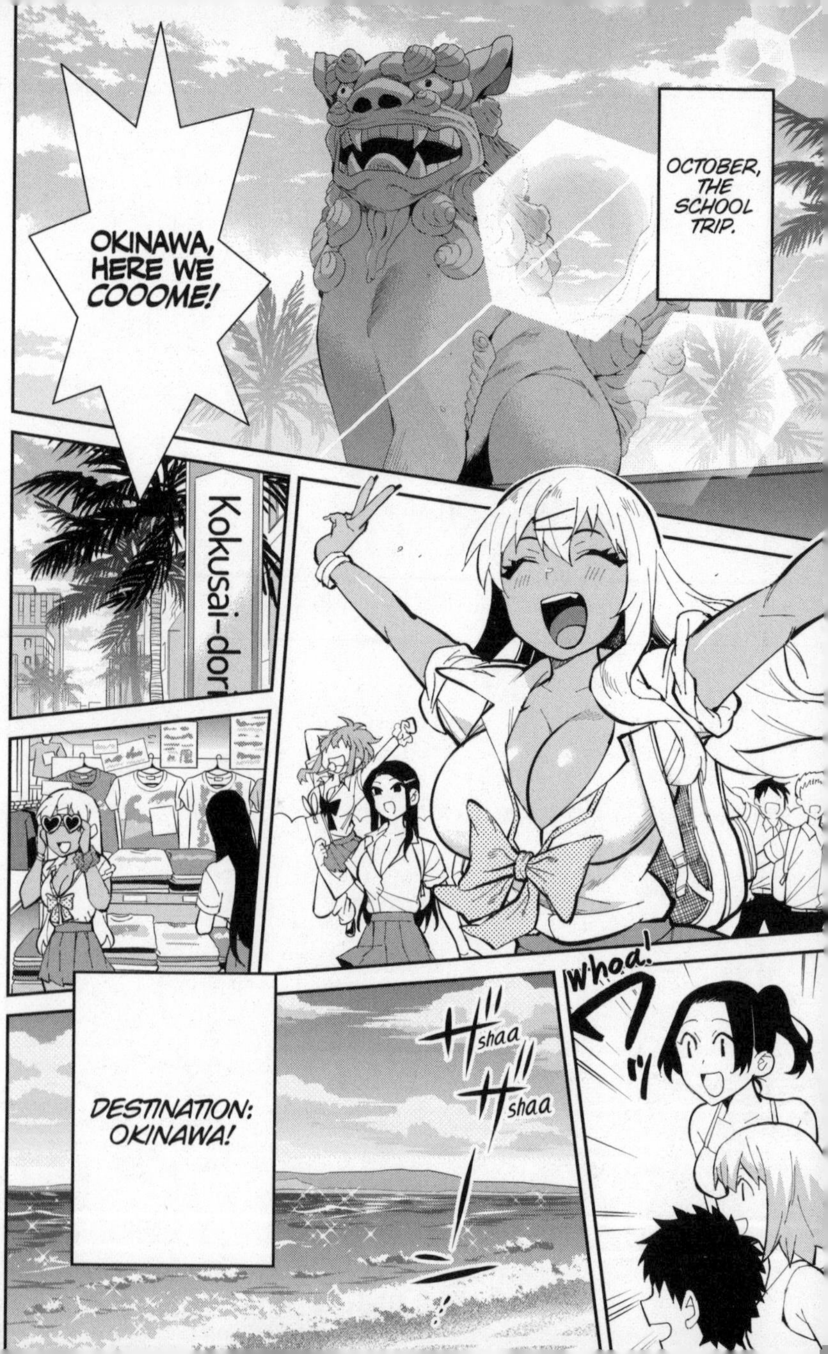
OCTOBER, THE SCHOOL TRIP.
OKINAWA, HERE WE COOOME!
Kokusai-dor
whoa!
shaa
shaa
DESTINATION: OKINAWA!

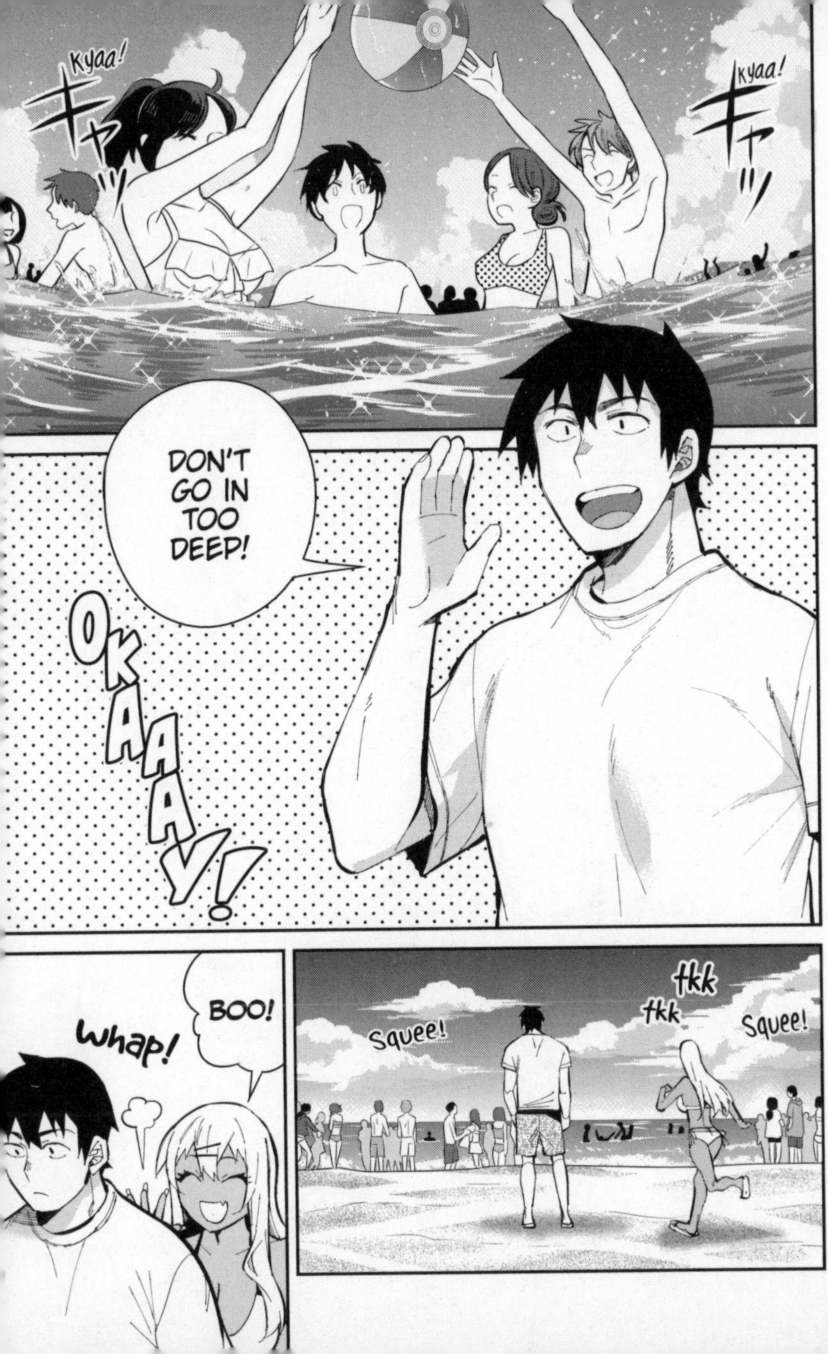
Kyaa!
キャッ
Kyaa!
キャッ
DON'T GO IN TOO DEEP!
OKAAAY!
tkk
tkk
Squee!
Squee!
BOO!
Whap!

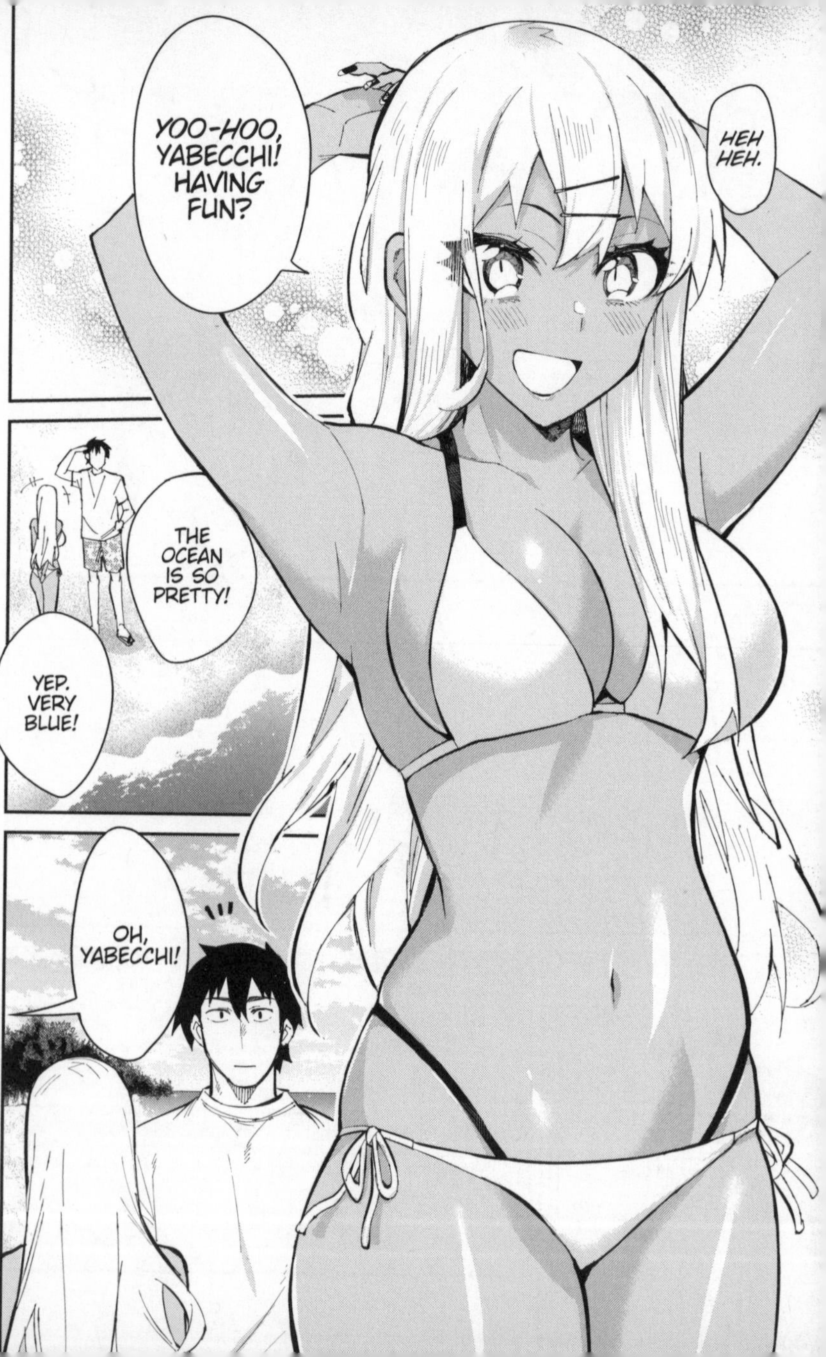
HEH HEH.
YOO-HOO, YABECCHI! HAVING FUN?
THE OCEAN IS SO PRETTY!
YEP. VERY BLUE!
OH, YABECCHI!

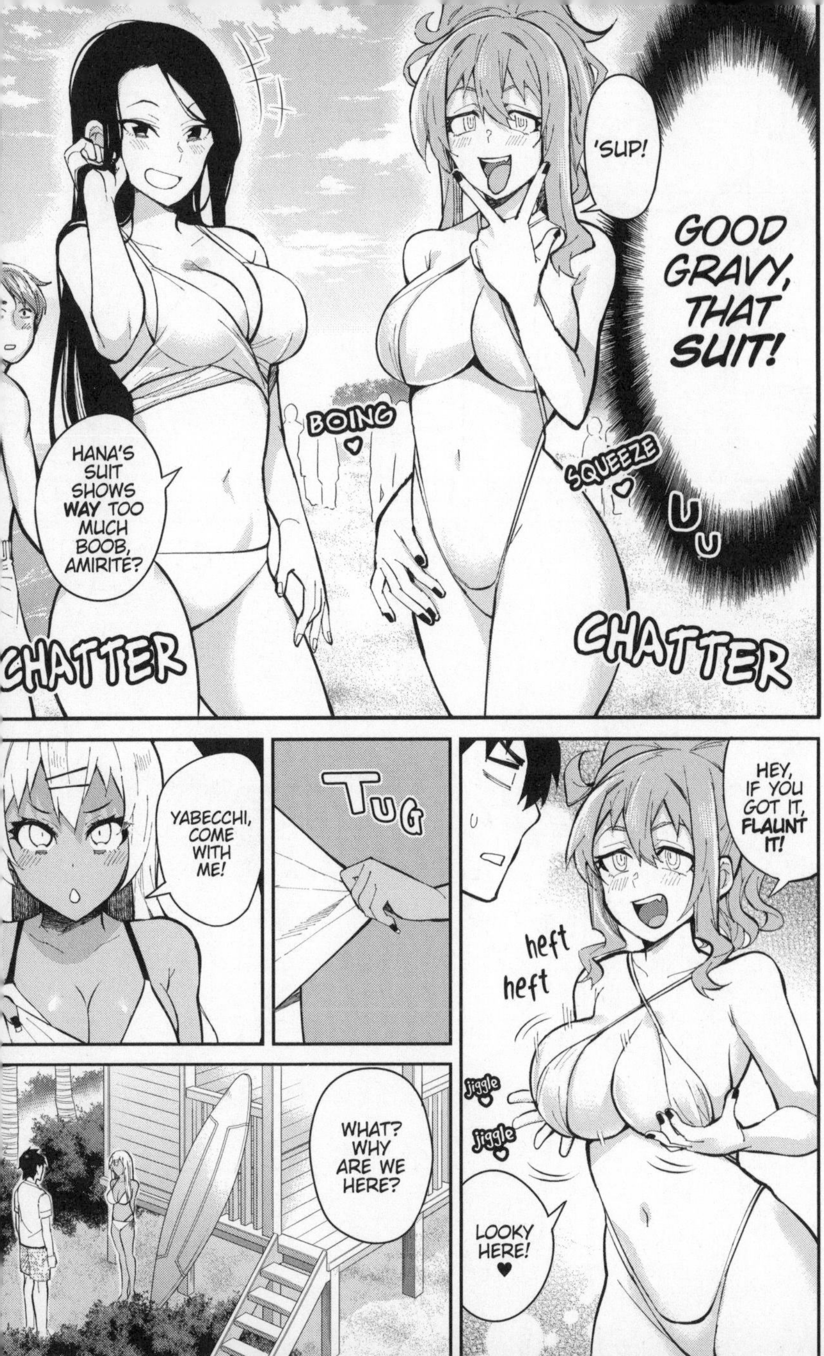
'SUP!
GOOD GRAVY, THAT SUIT!
SQUEEZE
U U
CHATTER
BOING
HANA'S SUIT SHOWS WAY TOO MUCH BOOB, AMIRITE?
CHATTER
HEY, IF YOU GOT IT, FLAUNT IT!
heft heft
jiggle
jiggle
LOOKY HERE!
TUG
YABECCHI, COME WITH ME!
WHAT? WHY ARE WE HERE?

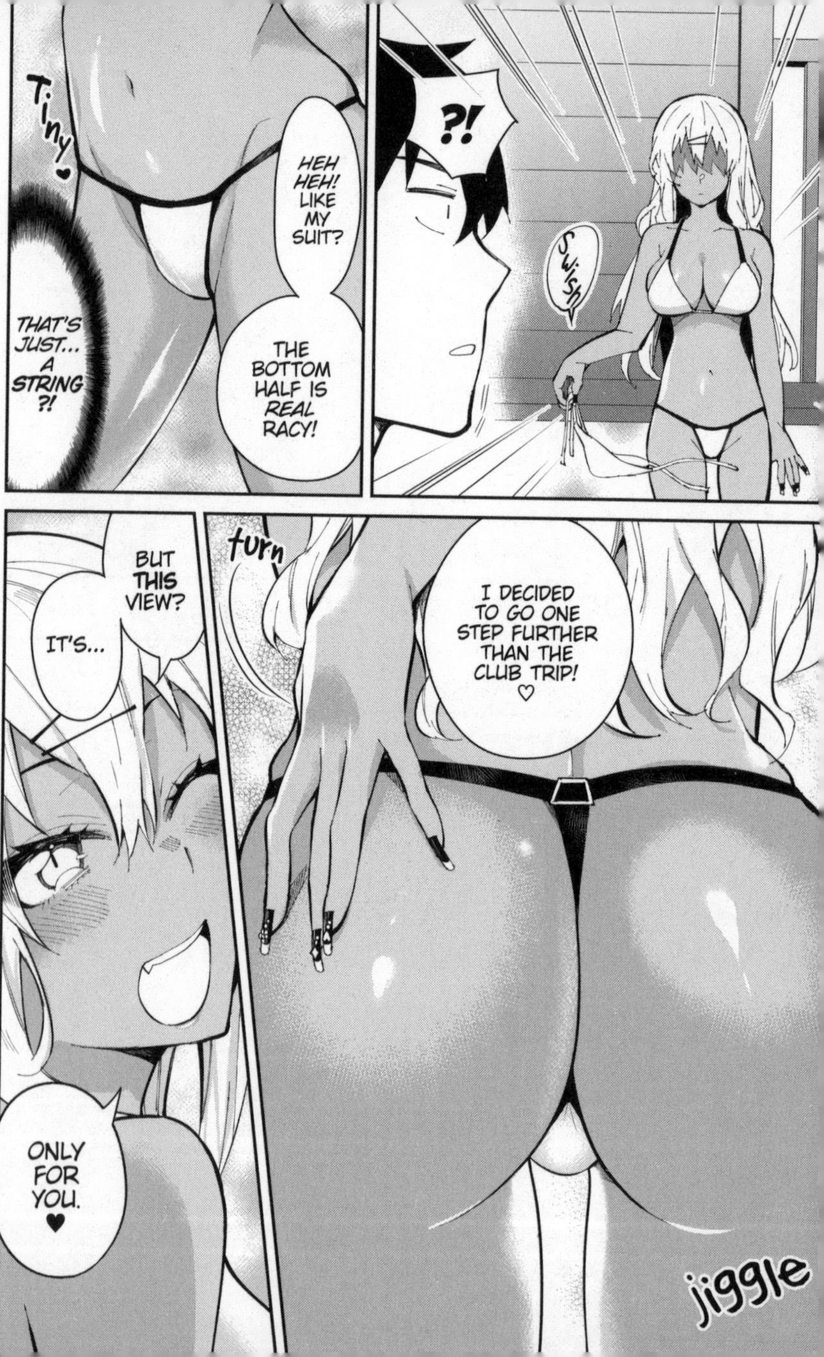
?!
Swish
HEH HEH! LIKE MY SUIT?
THE BOTTOM HALF IS REAL RACY!
Tiny ♥
THAT'S JUST... A STRING?!
turn
I DECIDED TO GO ONE STEP FURTHER THAN THE CLUB TRIP! ♡
jiggle
BUT THIS VIEW?
IT'S...
ONLY FOR YOU. ♥

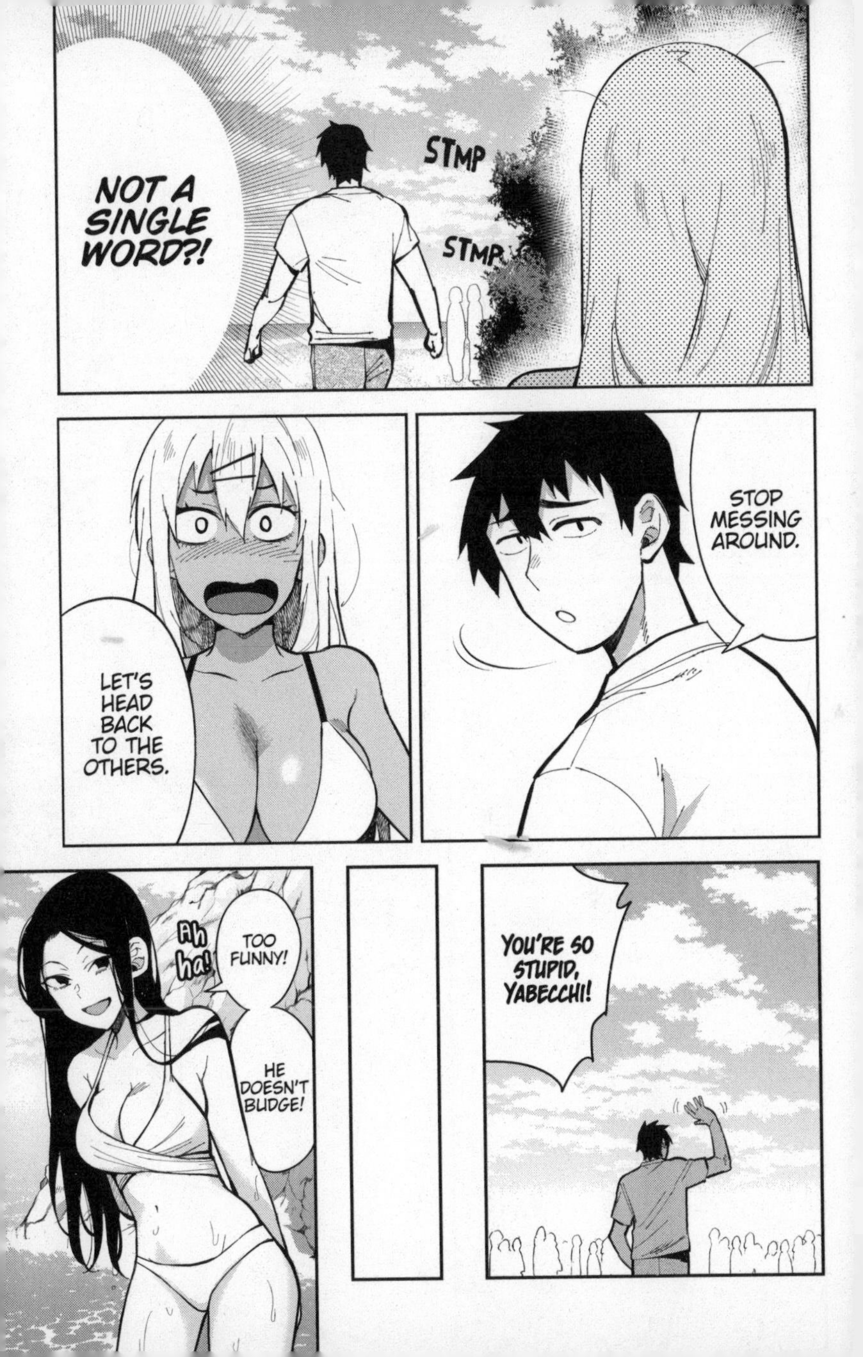
STMP
STMP
NOT A SINGLE WORD?!
STOP MESSING AROUND.
LET'S HEAD BACK TO THE OTHERS.
YOU'RE SO STUPID, YABECCHI!
TOO FUNNY!
Ah ha!
HE DOESN'T BUDGE!

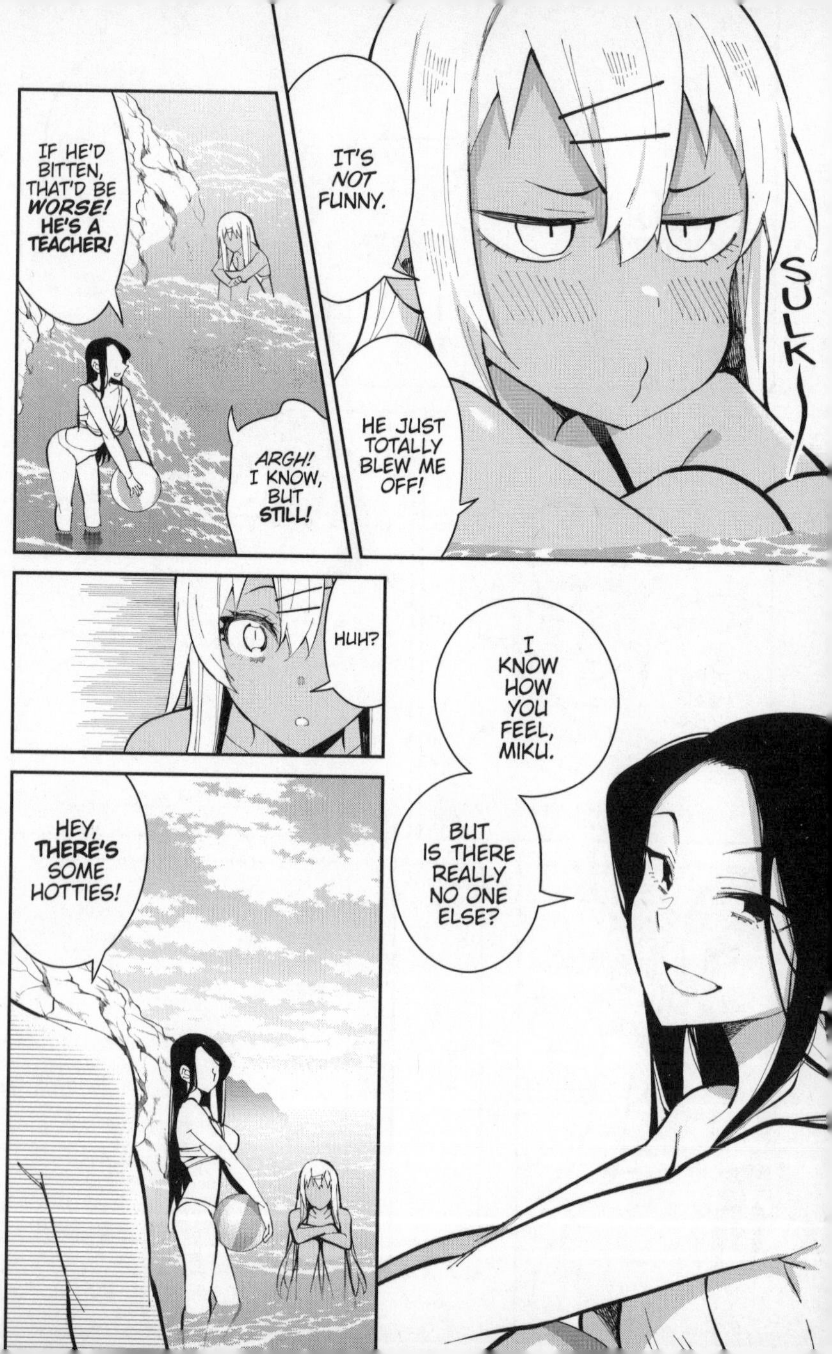
IT'S *NOT* FUNNY.
SULK
HE JUST TOTALLY BLEW ME OFF!
IF HE'D BITTEN, THAT'D BE ***WORSE!*** **HE'S A TEACHER!**
ARGH! I KNOW, BUT **STILL!**
I KNOW HOW YOU FEEL, MIKU.
BUT IS THERE REALLY NO ONE ELSE?
HUH?
HEY, **THERE'S** SOME HOTTIES!

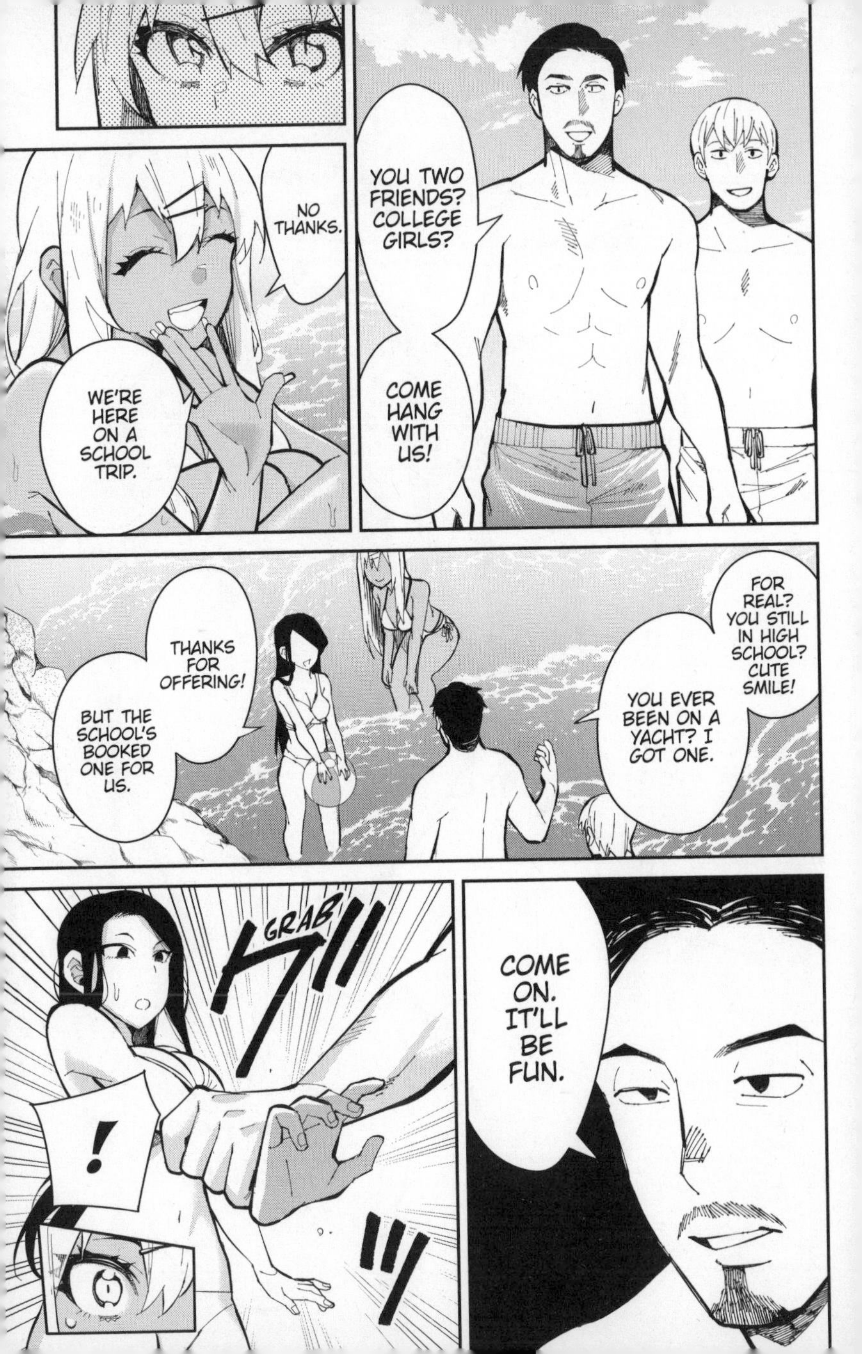
YOU TWO FRIENDS? COLLEGE GIRLS?
COME HANG WITH US!
NO THANKS.
WE'RE HERE ON A SCHOOL TRIP.
FOR REAL? YOU STILL IN HIGH SCHOOL? CUTE SMILE!
YOU EVER BEEN ON A YACHT? I GOT ONE.
THANKS FOR OFFERING!
BUT THE SCHOOL'S BOOKED ONE FOR US.
COME ON. IT'LL BE FUN.
GRAB
!

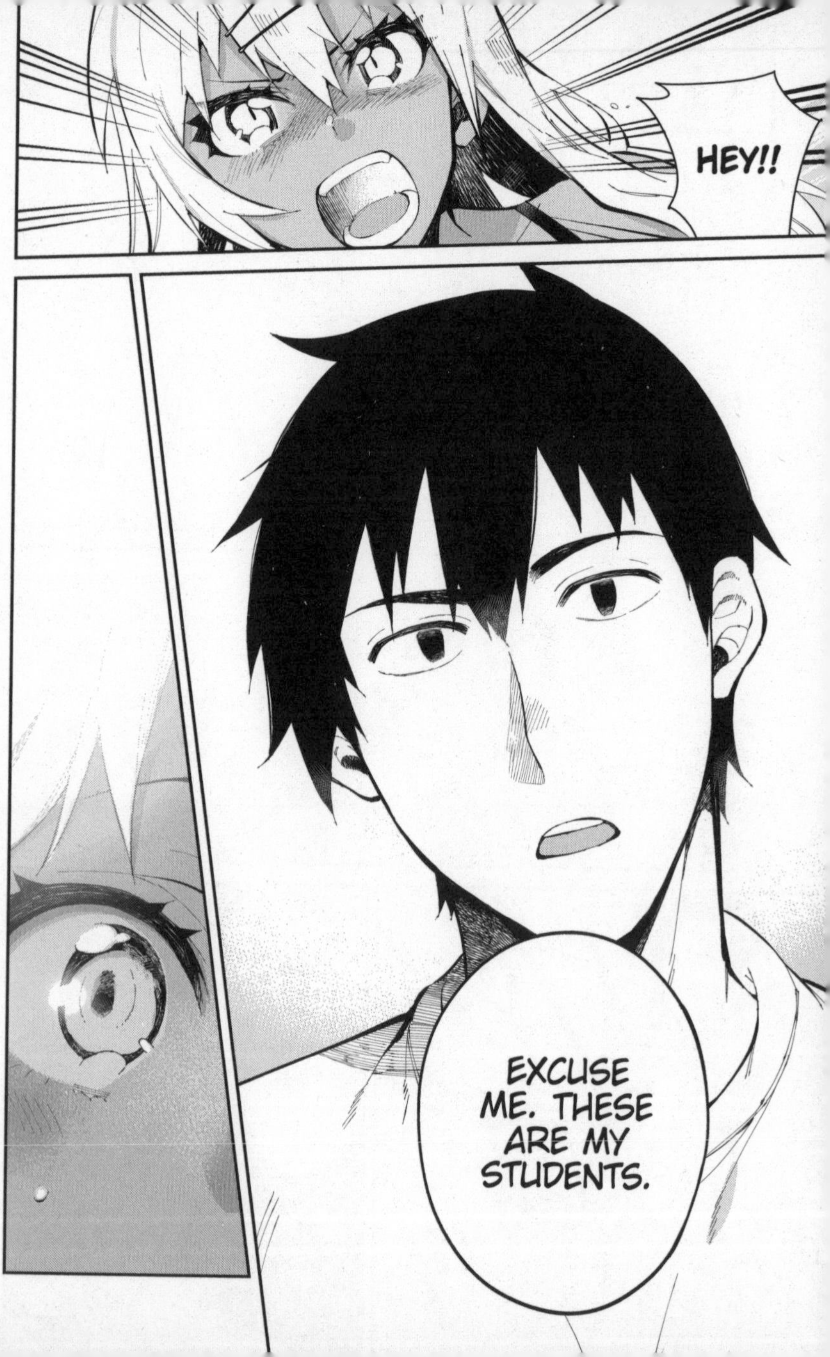
HEY!!
EXCUSE ME. THESE ARE MY STUDENTS.

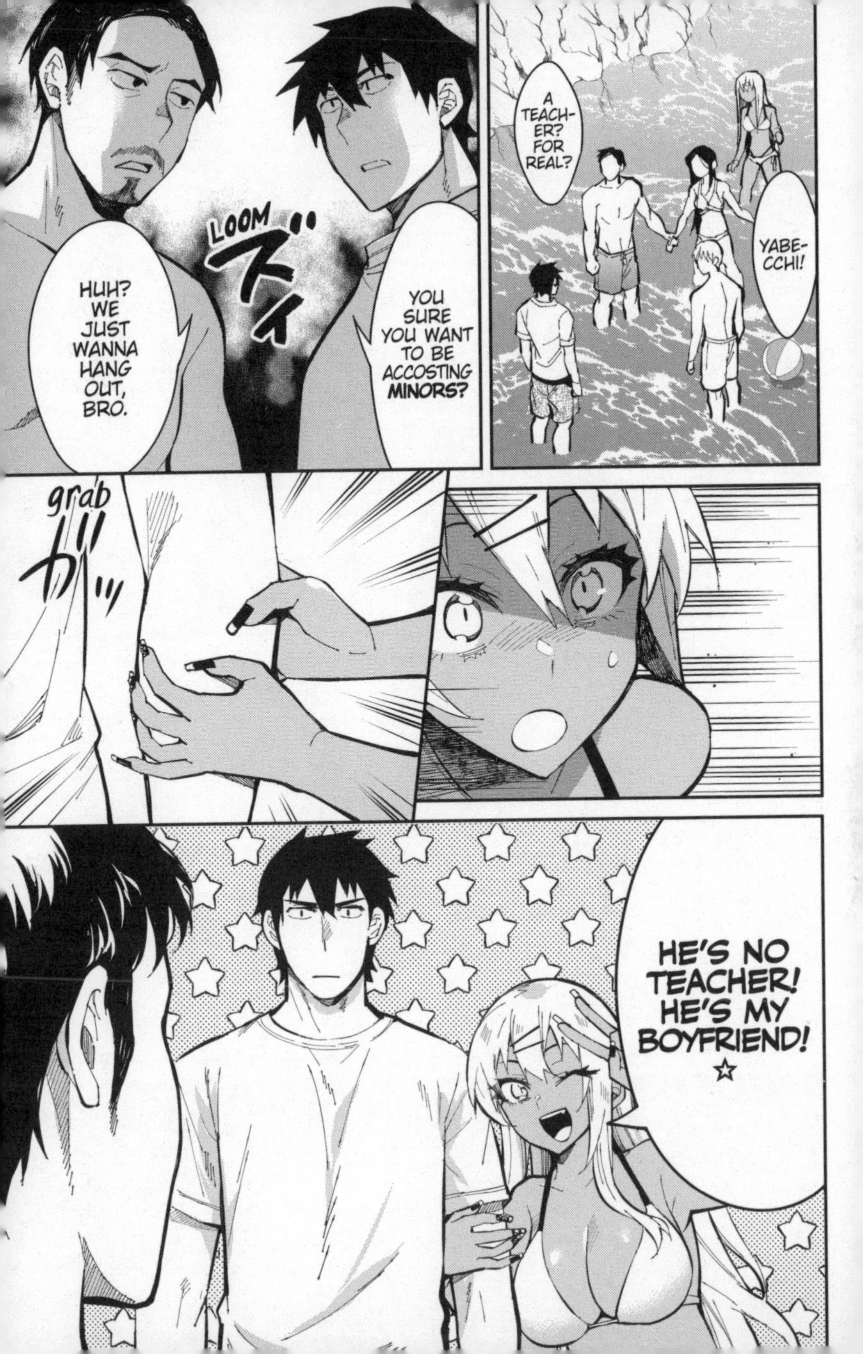
YABE-CCHI!
A TEACHER? FOR REAL?
YOU SURE YOU WANT TO BE ACCOSTING MINORS?
LOOM
HUH? WE JUST WANNA HANG OUT, BRO.
grab
HE'S NO TEACHER! HE'S MY BOYFRIEND! ☆

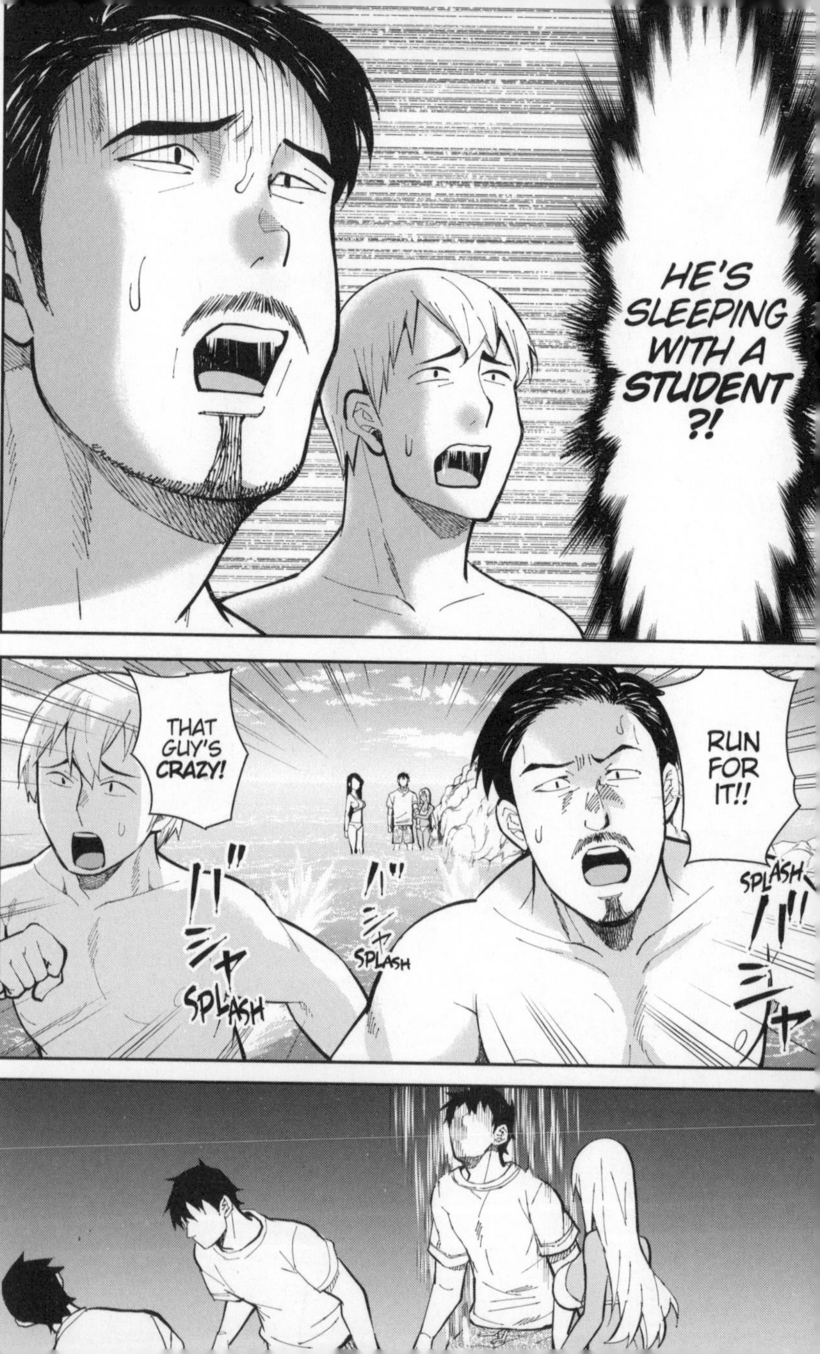
HE'S SLEEPING WITH A STUDENT?!
RUN FOR IT!!
SPLASH
バ!!
シャ
THAT GUY'S CRAZY!
バ!!
シャ
SPLASH
バ!!
シャ
SPLASH

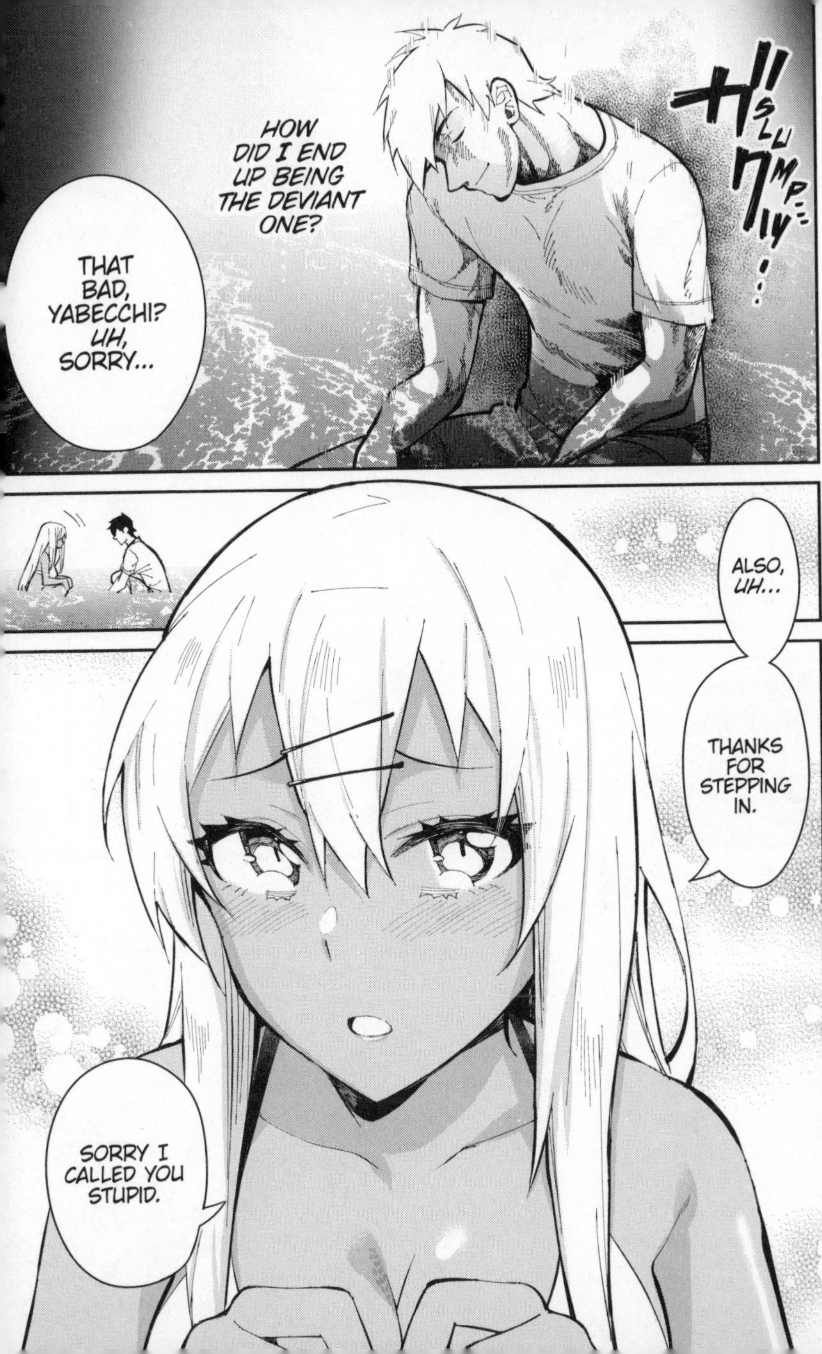
SLUMP
HOW DID I END UP BEING THE DEVIANT ONE?
THAT BAD, YABECCHI? UH, SORRY...
ALSO, UH...
THANKS FOR STEPPING IN.
SORRY I CALLED YOU STUPID.

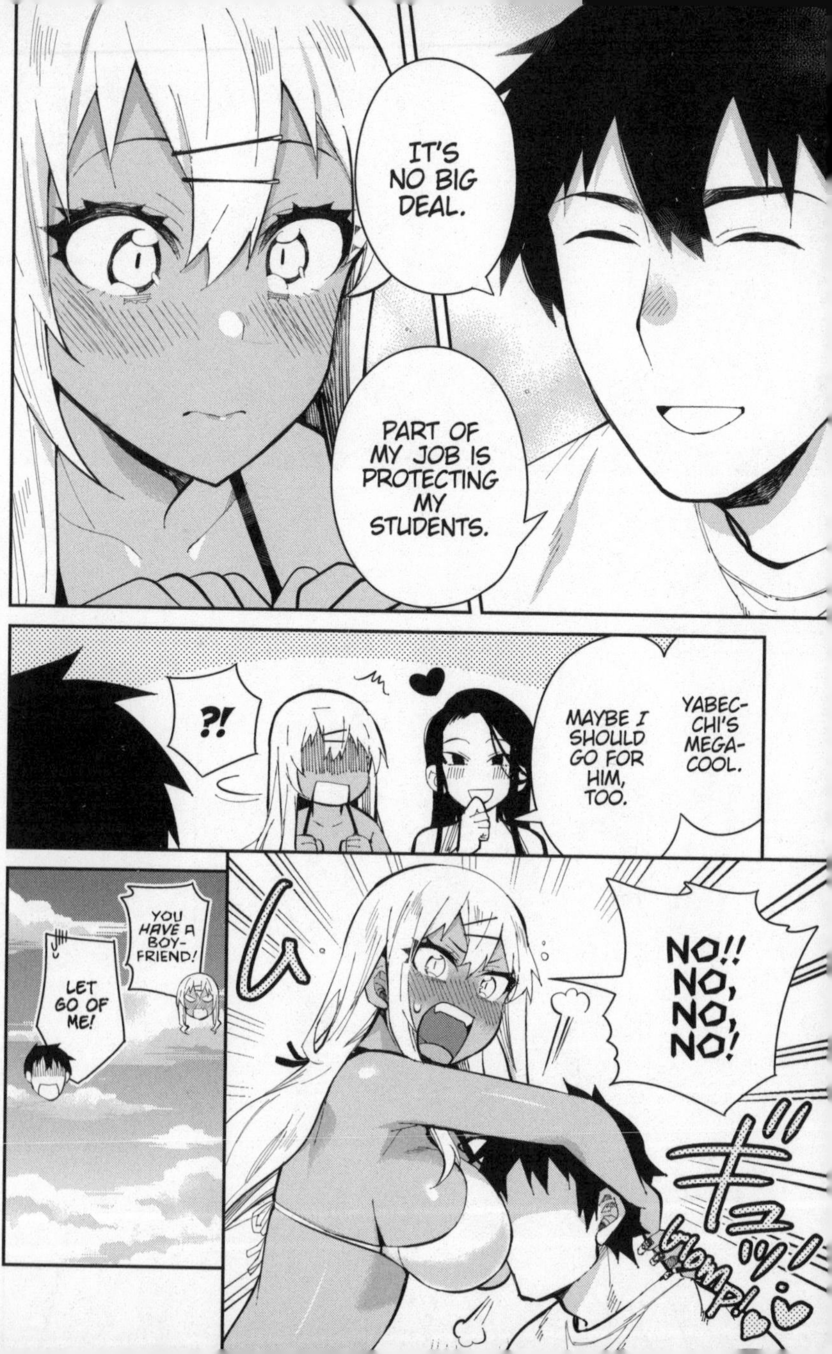
IT'S NO BIG DEAL.
PART OF MY JOB IS PROTECTING MY STUDENTS.
YABEC-CHI'S MEGA-COOL.
MAYBE I SHOULD GO FOR HIM, TOO.
?!
NO!! NO, NO, NO!
GLOMP!
YOU HAVE A BOY-FRIEND!
LET GO OF ME!

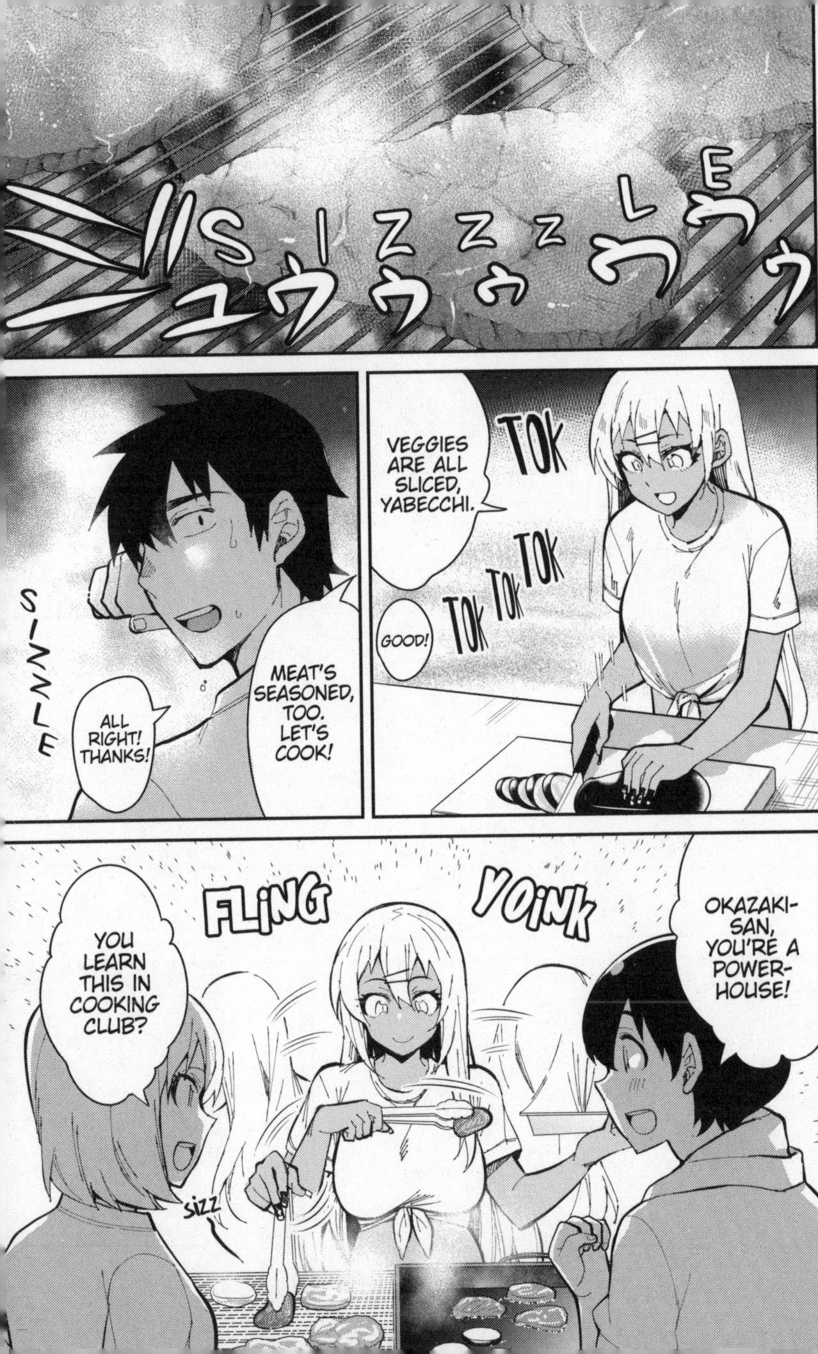
SIZZZZLE
VEGGIES ARE ALL SLICED, YABECCHI.
TOK
TOK TOK TOK
GOOD!
MEAT'S SEASONED, TOO. LET'S COOK!
ALL RIGHT! THANKS!
SIZZLE
OKAZAKI-SAN, YOU'RE A POWER-HOUSE!
YOINK
FLING
YOU LEARN THIS IN COOKING CLUB?
SIZZ

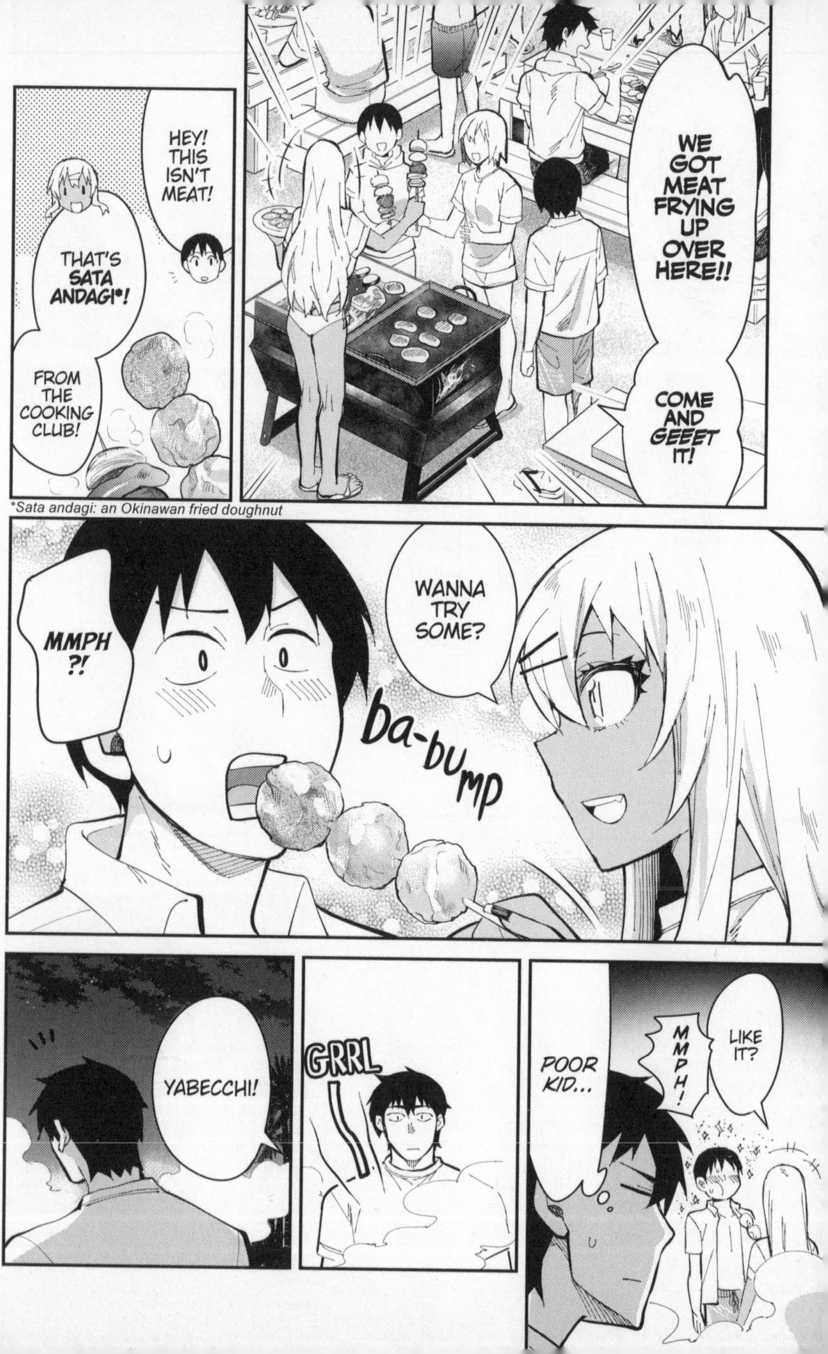
WE GOT MEAT FRYING UP OVER HERE!!
COME AND GEEET IT!
HEY! THIS ISN'T MEAT!
THAT'S SATA ANDAGI*!
FROM THE COOKING CLUB!
WANNA TRY SOME?
ba-bump
MMPH ?!
LIKE IT?
MMPH!
POOR KID...
GRRL
YABECCHI!

*Sata andagi: an Okinawan fried doughnut

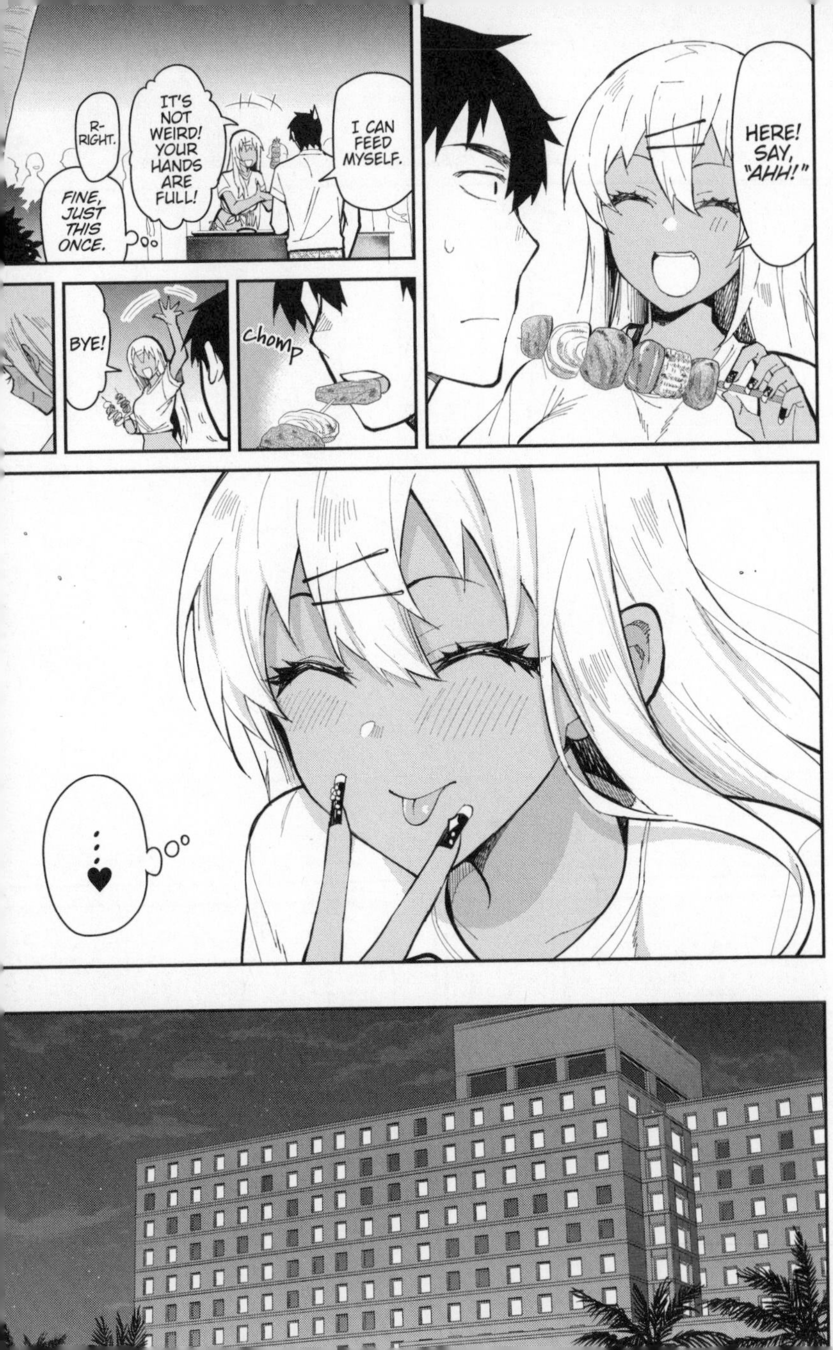
HERE! SAY, "AHH!"
I CAN FEED MYSELF.
IT'S NOT WEIRD! YOUR HANDS ARE FULL!
R-RIGHT.
FINE, JUST THIS ONCE.
chomp
BYE!
...♥

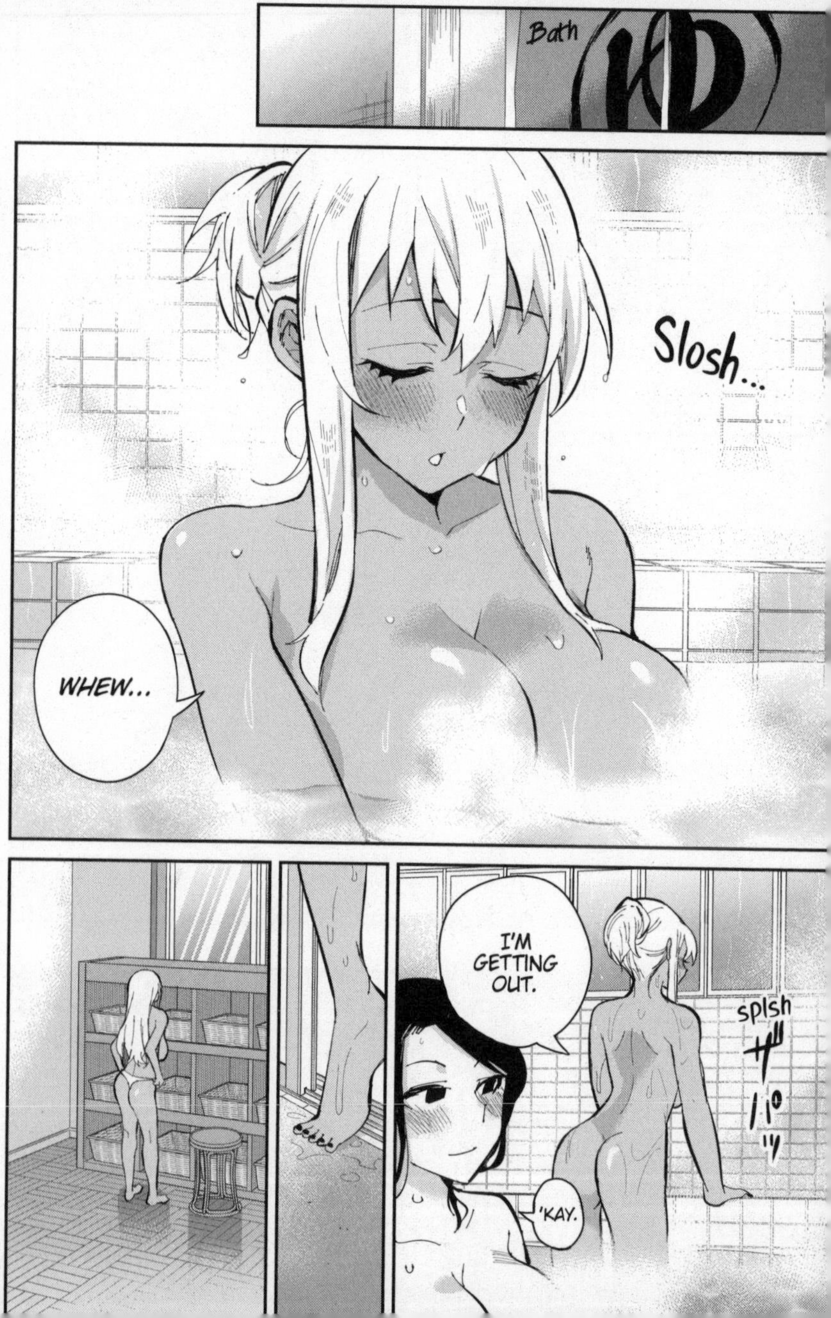
Bath
Slosh...
WHEW...
I'M GETTING OUT.
splsh
'KAY.

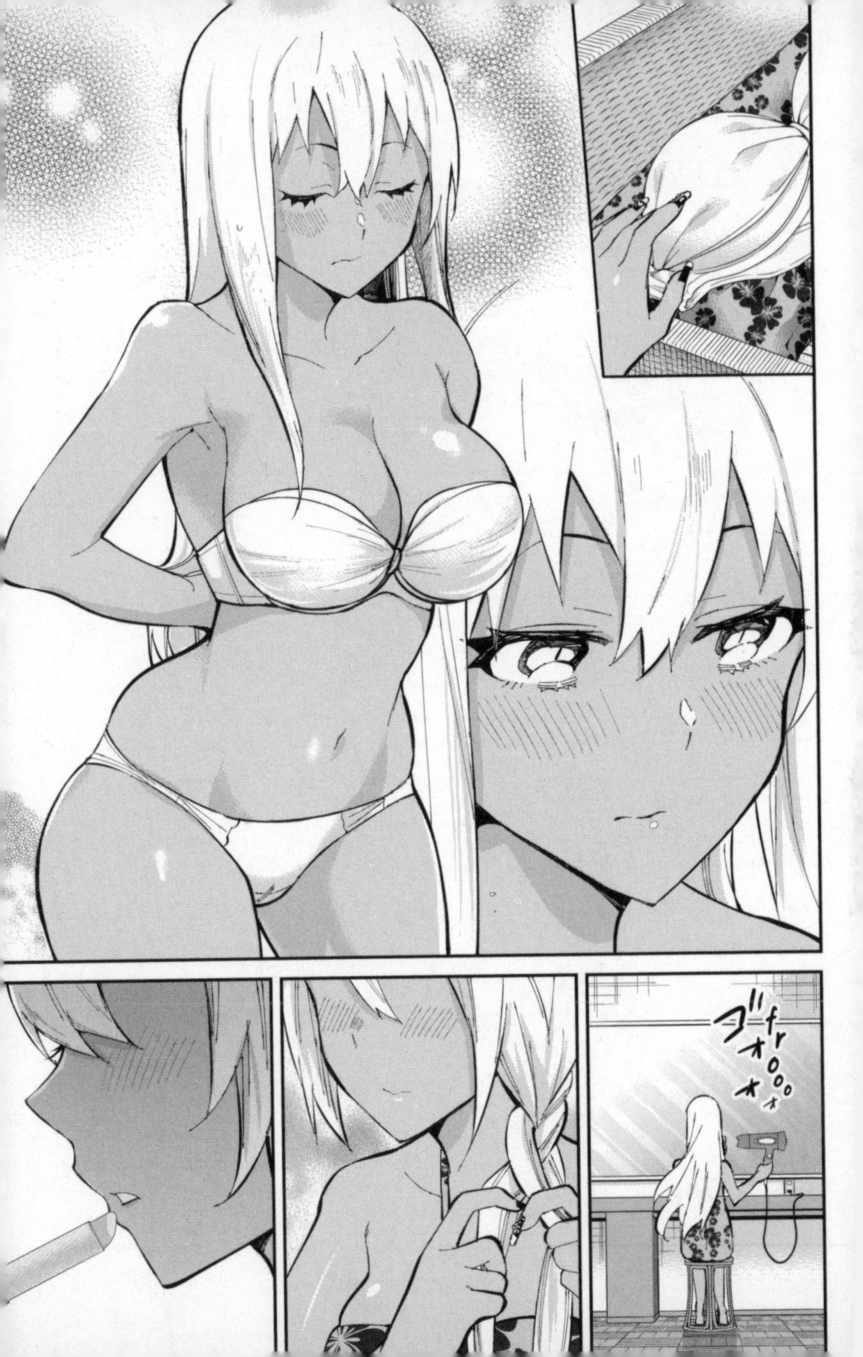
ゴォォォ
frooo

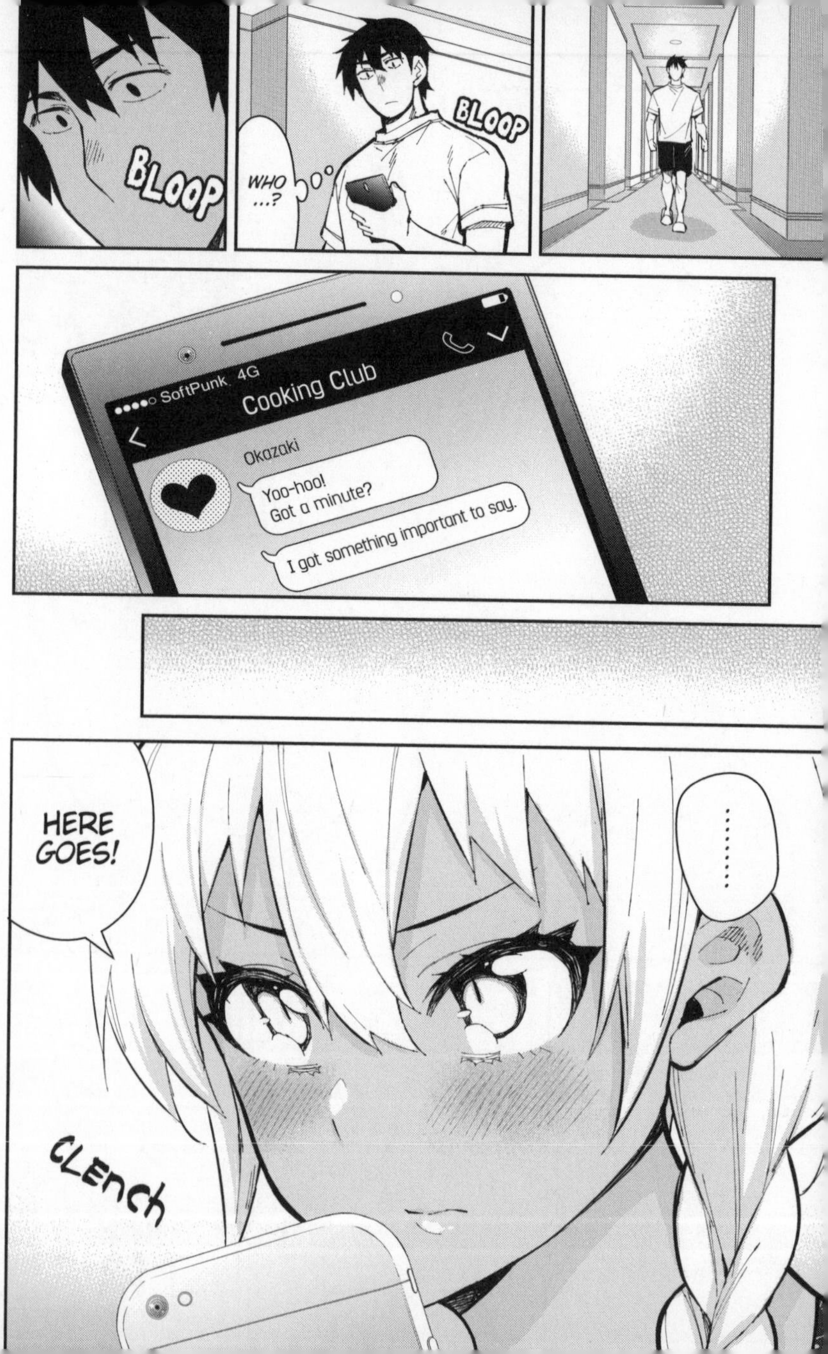

BLOOP
WHO ...?
BLOOP
SoftPunk 4G
Cooking Club
Okazaki
Yoo-hoo!
Got a minute?
I got something important to say.
......
HERE GOES!
CLENCH

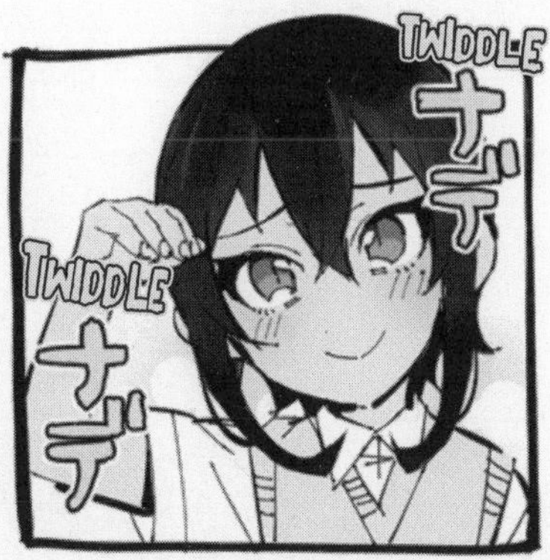
TWIDDLE
ナデ
TWIDDLE
ナデ

Gal
Gohan

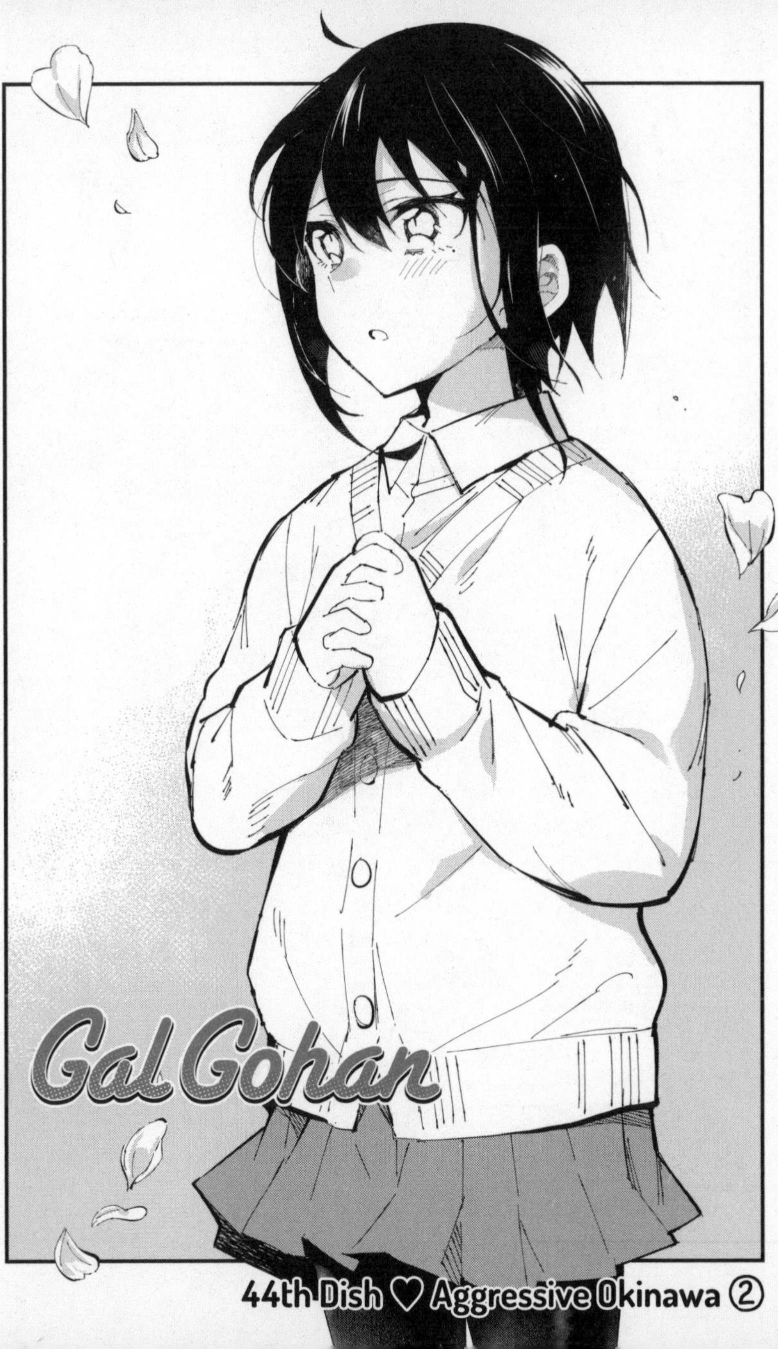
Gal Gohan
44th Dish ♡ Aggressive Okinawa ②

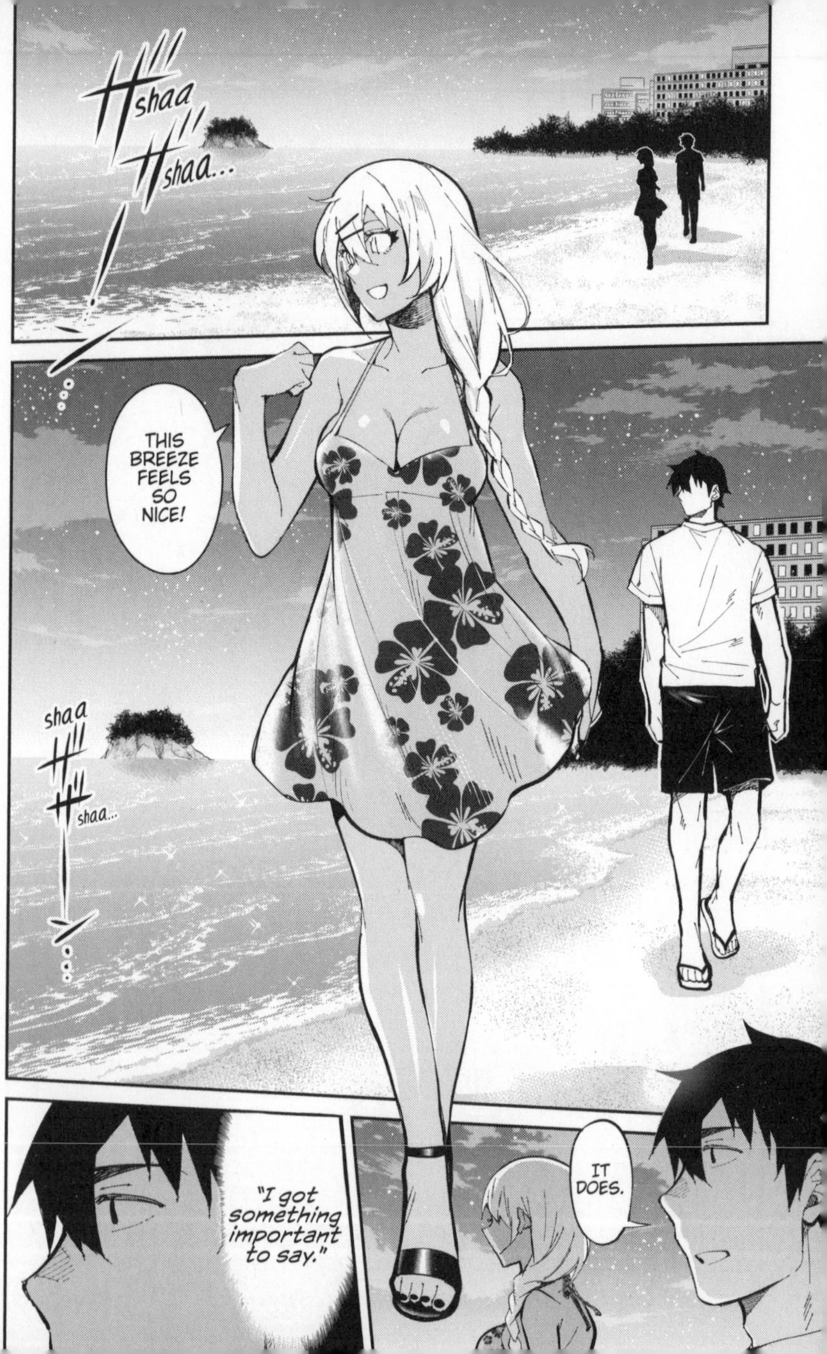
shaa
shaa...
THIS BREEZE FEELS SO NICE!
shaa
shaa...
IT DOES.
"I got something important to say."

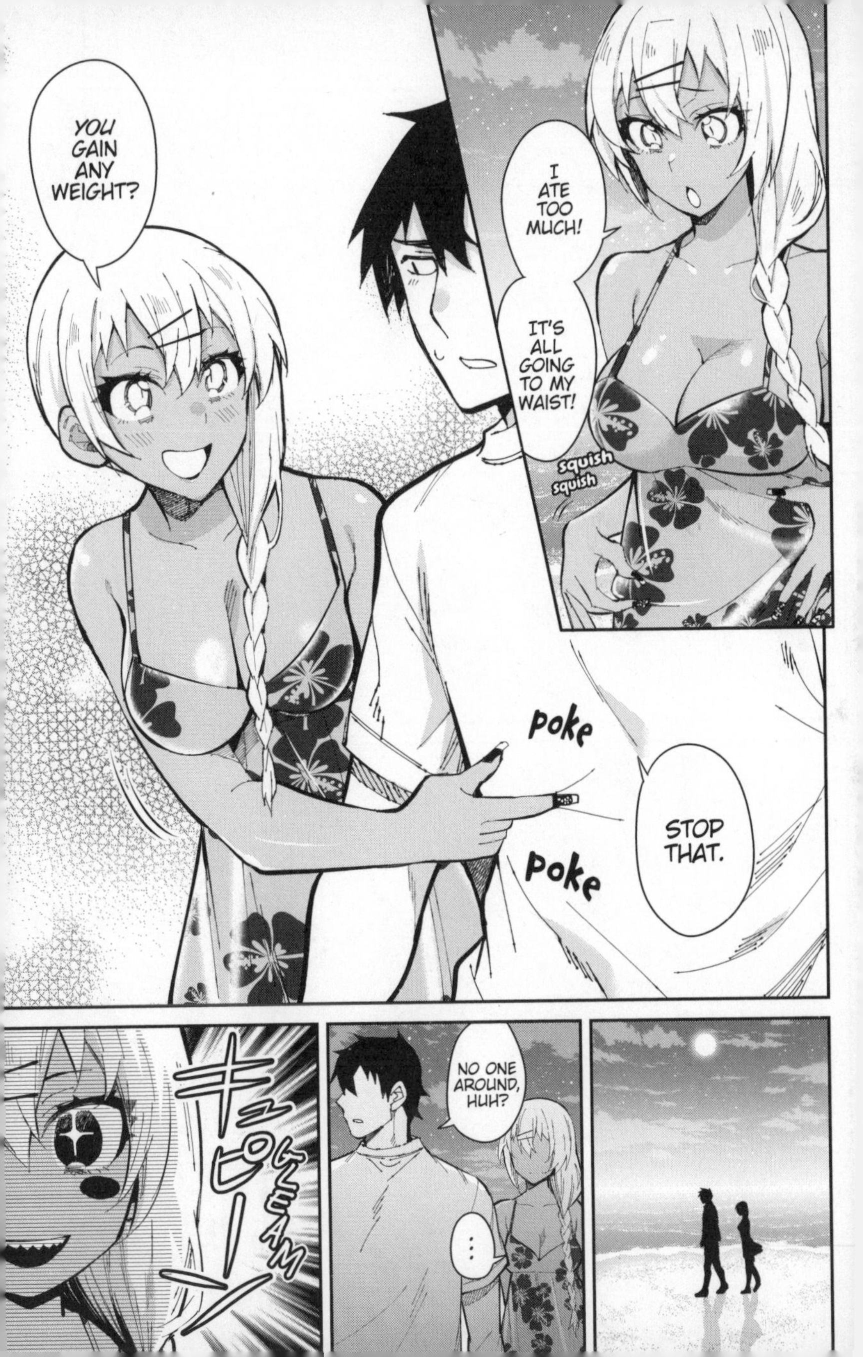
I ATE TOO MUCH!
IT'S ALL GOING TO MY WAIST!
squish squish
YOU GAIN ANY WEIGHT?
poke
poke
STOP THAT.
NO ONE AROUND, HUH?
...
GLEAM

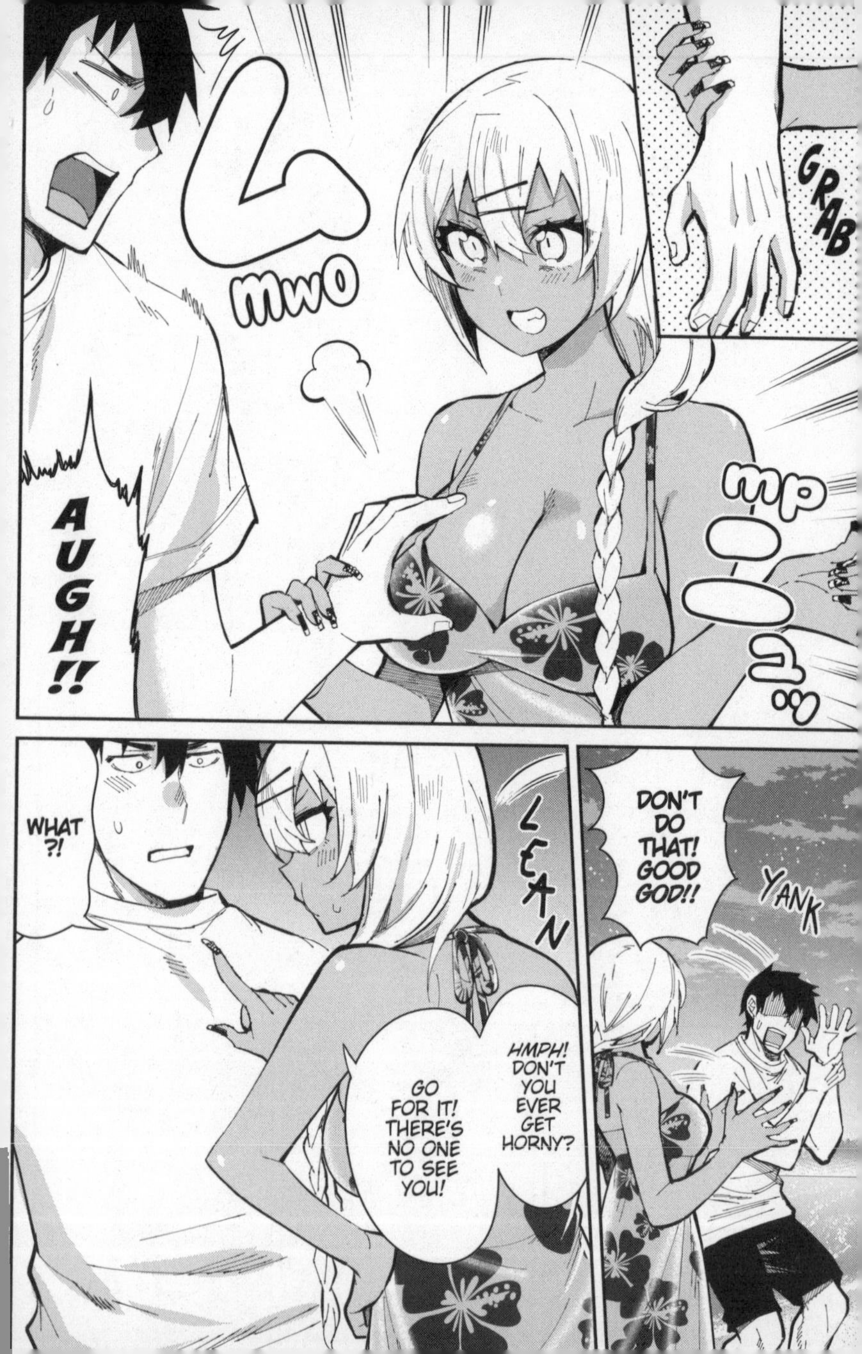
GRAB
mwo
mp
AUGH!!
DON'T DO THAT! GOOD GOD!!
YANK
LEAN
WHAT ?!
HMPH! DON'T YOU EVER GET HORNY?
GO FOR IT! THERE'S NO ONE TO SEE YOU!

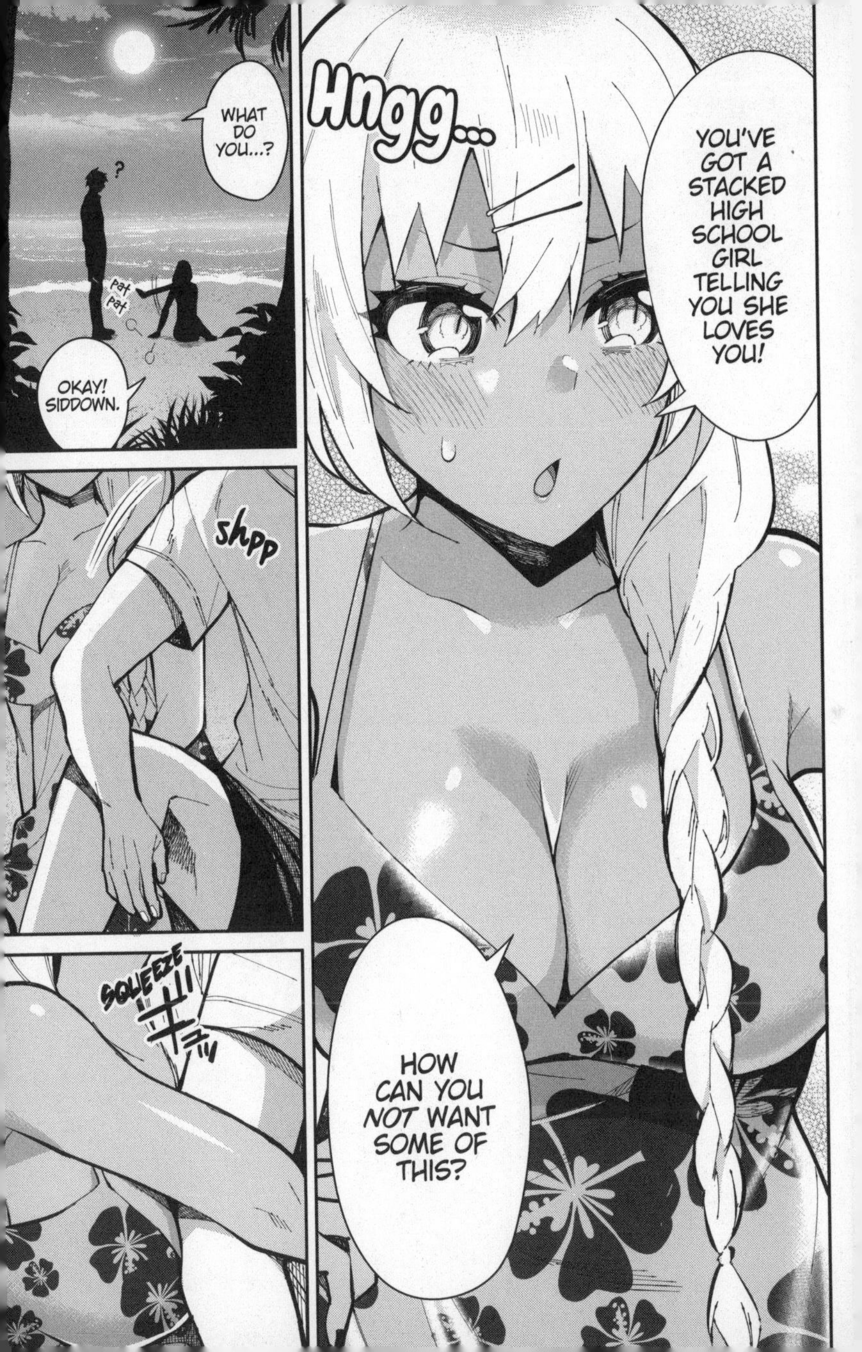
Hngg...
YOU'VE GOT A STACKED HIGH SCHOOL GIRL TELLING YOU SHE LOVES YOU!
HOW CAN YOU *NOT* WANT SOME OF THIS?
WHAT DO YOU...?
?
pat pat
OKAY! SIDDOWN.
shpp
SQUEEZE

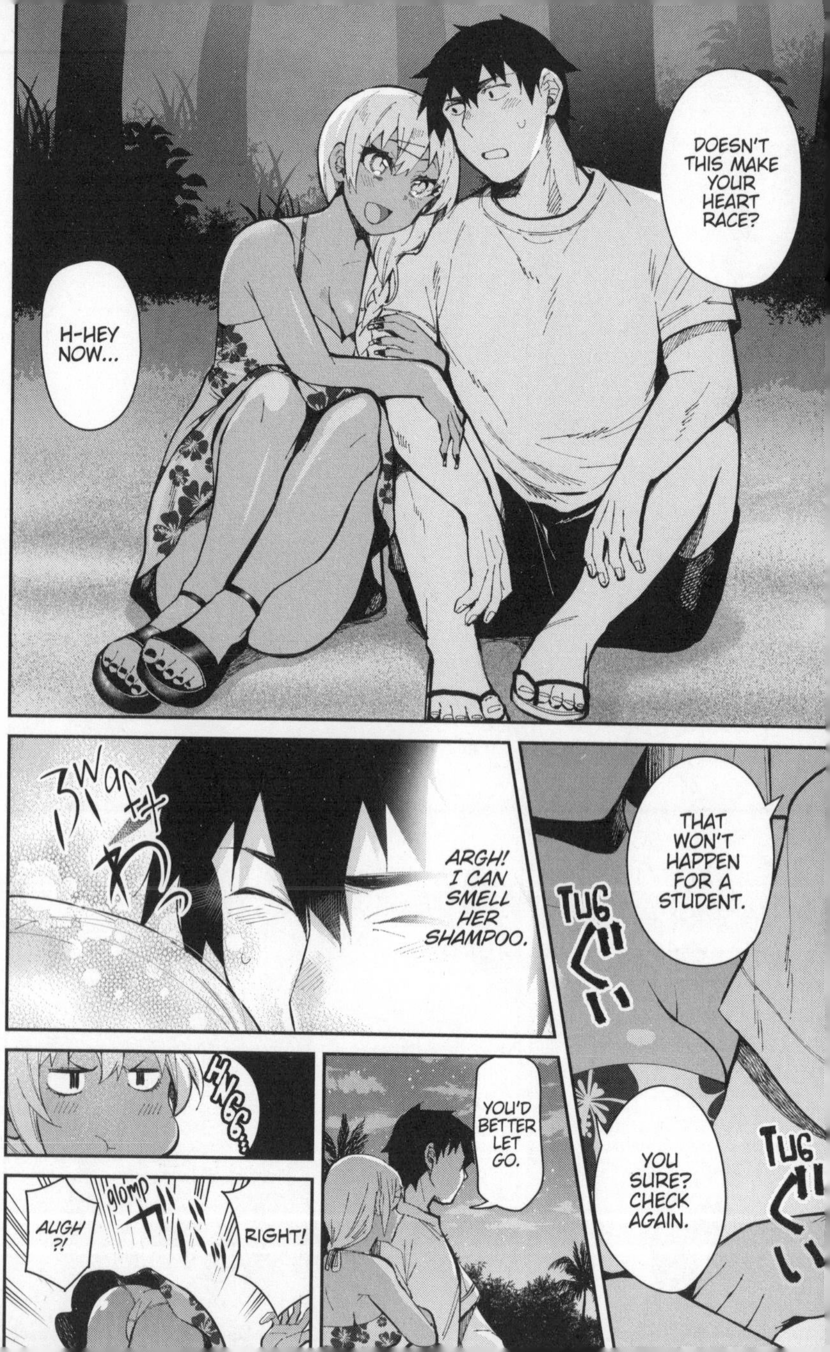
DOESN'T THIS MAKE YOUR HEART RACE?
H-HEY NOW...
THAT WON'T HAPPEN FOR A STUDENT.
TUG
ARGH! I CAN SMELL HER SHAMPOO.
WAFT
TUG
YOU SURE? CHECK AGAIN.
YOU'D BETTER LET GO.
HNGG...
RIGHT!
glomp
AUGH?!

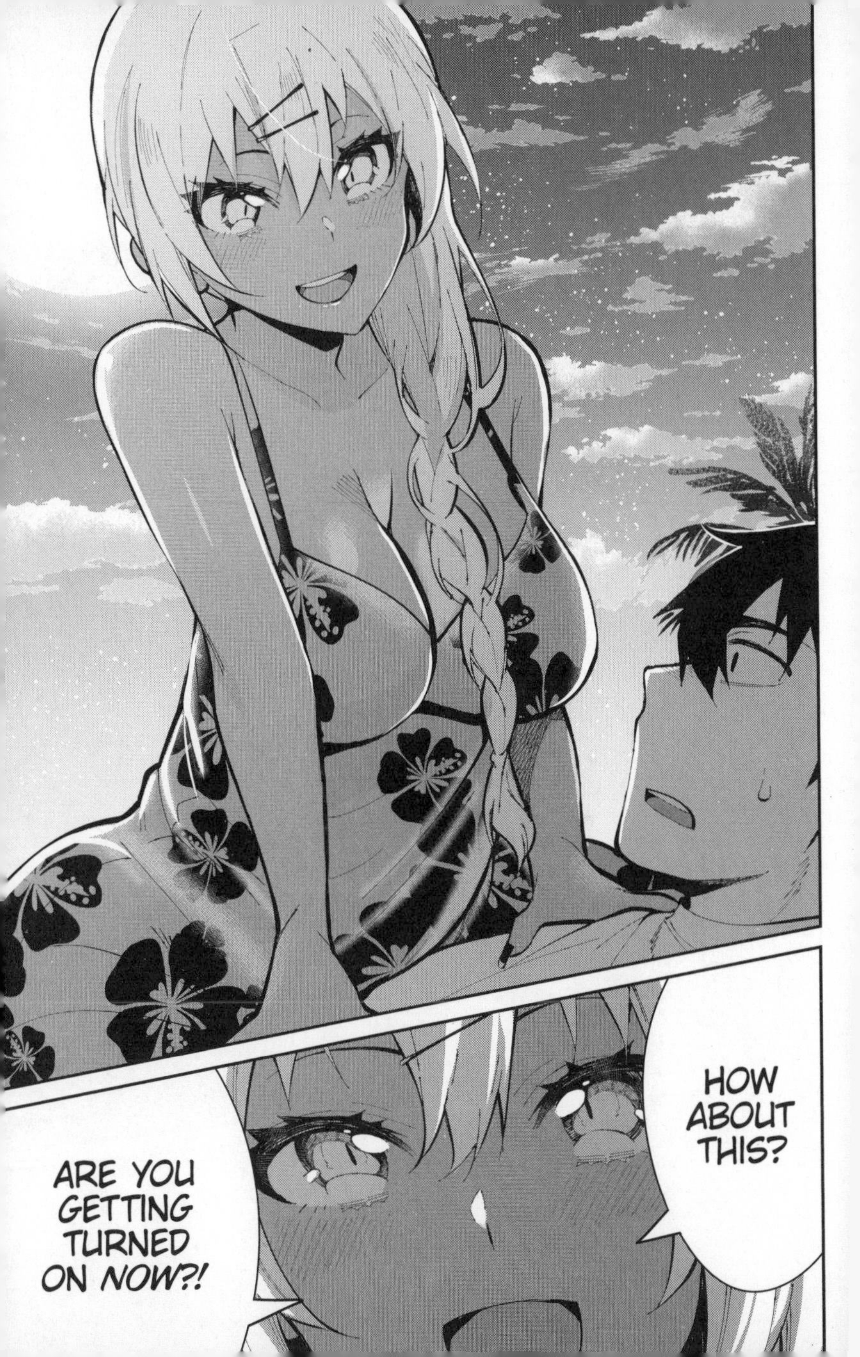
HOW ABOUT THIS?
ARE YOU GETTING TURNED ON *NOW*?!

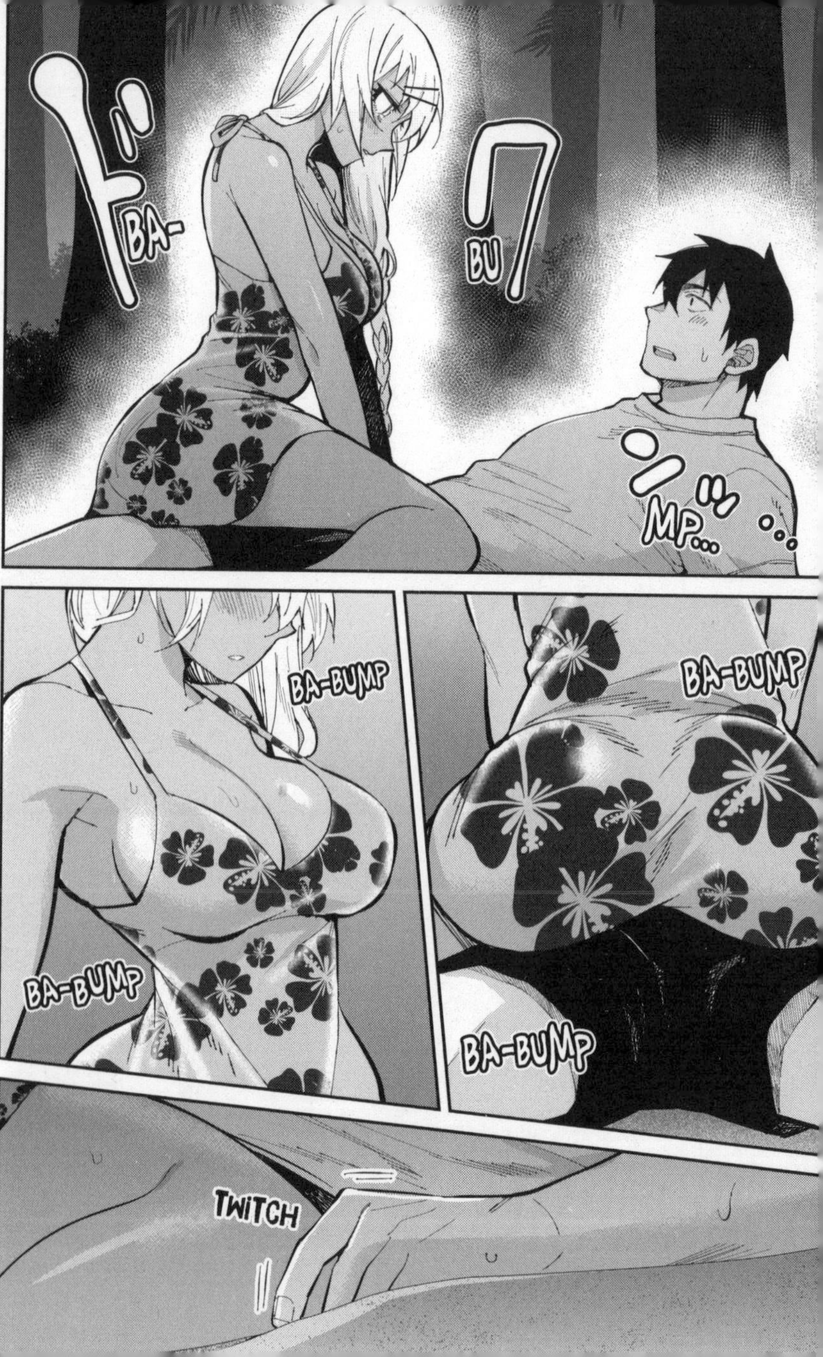
BA-
BU
MP...
...
BA-BUMP
BA-BUMP
BA-BUMP
BA-BUMP
TWITCH

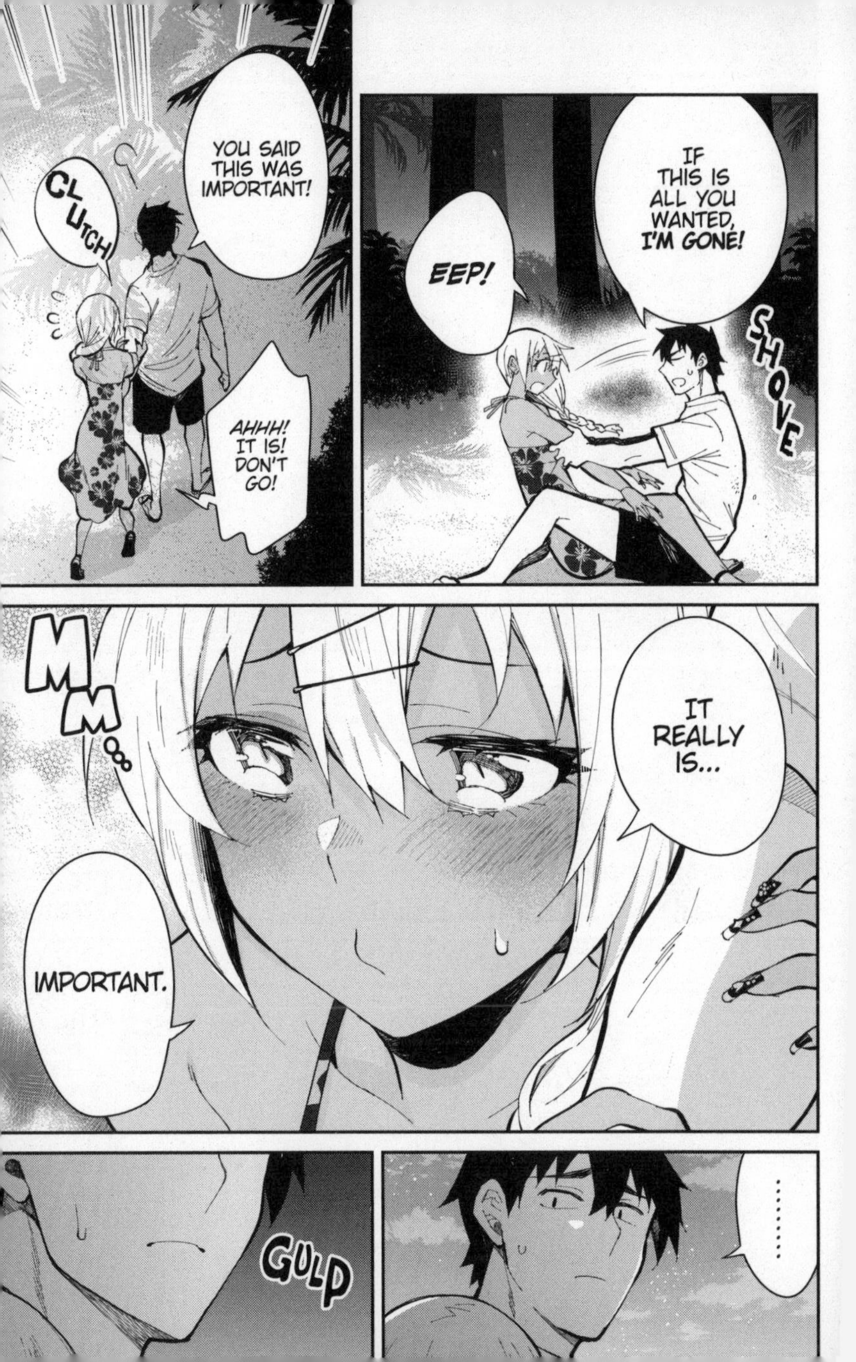
IF THIS IS ALL YOU WANTED, I'M GONE!
SHOVE
EEP!
YOU SAID THIS WAS IMPORTANT!
CLUTCH
AHHH! IT IS! DON'T GO!
IT REALLY IS...
MMM
IMPORTANT.
......
GULP

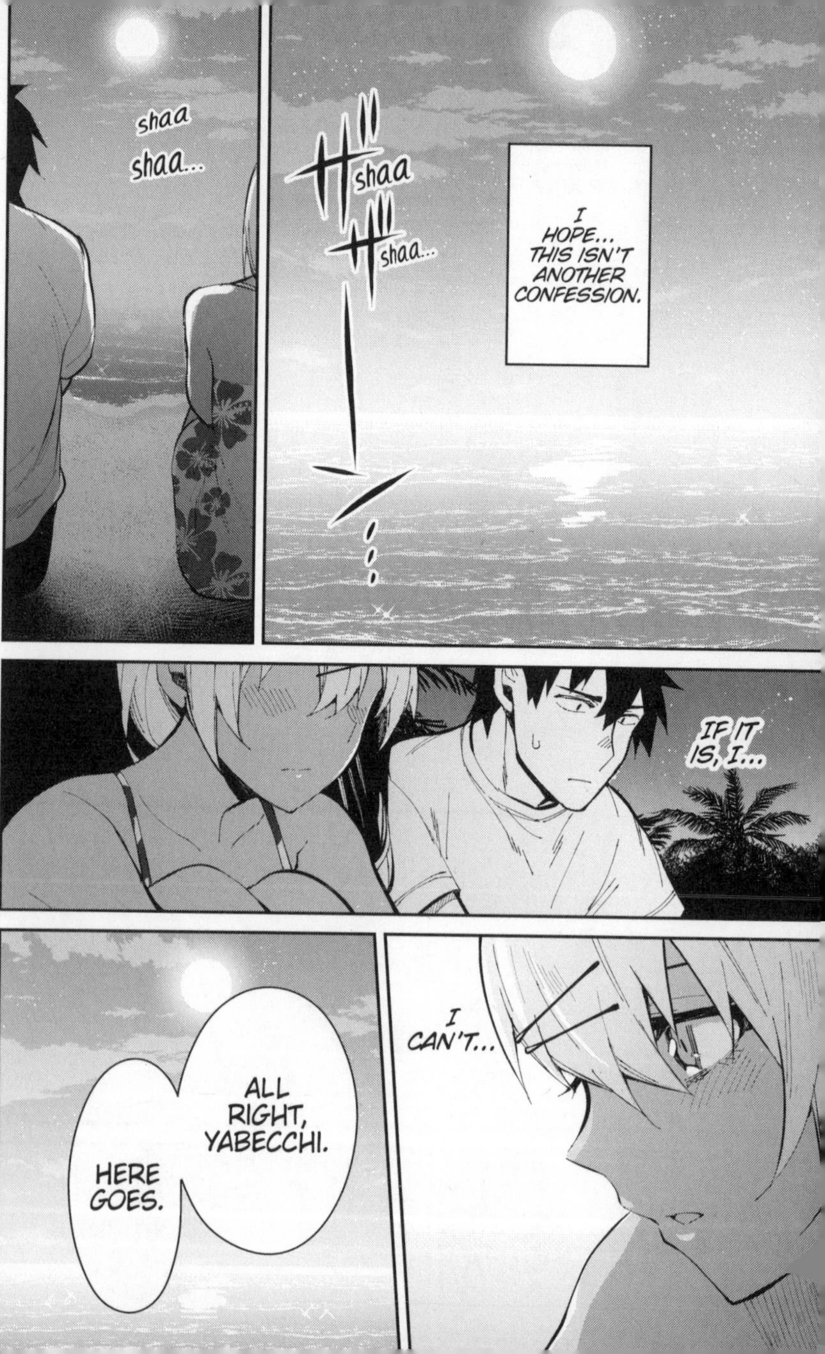
shaa
shaa...
I HOPE... THIS ISN'T ANOTHER CONFESSION.
shaa
shaa...
IF IT IS, I...
I CAN'T...
ALL RIGHT, YABECCHI.
HERE GOES.

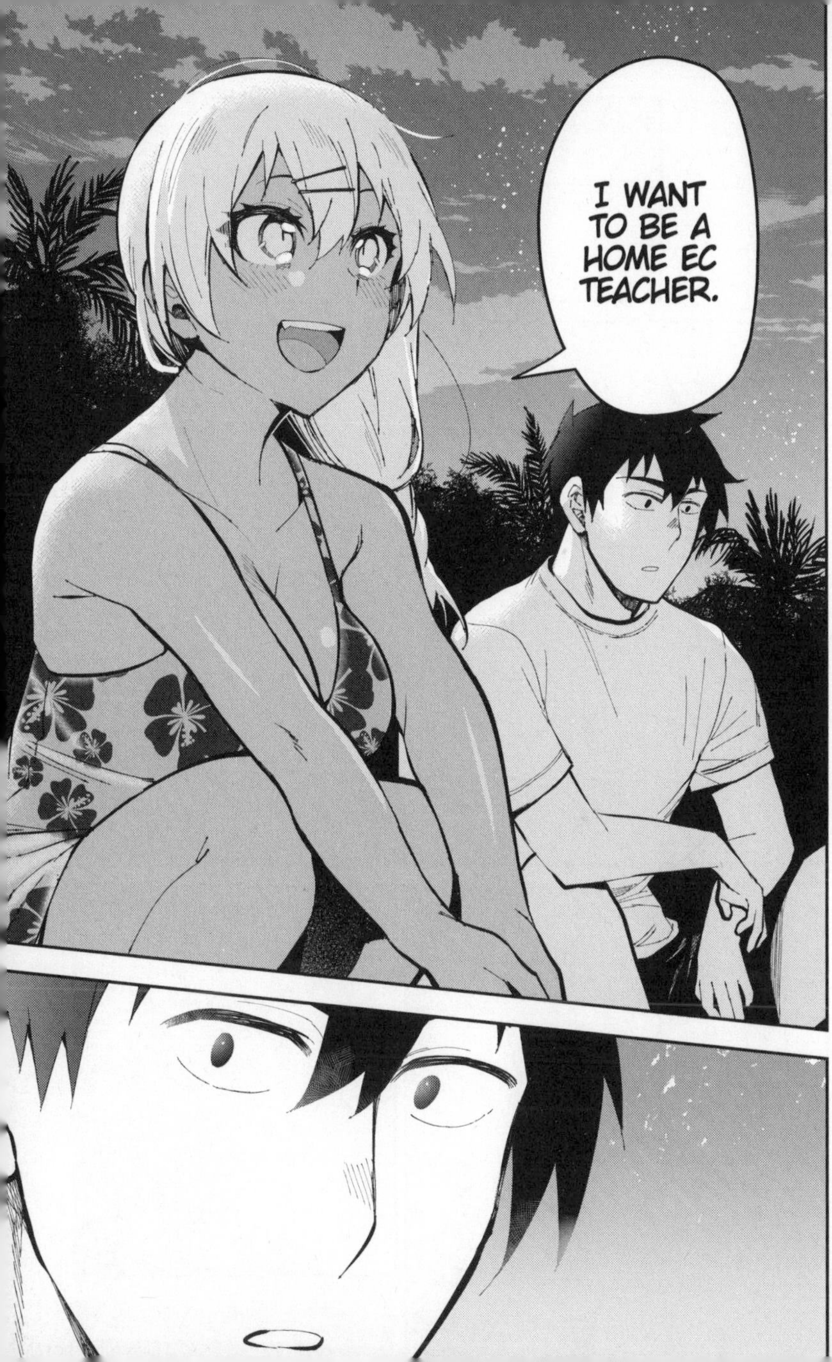
I WANT TO BE A HOME EC TEACHER.

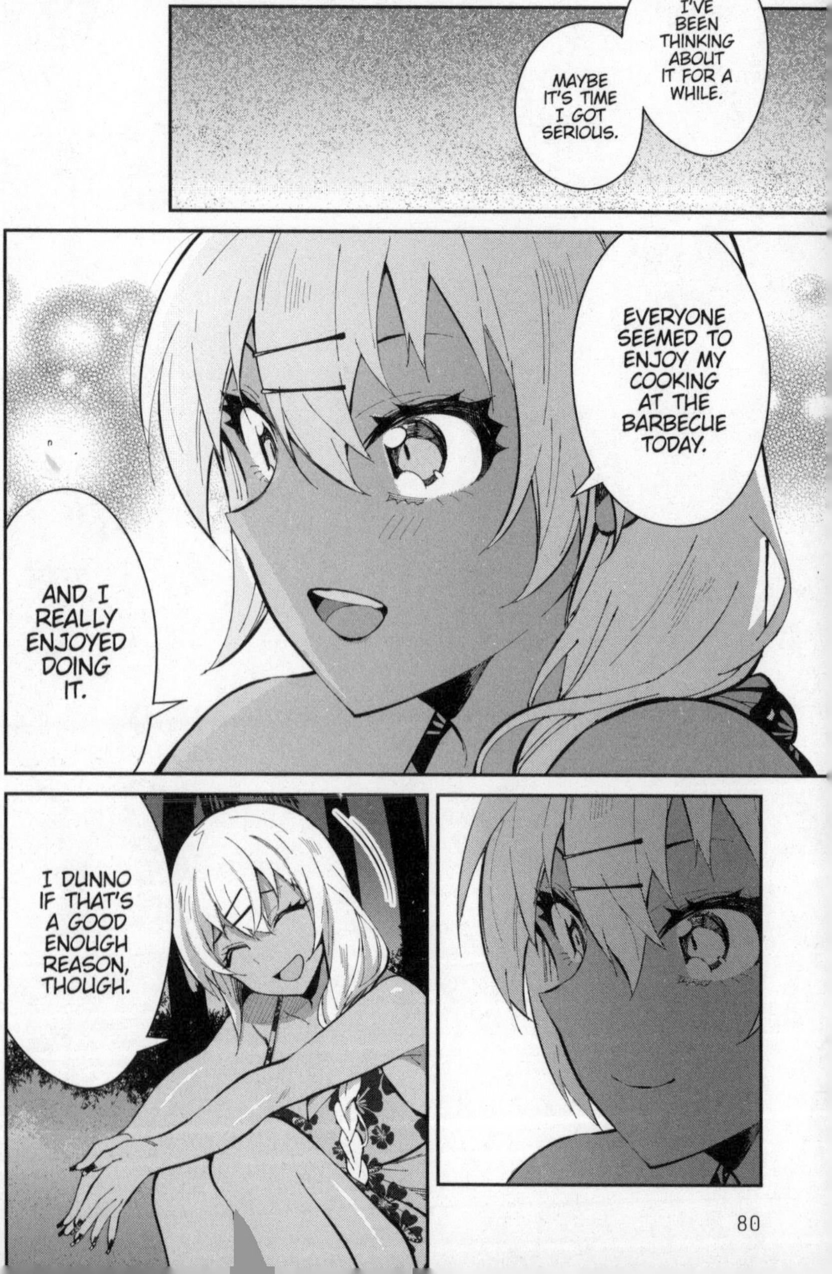
I'VE BEEN THINKING ABOUT IT FOR A WHILE.
MAYBE IT'S TIME I GOT SERIOUS.
EVERYONE SEEMED TO ENJOY MY COOKING AT THE BARBECUE TODAY.
AND I REALLY ENJOYED DOING IT.
I DUNNO IF THAT'S A GOOD ENOUGH REASON, THOUGH.

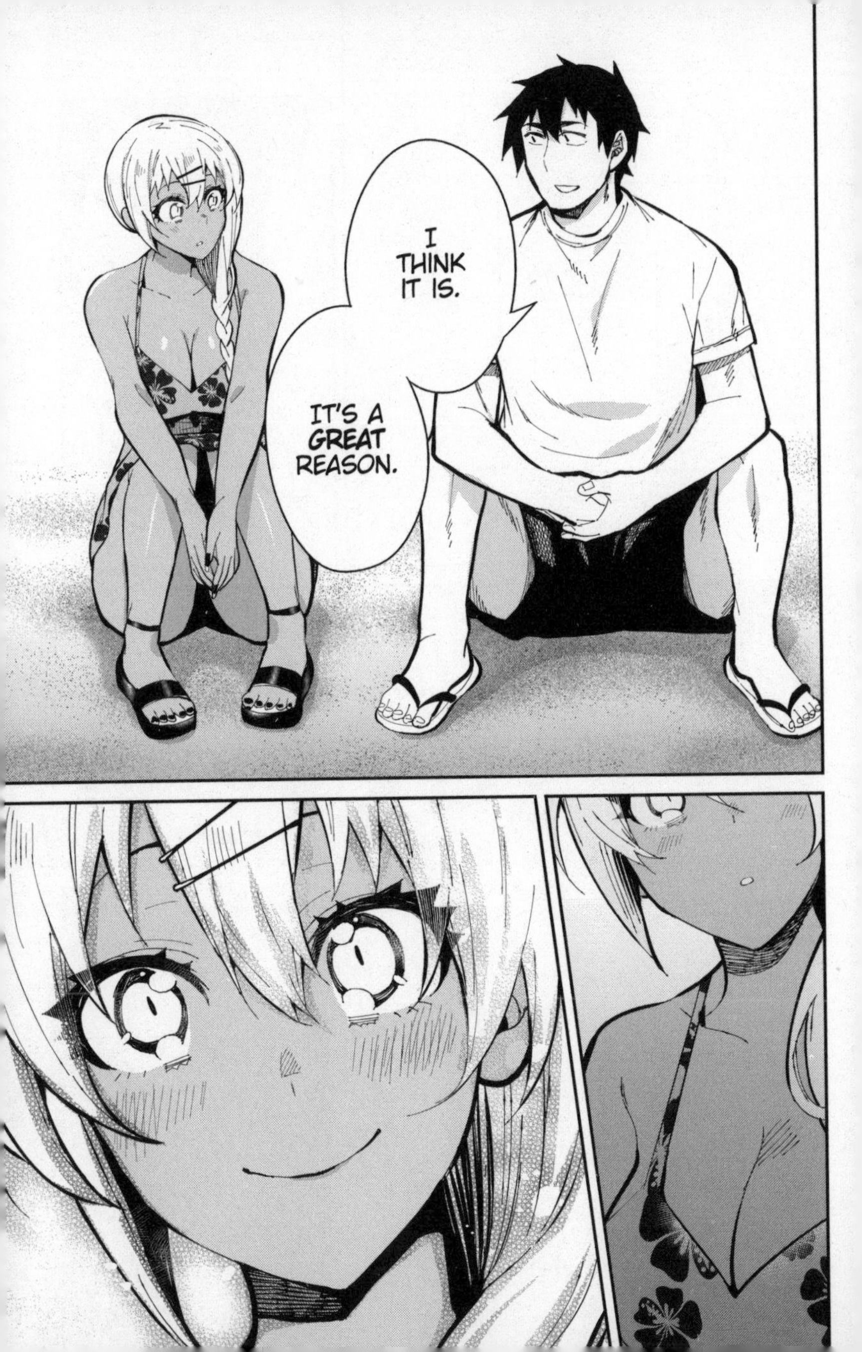
I THINK IT IS.
IT'S A GREAT REASON.

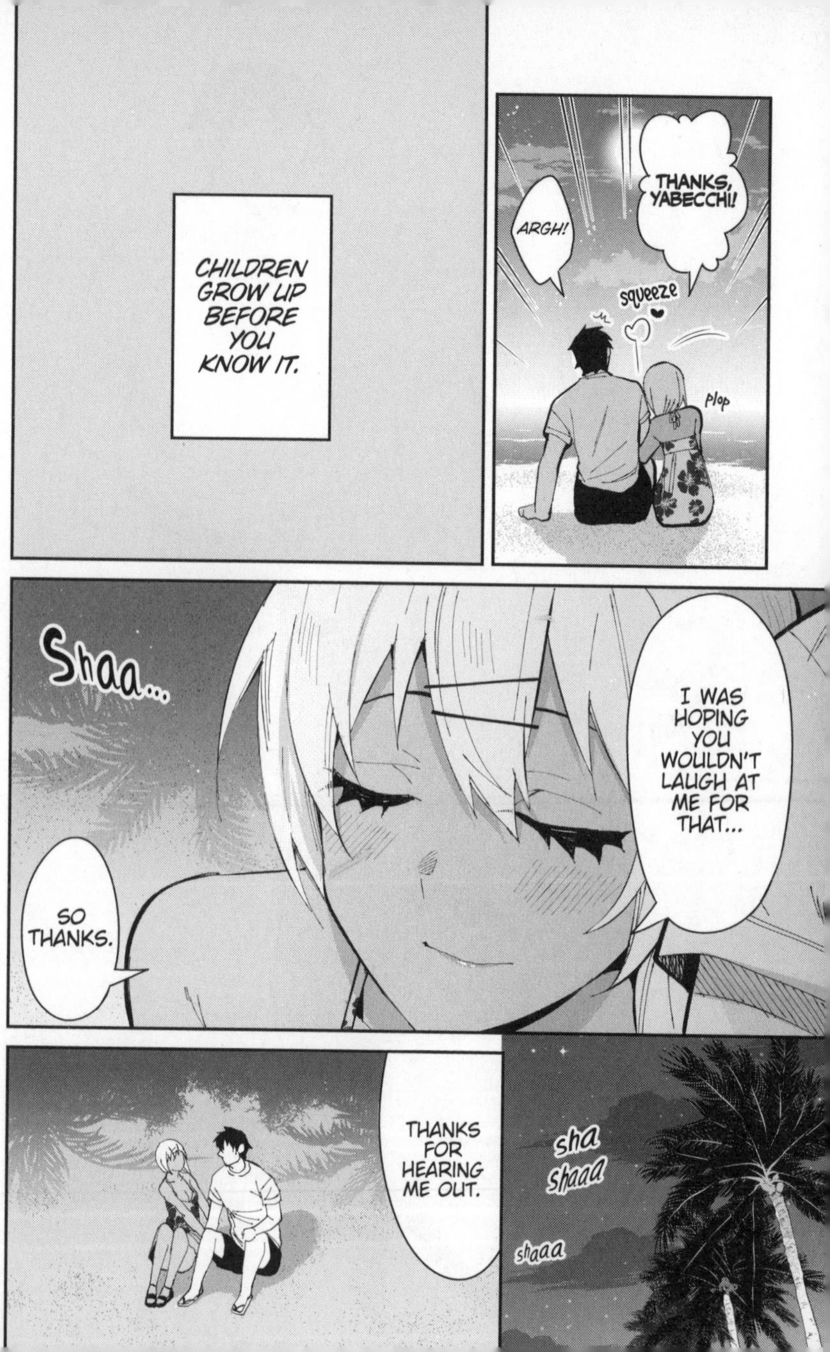
THANKS, YABECCHI!
ARGH!
squeeze
plop
CHILDREN GROW UP BEFORE YOU KNOW IT.
I WAS HOPING YOU WOULDN'T LAUGH AT ME FOR THAT...
Shaa...
SO THANKS.
sha shaaa
shaaa
THANKS FOR HEARING ME OUT.

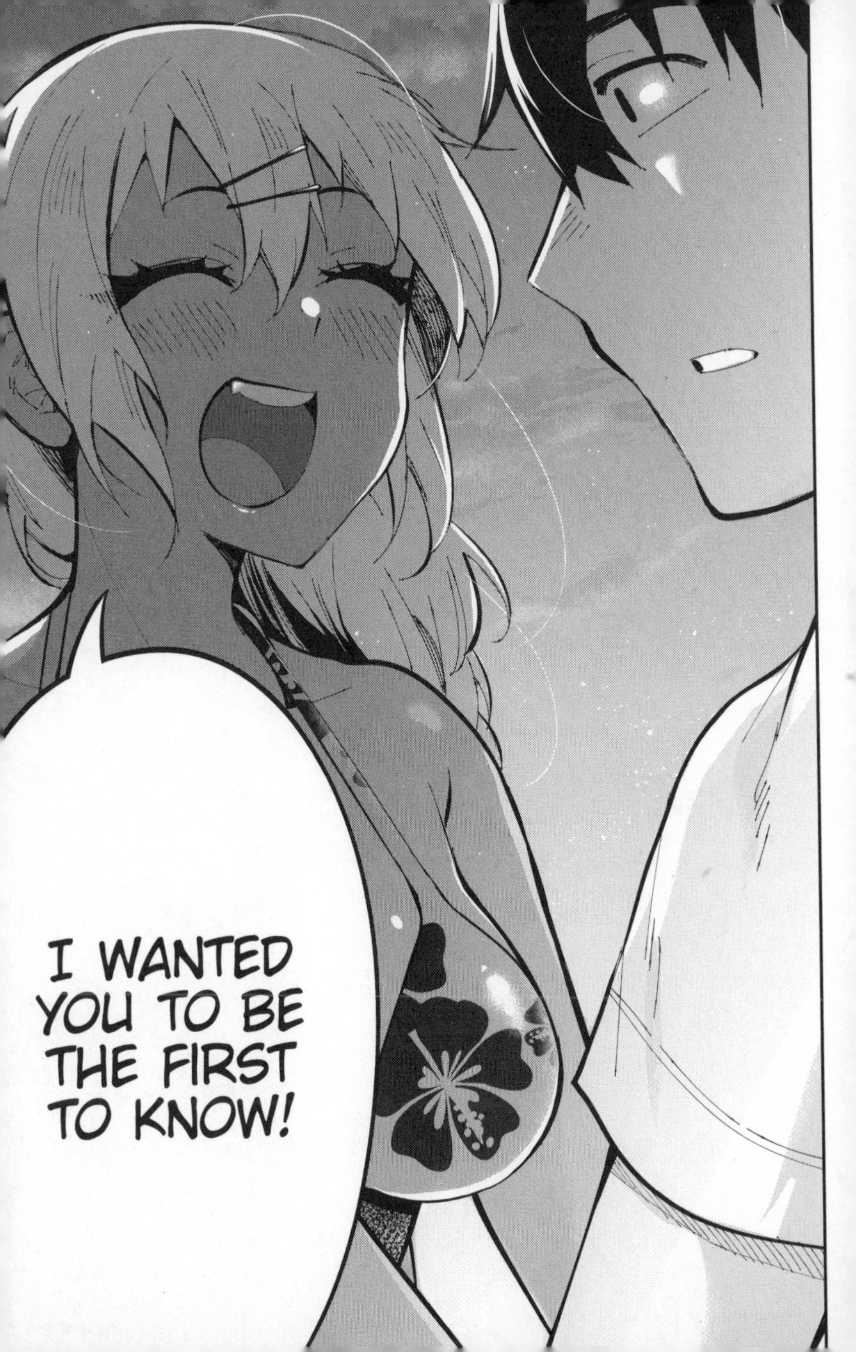
I WANTED YOU TO BE THE FIRST TO KNOW!

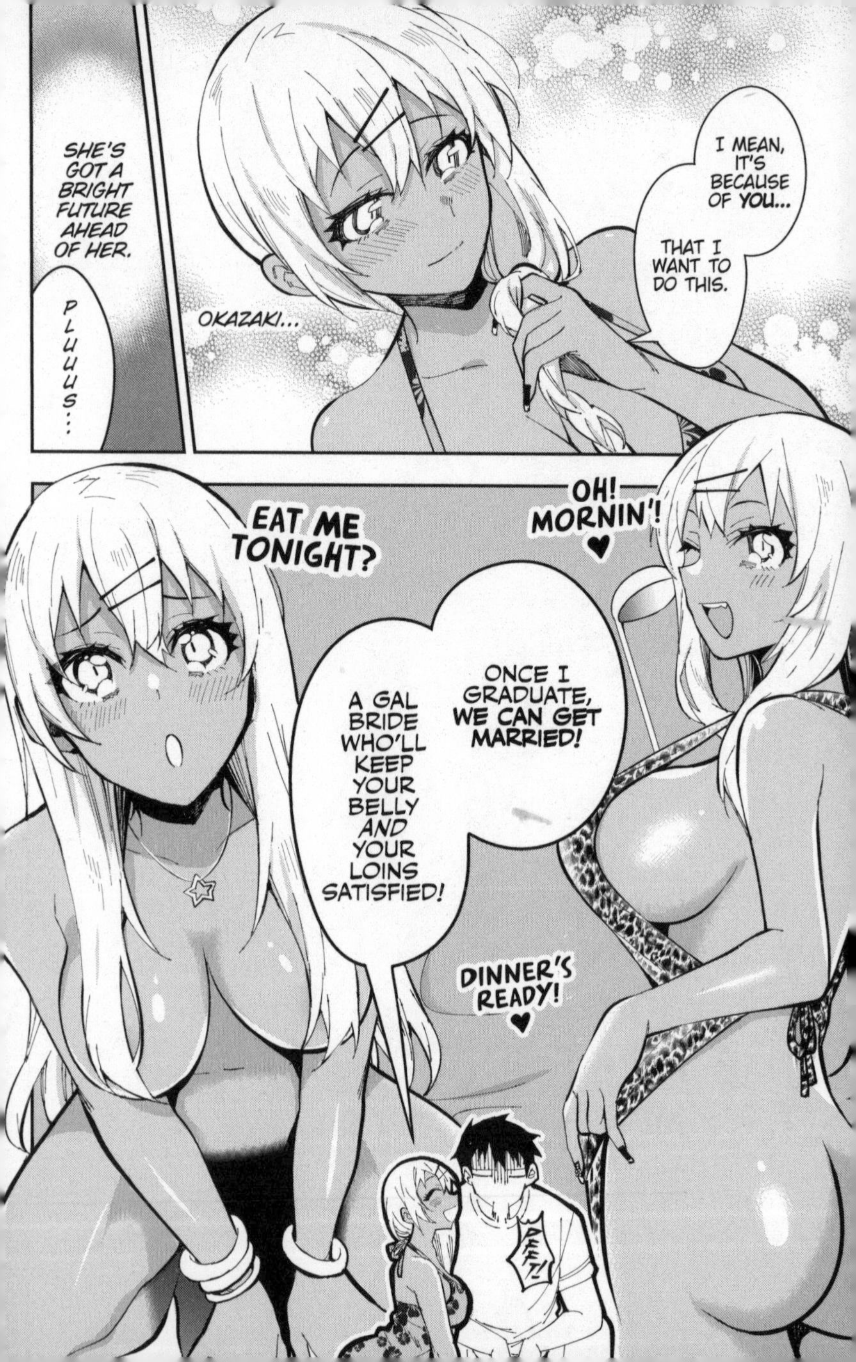
I MEAN, IT'S BECAUSE OF YOU...
THAT I WANT TO DO THIS.
SHE'S GOT A BRIGHT FUTURE AHEAD OF HER.
OKAZAKI...
PLUUUS...
OH! MORNIN'! ♥
EAT ME TONIGHT?
ONCE I GRADUATE, WE CAN GET MARRIED!
A GAL BRIDE WHO'LL KEEP YOUR BELLY AND YOUR LOINS SATISFIED!
DINNER'S READY! ♥
DEFT!

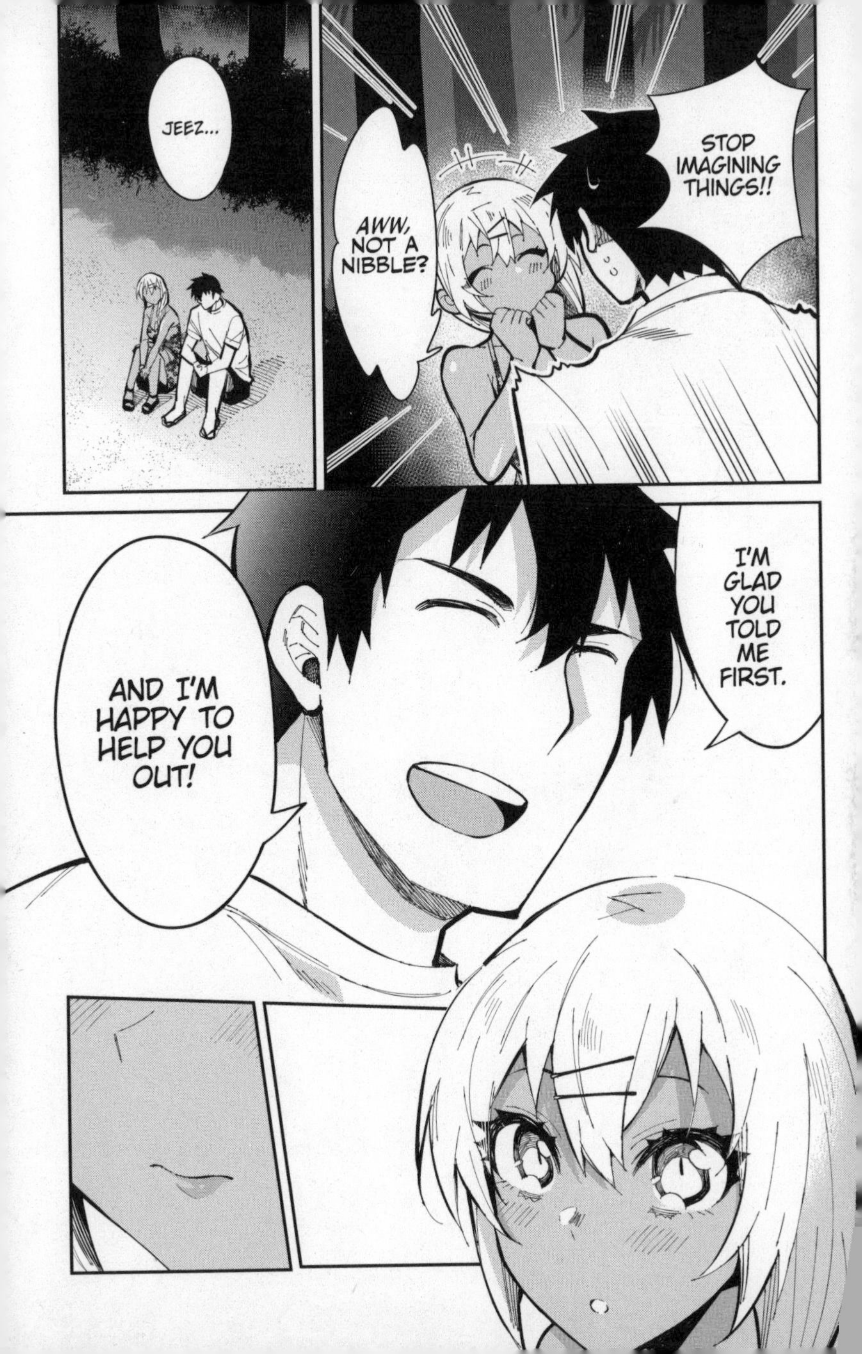
STOP IMAGINING THINGS!!
AWW, NOT A NIBBLE?
JEEZ...
I'M GLAD YOU TOLD ME FIRST.
AND I'M HAPPY TO HELP YOU OUT!

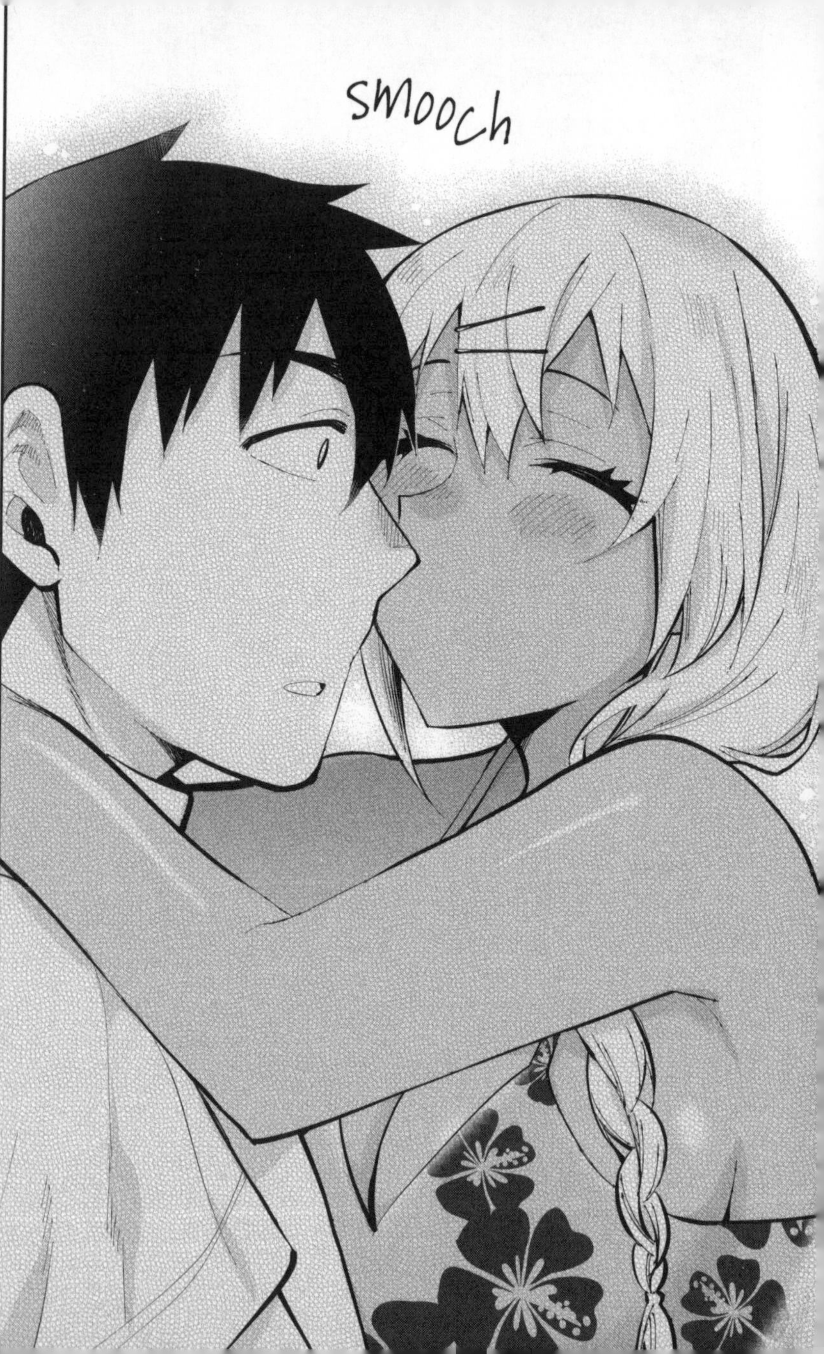
smooch

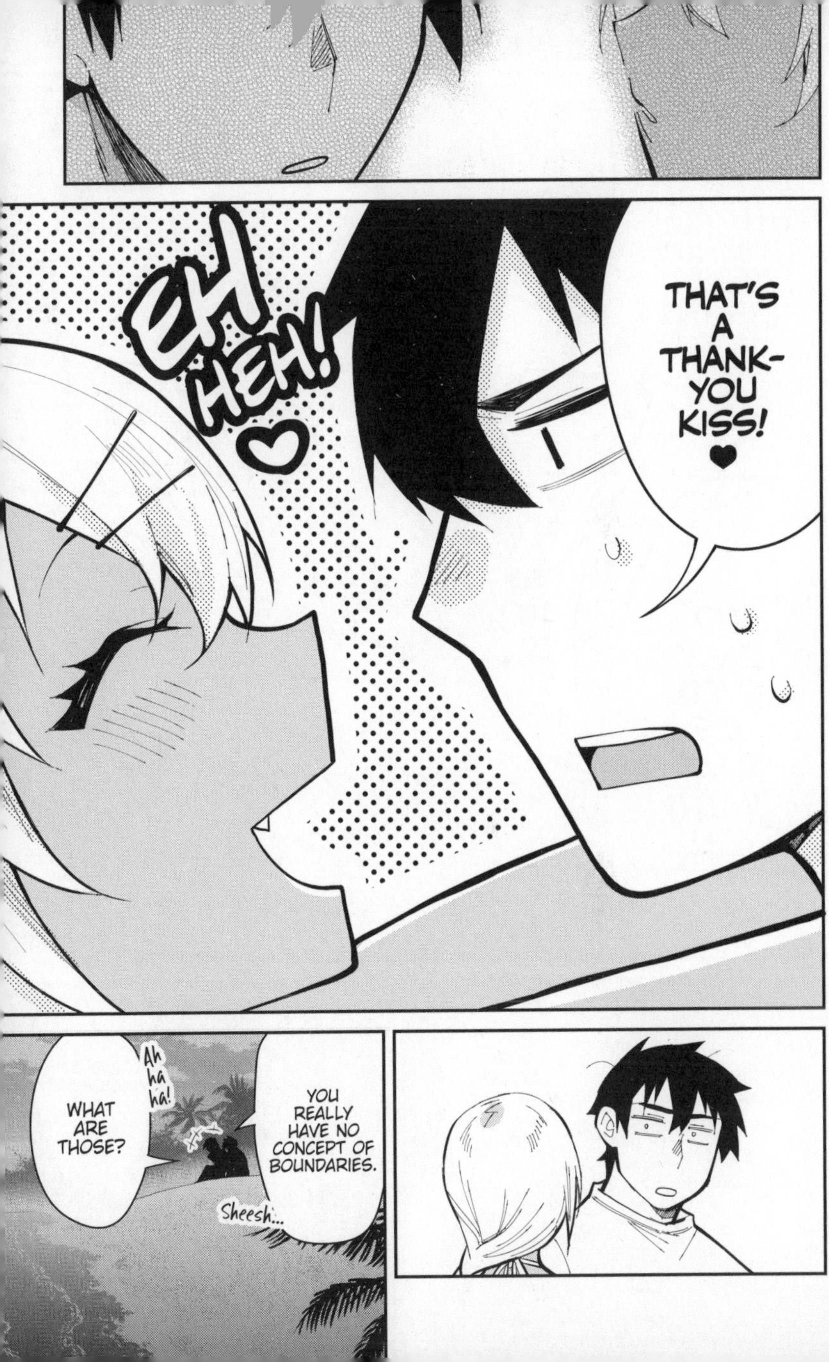
THAT'S A THANK-YOU KISS! ♥
EH HEH! ♥
YOU REALLY HAVE NO CONCEPT OF BOUNDARIES.
Sheesh...
Ah ha ha!
WHAT ARE THOSE?

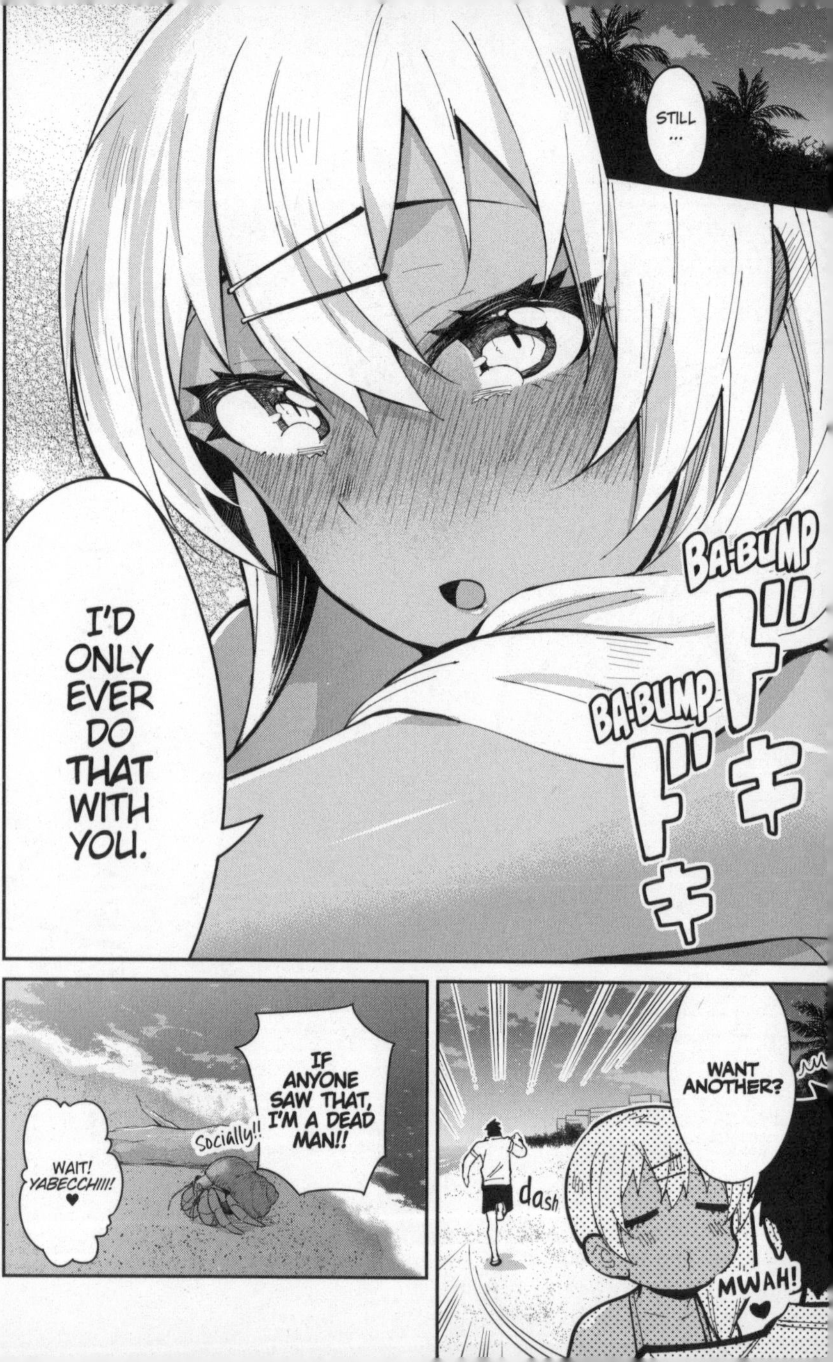
STILL ...
I'D ONLY EVER DO THAT WITH YOU.
BA-BUMP
ドキ
BA-BUMP
ドキ
WANT ANOTHER?
dash
MWAH! ♥
IF ANYONE SAW THAT, I'M A DEAD MAN!!
Socially!!
WAIT! YABECCHIIII! ♥

Gal Gohan

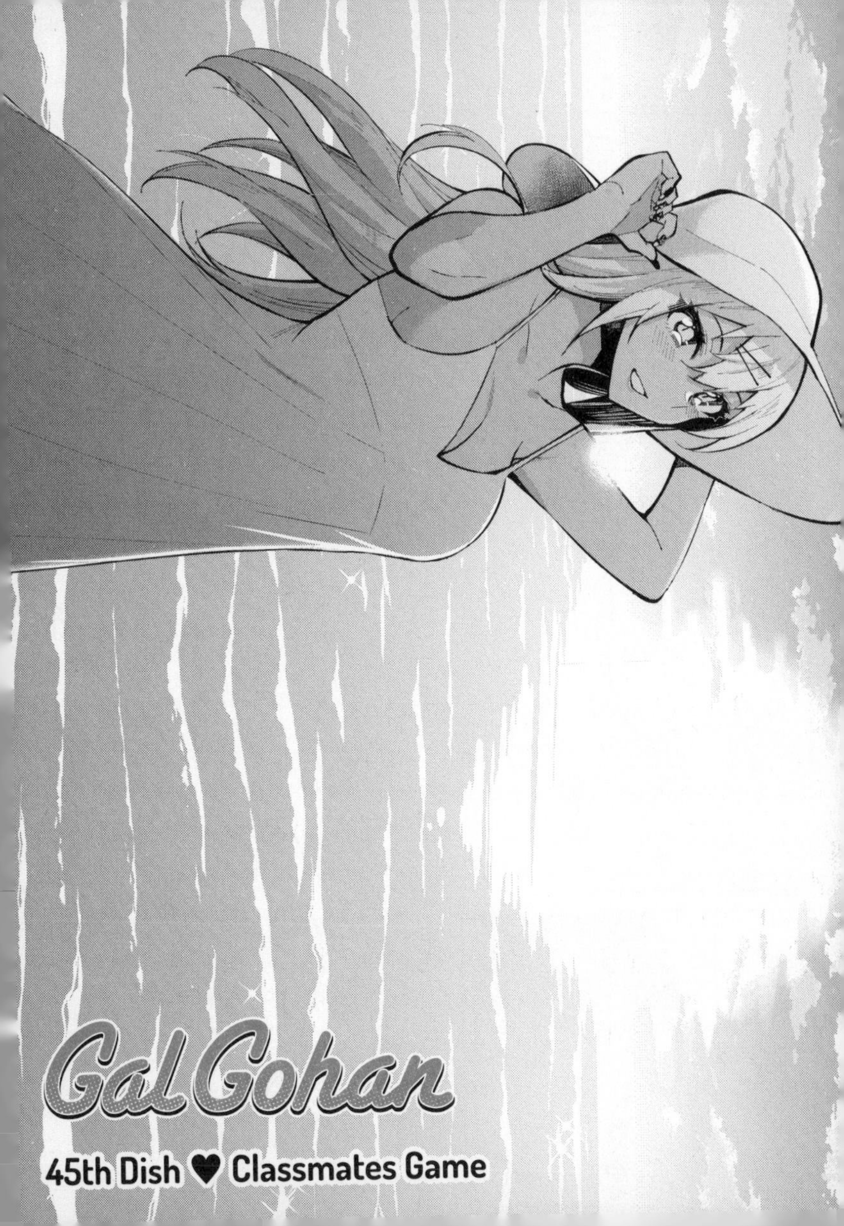
Gal Gohan
45th Dish ♥ Classmates Game

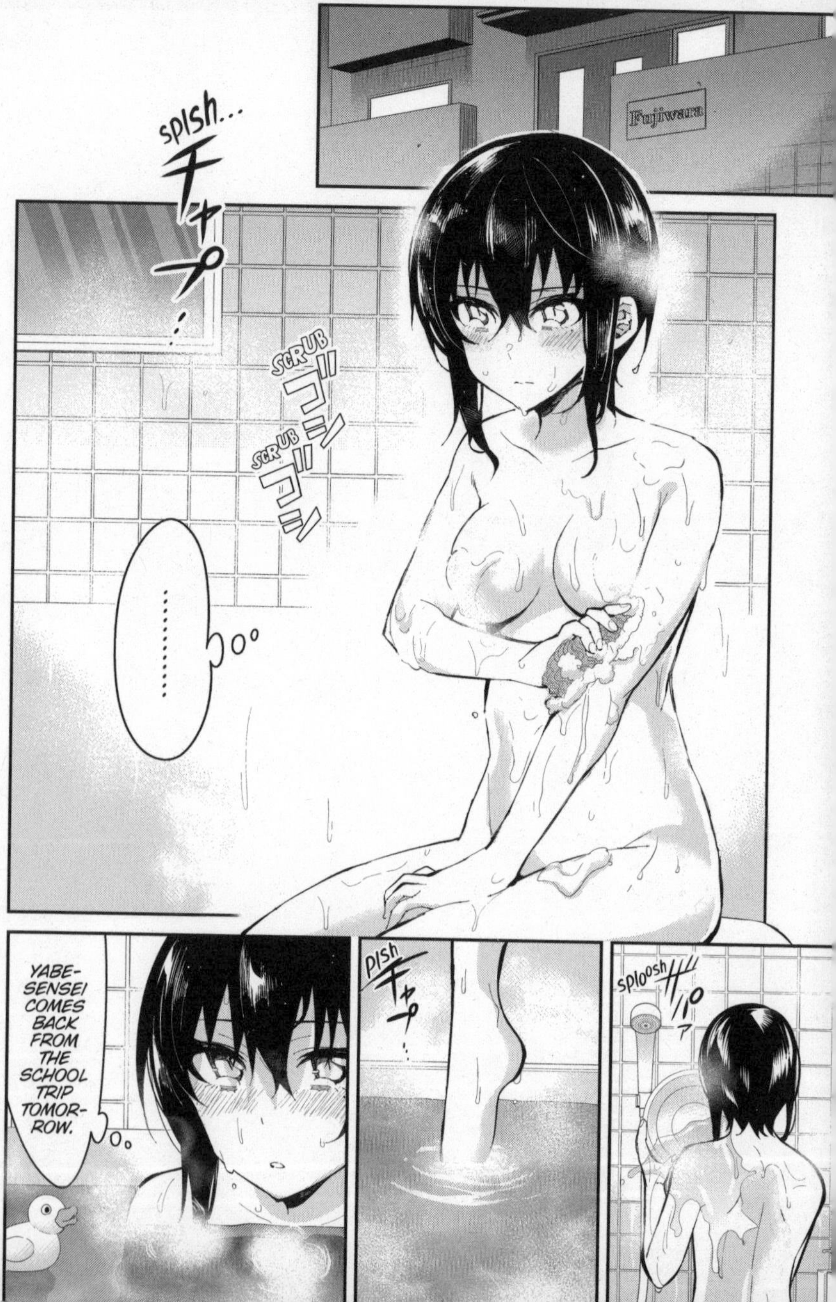
Fujiwara
splsh...
チャプ…
SCRUB
ゴシ
SCRUB
ゴシ
……
sploosh
パア
plsh
チャプ…
YABE-SENSEI COMES BACK FROM THE SCHOOL TRIP TOMORROW.

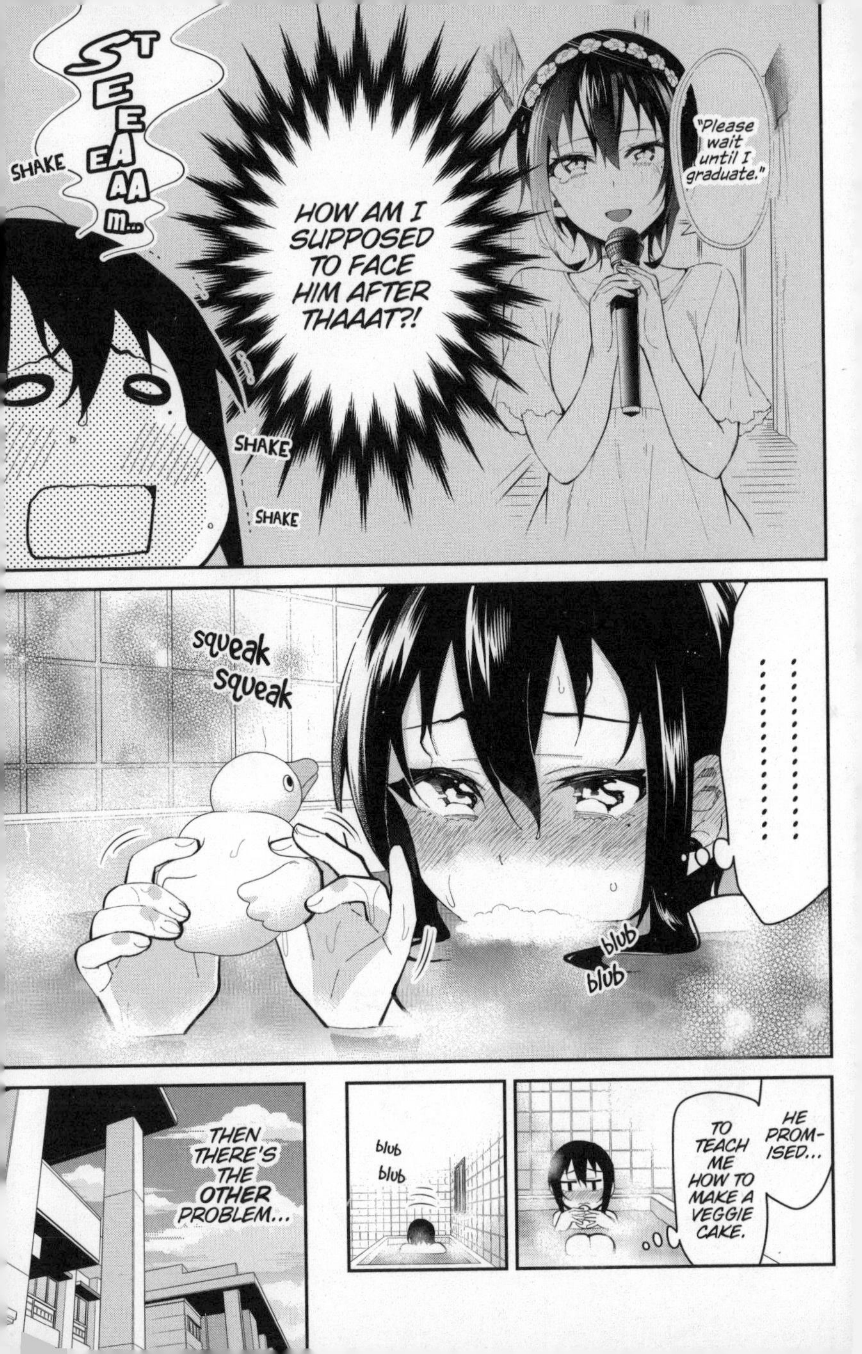
"Please wait until I graduate."
HOW AM I SUPPOSED TO FACE HIM AFTER THAAAT?!
STEEEAAAm...
SHAKE
SHAKE
SHAKE
......
squeak squeak
blub blub
HE PROMISED...
TO TEACH ME HOW TO MAKE A VEGGIE CAKE.
blub blub
THEN THERE'S THE OTHER PROBLEM...

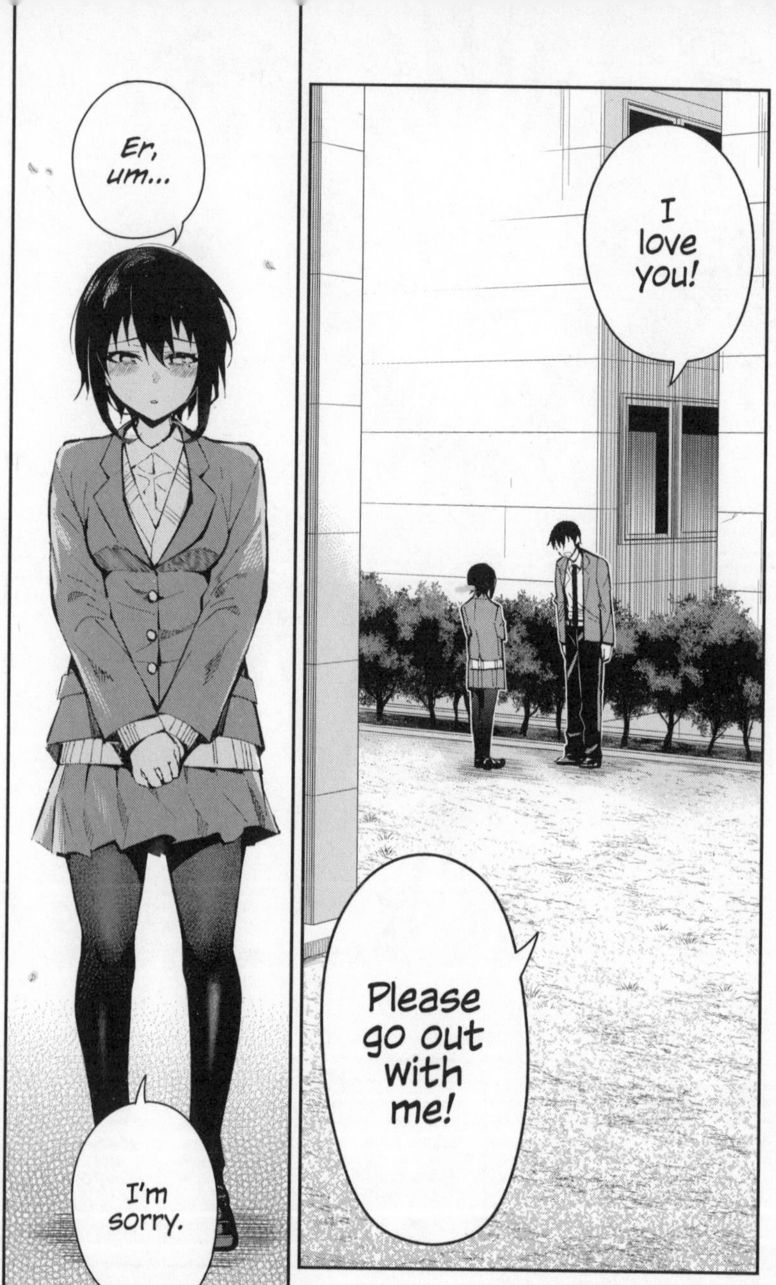
I love you!
Please go out with me!
Er, um...
I'm sorry.

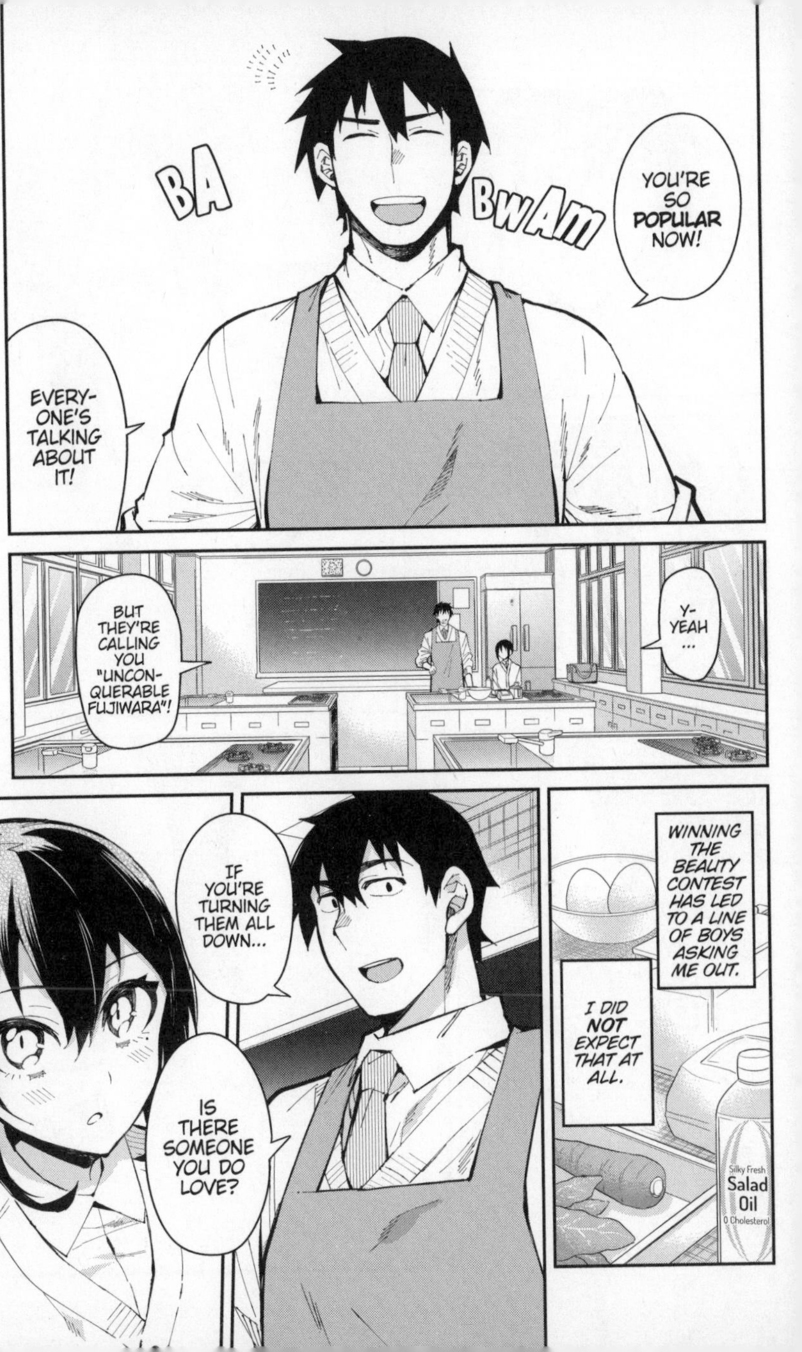

YOU'RE SO POPULAR NOW!
BA BwAm
EVERYONE'S TALKING ABOUT IT!
Y-YEAH...
BUT THEY'RE CALLING YOU "UNCONQUERABLE FUJIWARA"!
WINNING THE BEAUTY CONTEST HAS LED TO A LINE OF BOYS ASKING ME OUT.
I DID NOT EXPECT THAT AT ALL.
Silky Fresh Salad Oil 0 Cholesterol
IF YOU'RE TURNING THEM ALL DOWN...
IS THERE SOMEONE YOU DO LOVE?

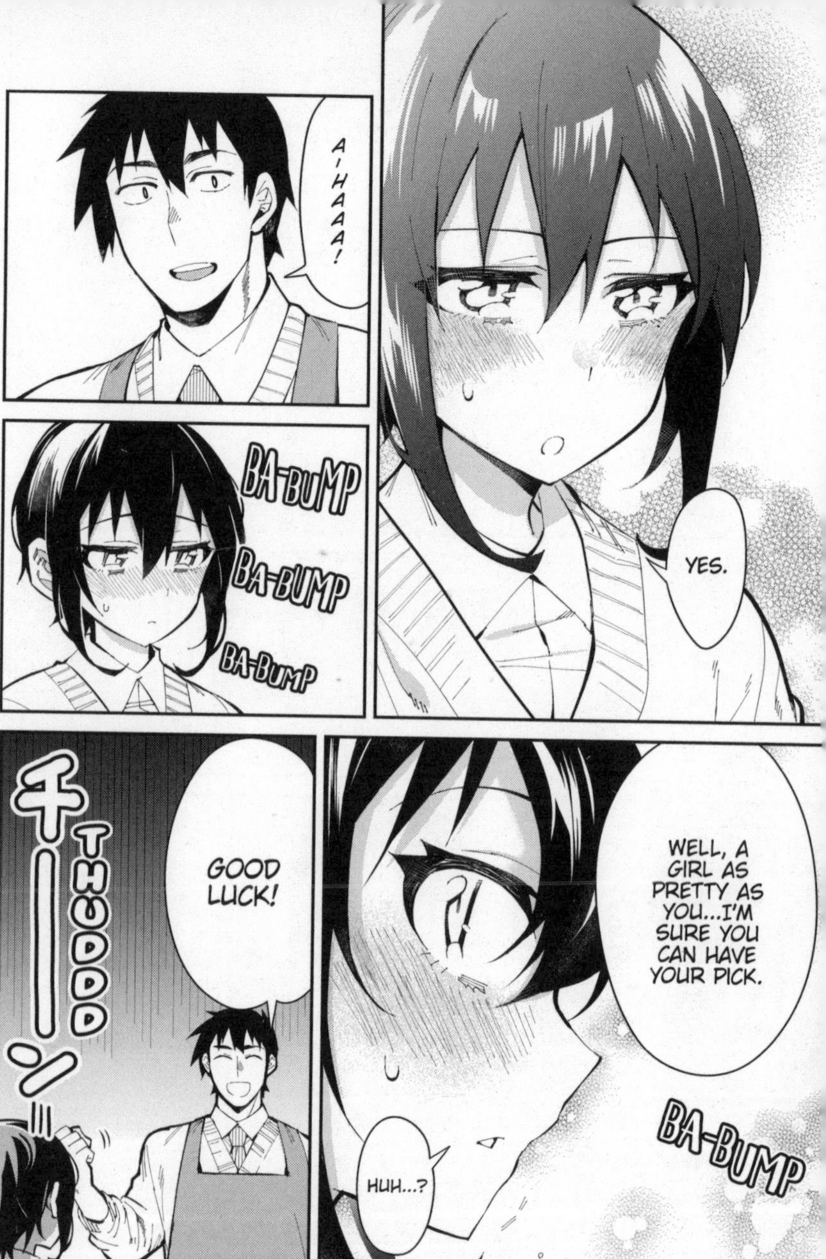
YES.
A-HAAAA!
BA-BUMP
BA-BUMP
BA-BUMP
WELL, A GIRL AS PRETTY AS YOU...I'M SURE YOU CAN HAVE YOUR PICK.
BA-BUMP
HUH...?
GOOD LUCK!
チーン
THUDDD

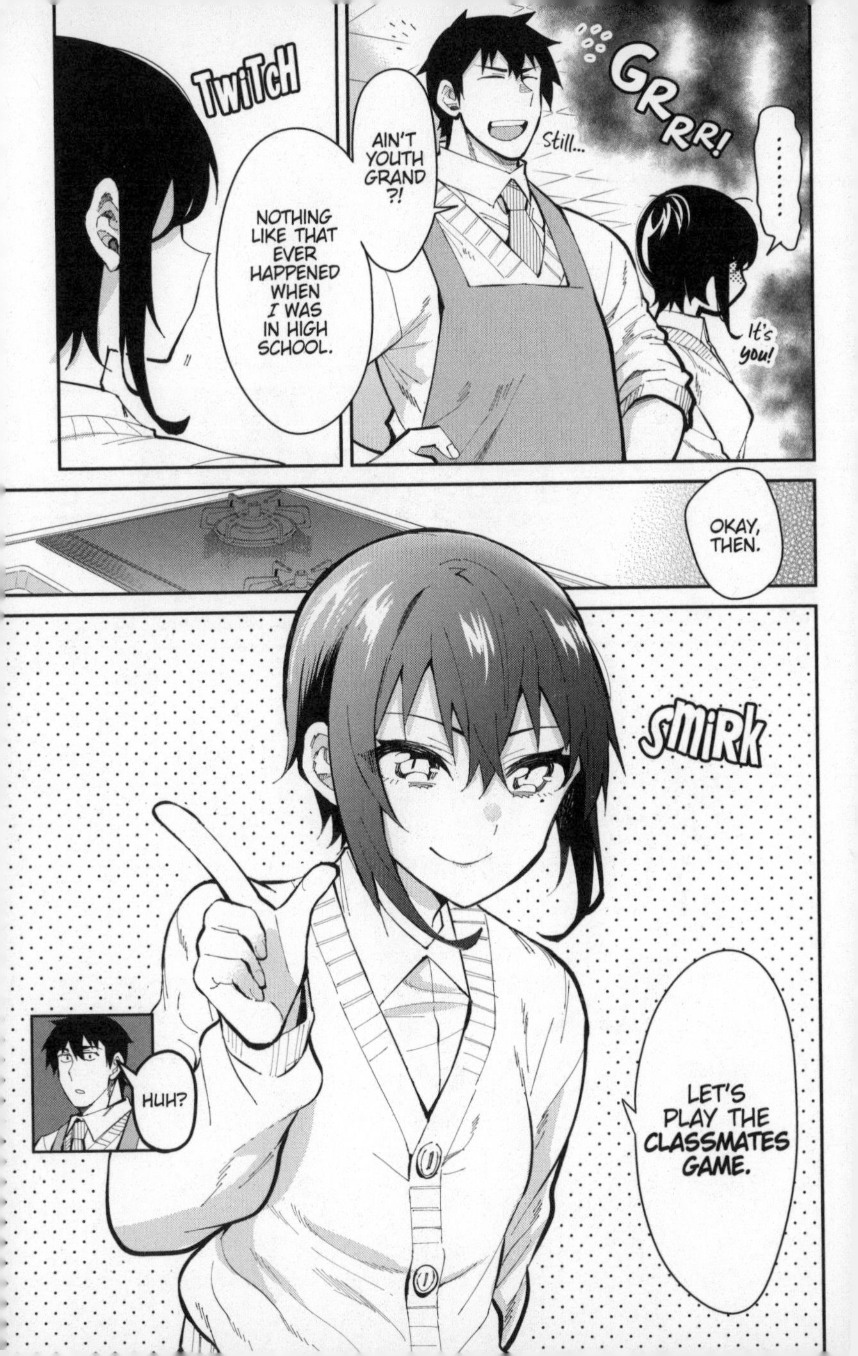
......
GRRR!
Still...
AIN'T YOUTH GRAND?!
NOTHING LIKE THAT EVER HAPPENED WHEN I WAS IN HIGH SCHOOL.
It's you!
TWITCH
OKAY, THEN.
SMIRK
LET'S PLAY THE CLASSMATES GAME.
HUH?

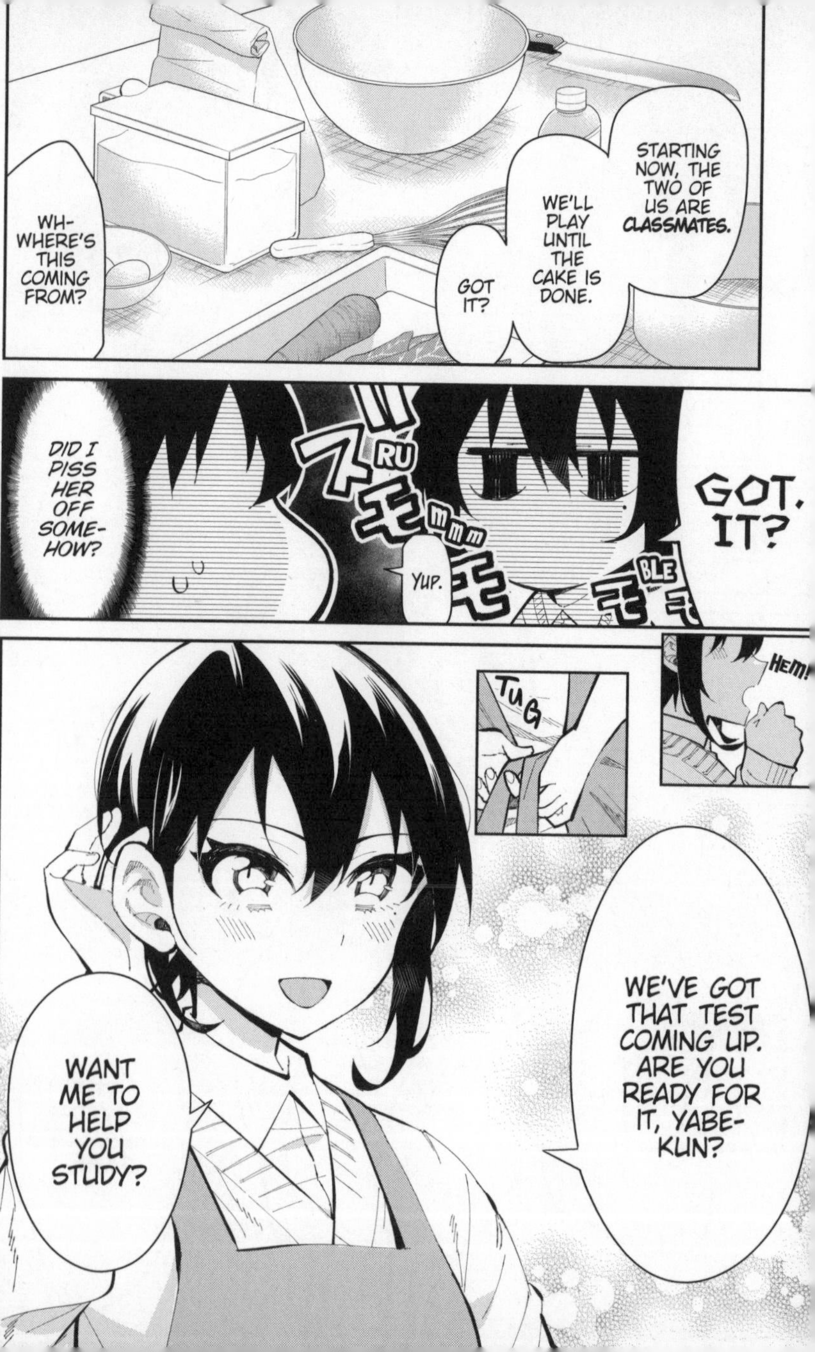

STARTING NOW, THE TWO OF US ARE **CLASSMATES.**
WE'LL PLAY UNTIL THE CAKE IS DONE.
GOT IT?
WH-WHERE'S THIS COMING FROM?
GOT. IT?
RU
mmm
BLE
YUP.
DID I PISS HER OFF SOMEHOW?
HEM!
TUG
WE'VE GOT THAT TEST COMING UP. ARE YOU READY FOR IT, YABE-KUN?
WANT ME TO HELP YOU STUDY?

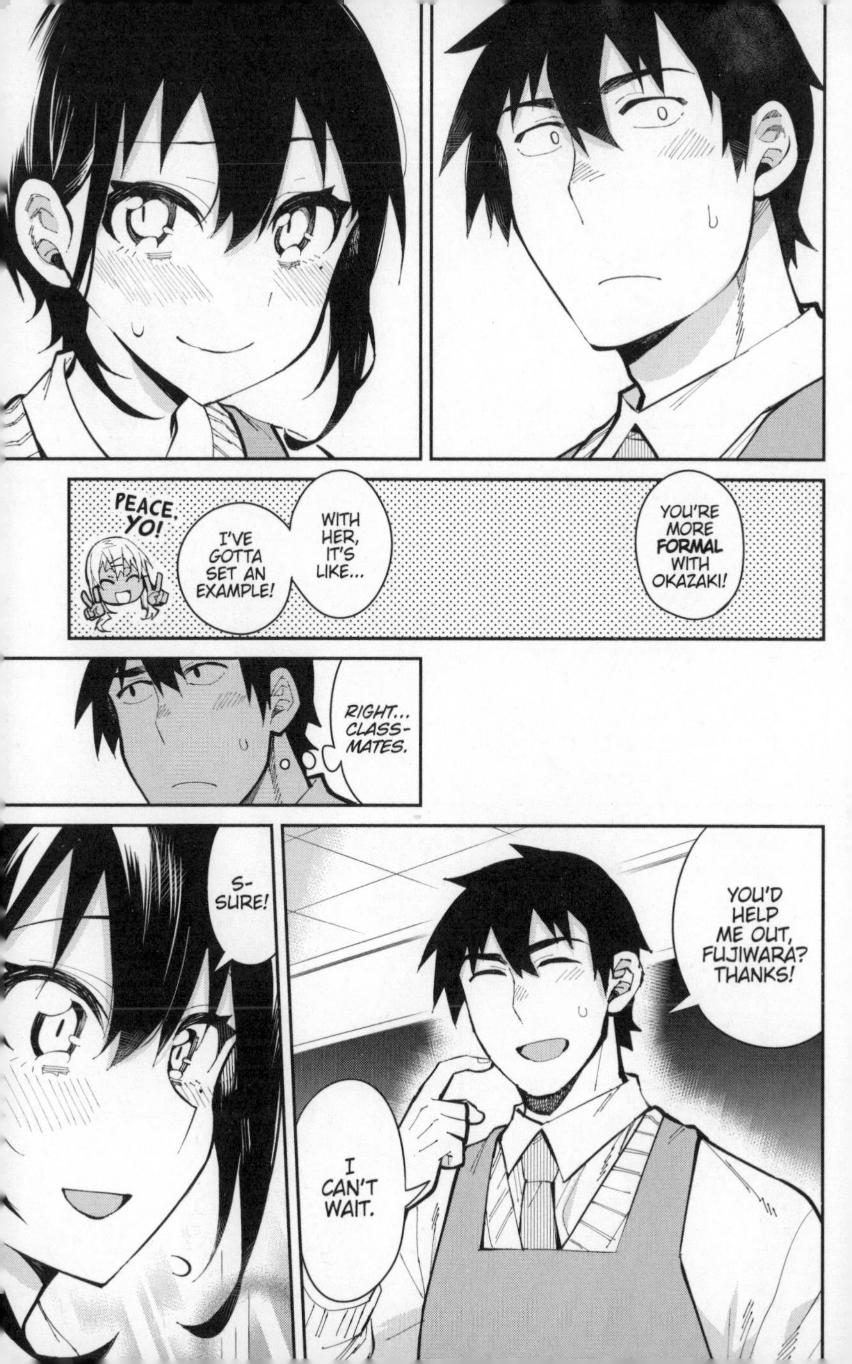
YOU'RE MORE FORMAL WITH OKAZAKI!
WITH HER, IT'S LIKE...
I'VE GOTTA SET AN EXAMPLE!
PEACE. YO!
RIGHT... CLASSMATES.
YOU'D HELP ME OUT, FUJIWARA? THANKS!
I CAN'T WAIT.
S-SURE!

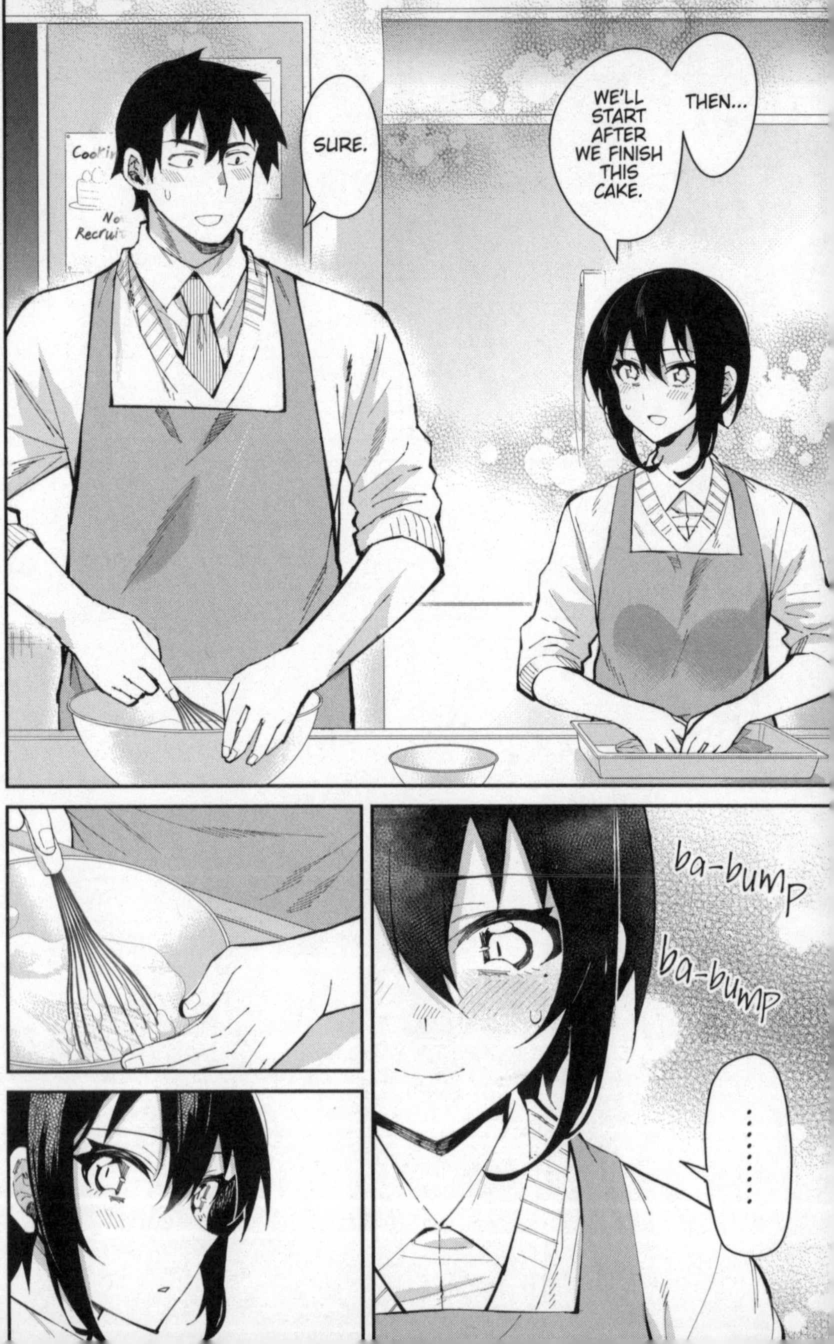
THEN...
WE'LL START AFTER WE FINISH THIS CAKE.
SURE.
ba-bump
ba-bump
....

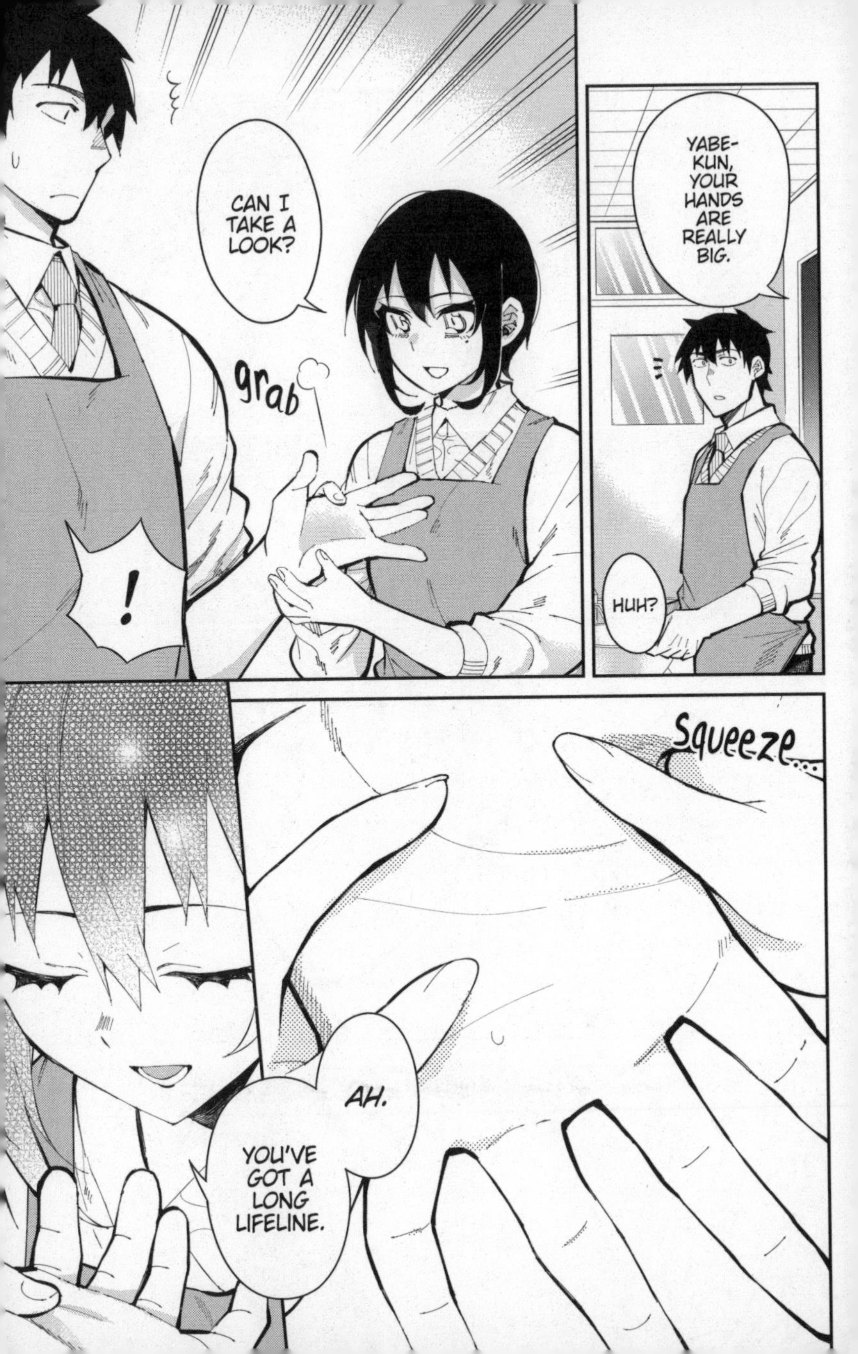
YABE-KUN, YOUR HANDS ARE REALLY BIG.
HUH?
CAN I TAKE A LOOK?
grab
!
Squeeze
AH.
YOU'VE GOT A LONG LIFELINE.

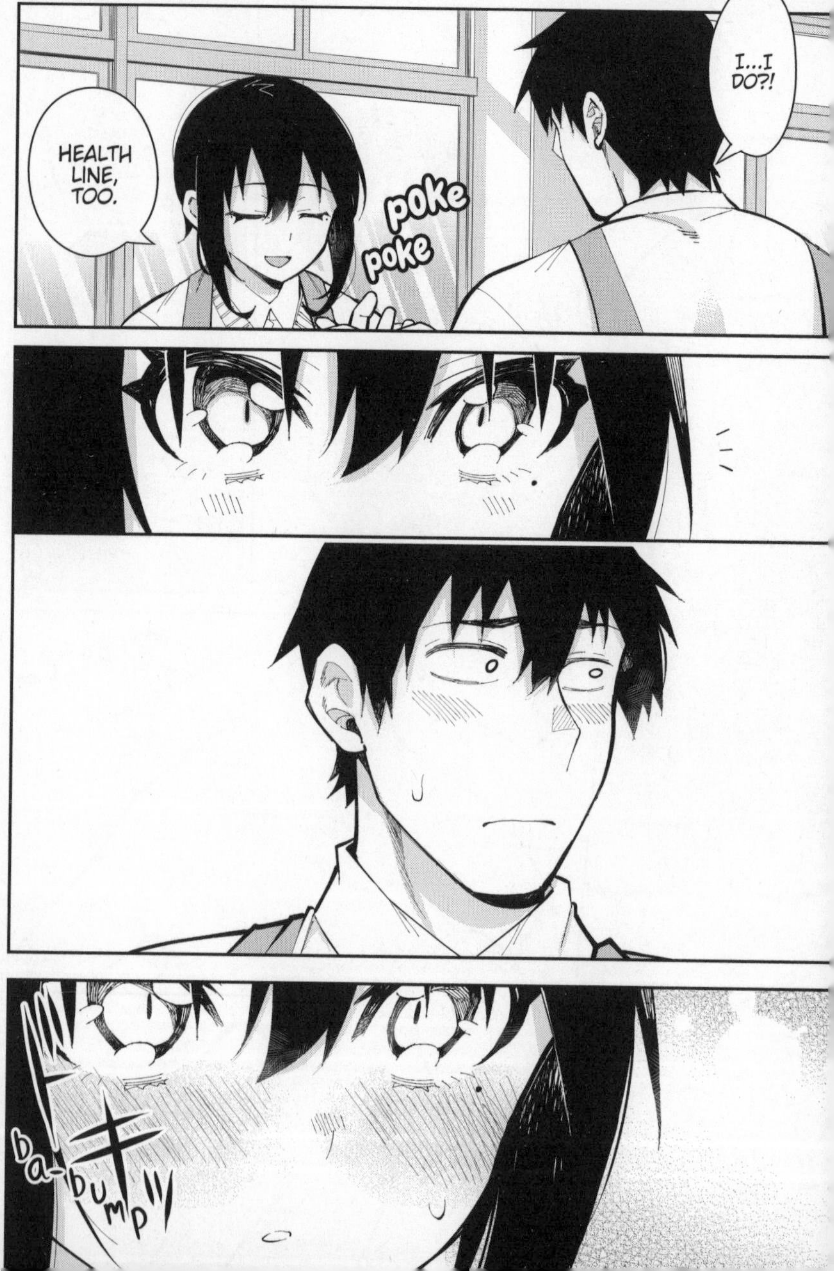
I...I DO?!
HEALTH LINE, TOO.
poke poke
ba-bump

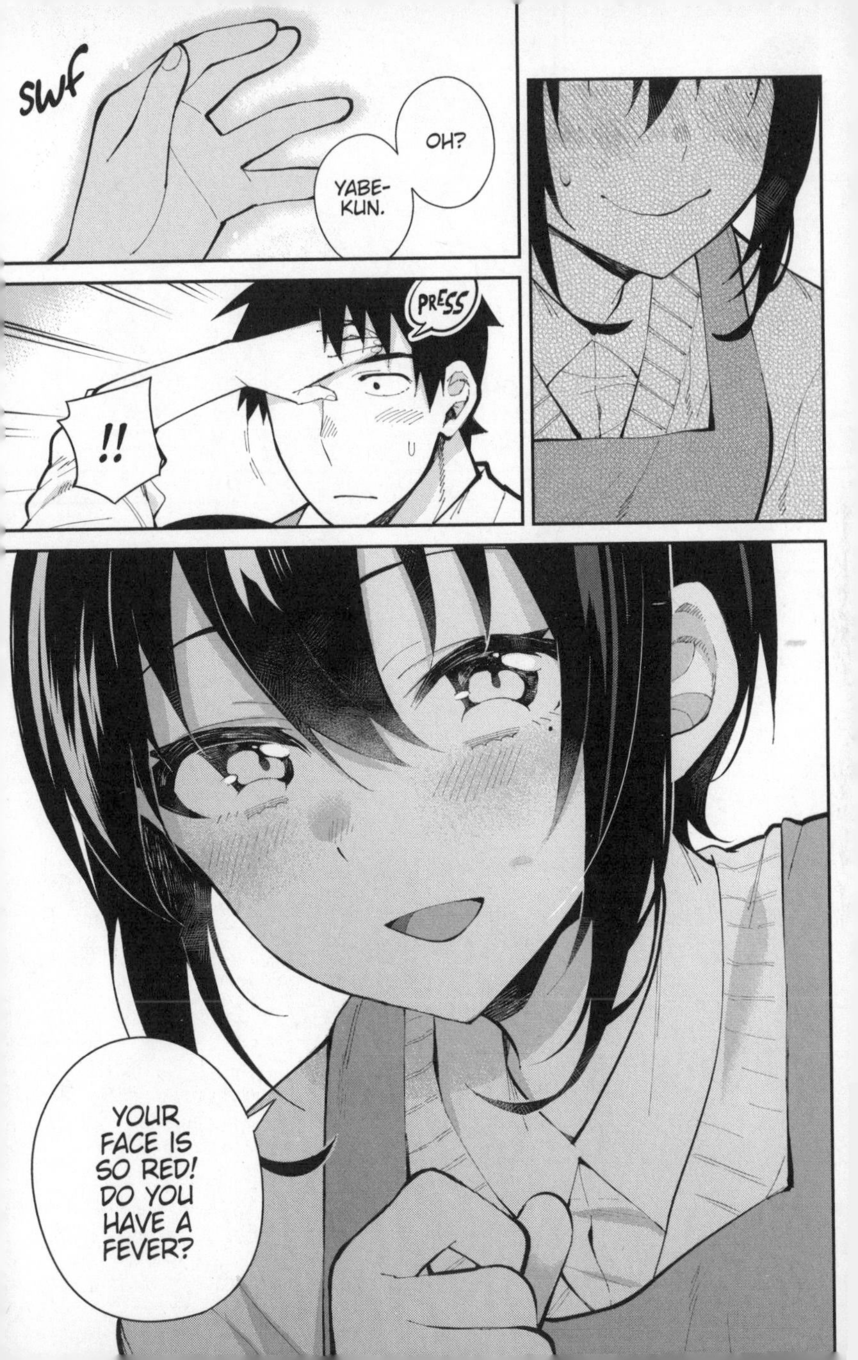
OH?
YABE-KUN.
SWF
PRESS
!!
YOUR FACE IS SO RED! DO YOU HAVE A FEVER?

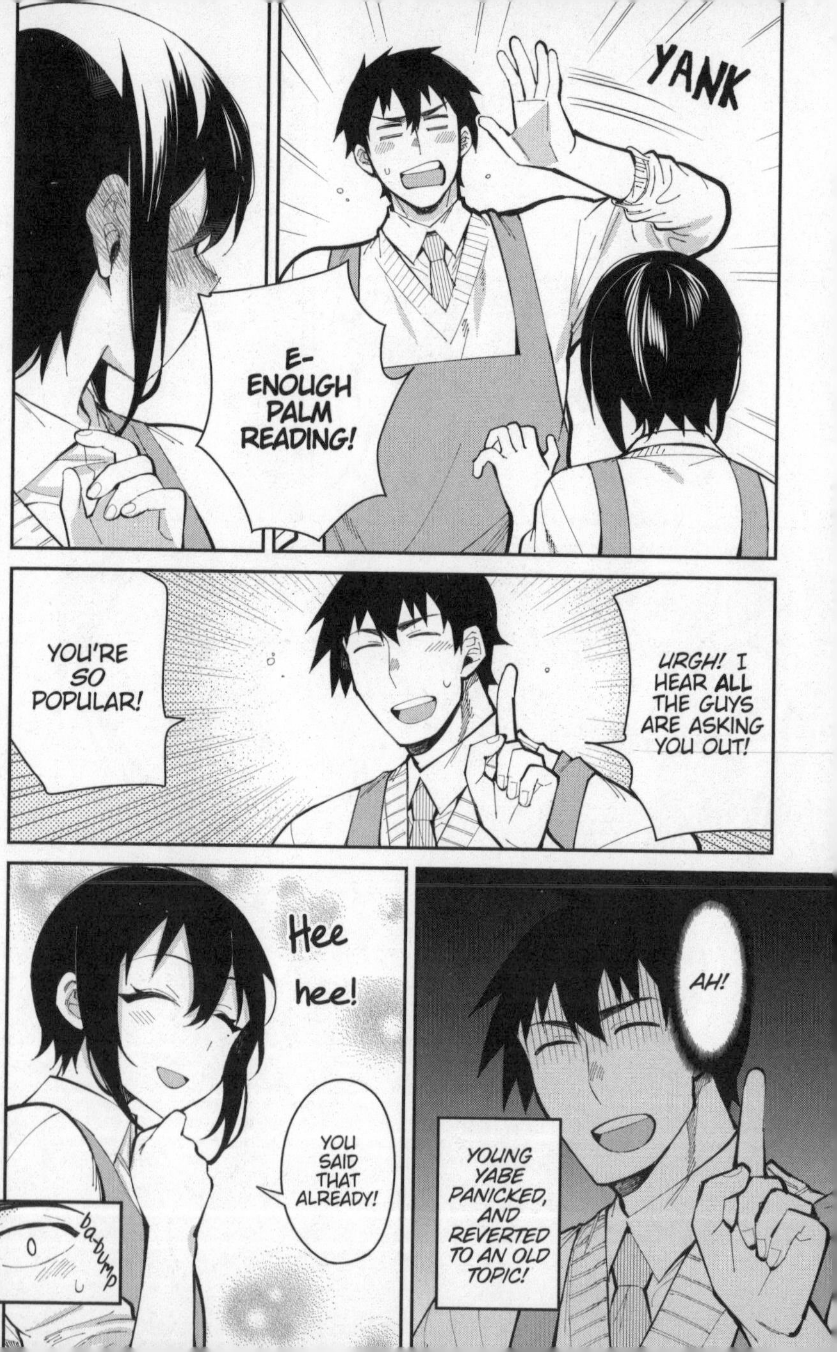
YANK
E-ENOUGH PALM READING!
URGH! I HEAR ALL THE GUYS ARE ASKING YOU OUT!
YOU'RE SO POPULAR!
AH!
YOUNG YABE PANICKED, AND REVERTED TO AN OLD TOPIC!
Hee hee!
YOU SAID THAT ALREADY!
ba-bump

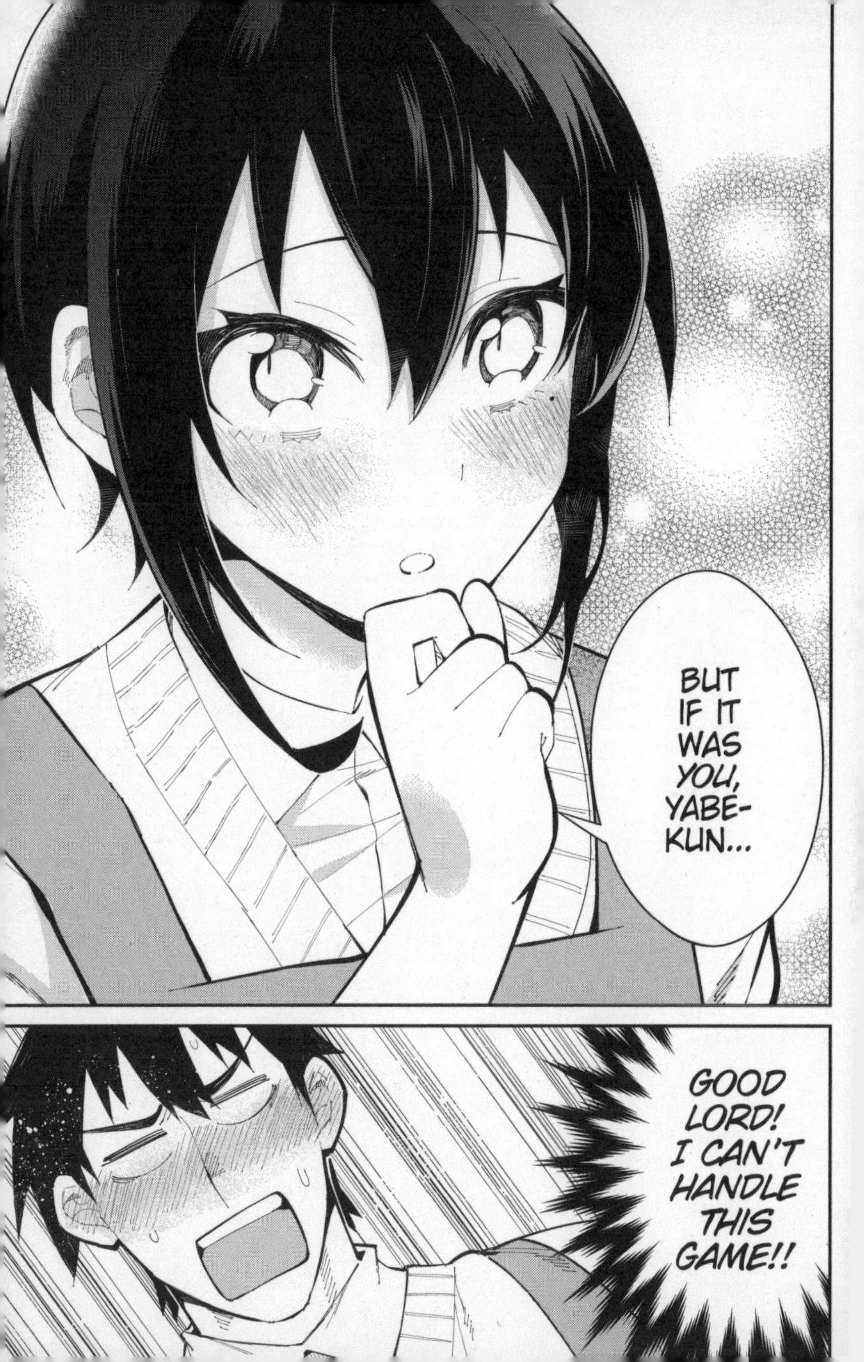
BUT IF IT WAS YOU, YABE-KUN...
GOOD LORD! I CAN'T HANDLE THIS GAME!!

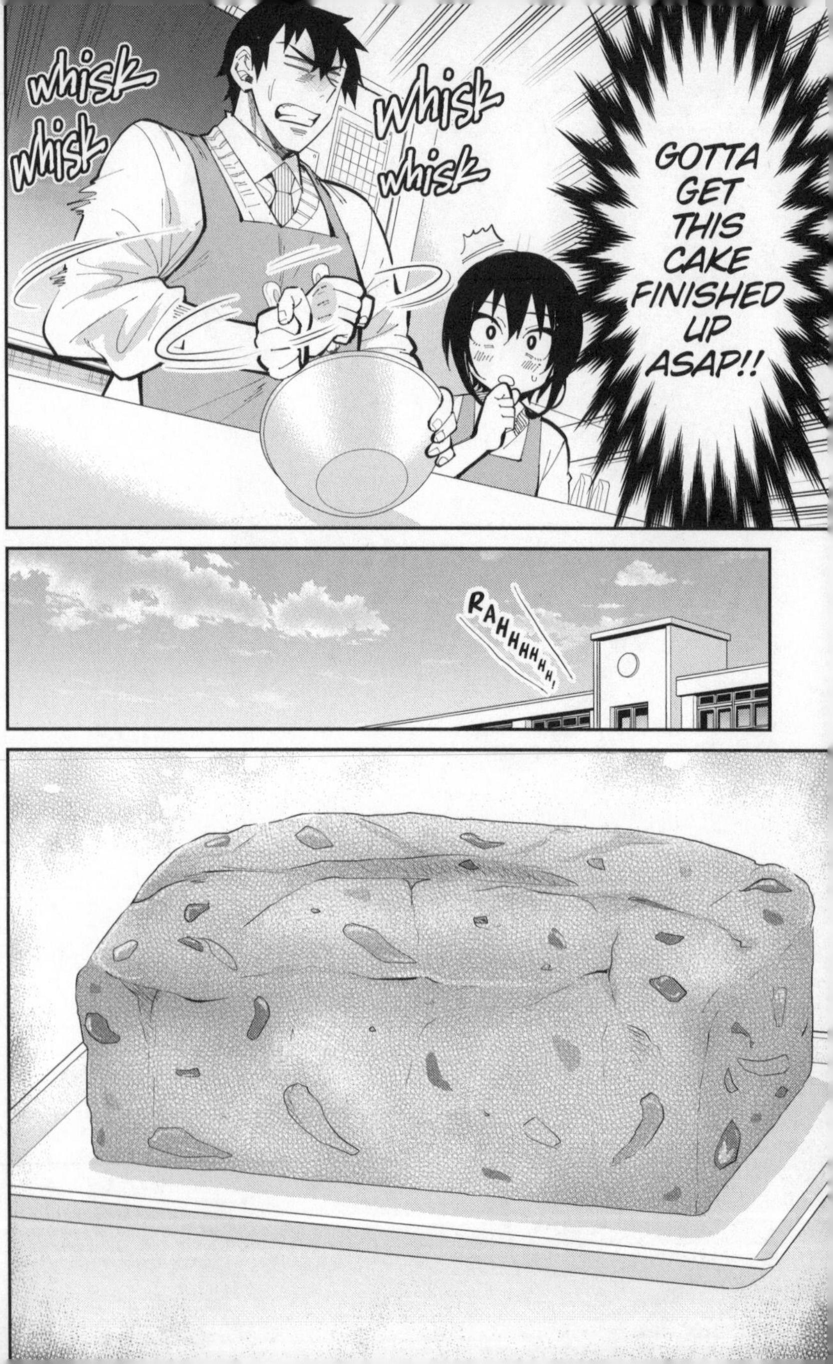
GOTTA GET THIS CAKE FINISHED UP ASAP!!
whisk whisk
whisk whisk
RAHHHHHHH!

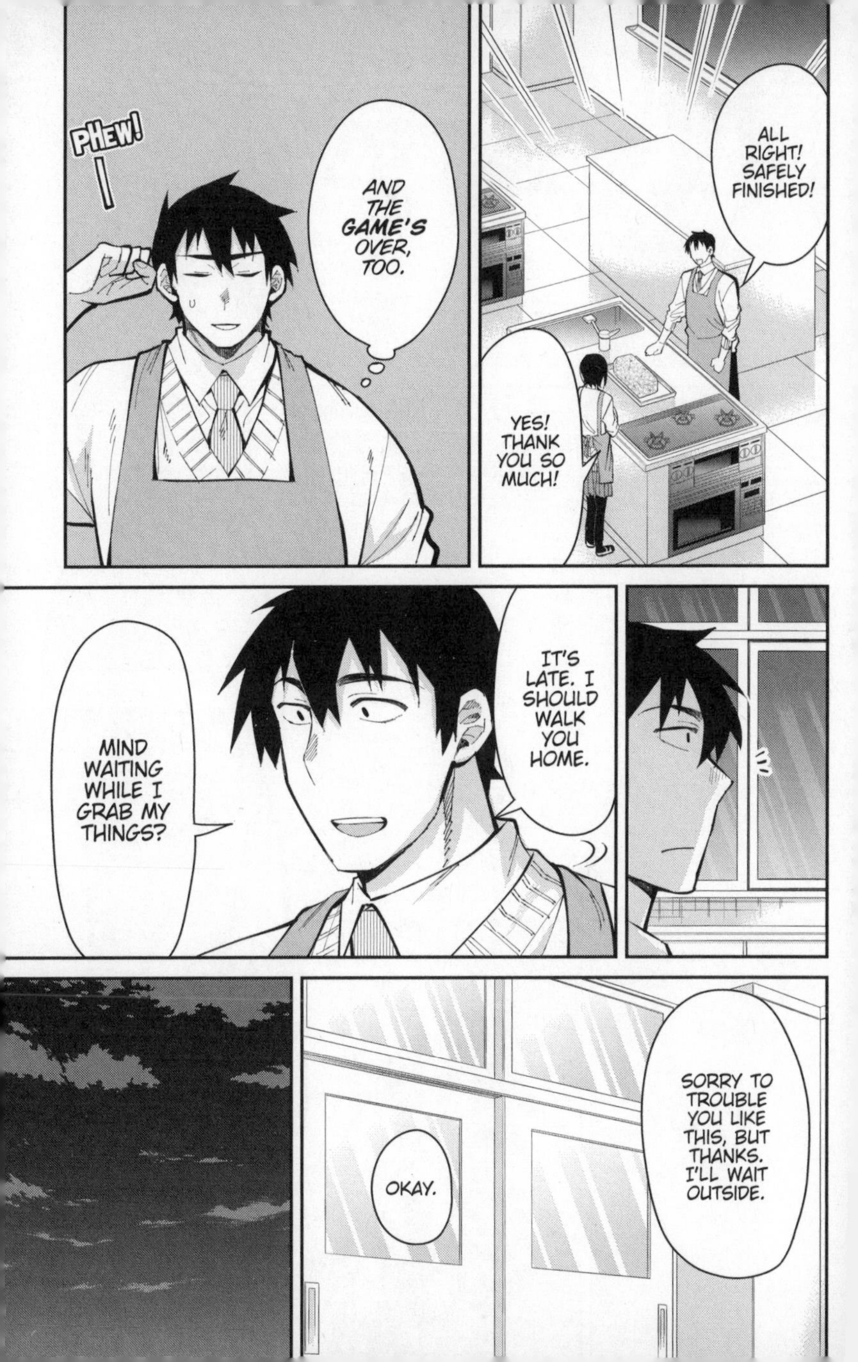
ALL RIGHT! SAFELY FINISHED!
YES! THANK YOU SO MUCH!
PHEW!
AND THE GAME'S OVER, TOO.
IT'S LATE. I SHOULD WALK YOU HOME.
MIND WAITING WHILE I GRAB MY THINGS?
SORRY TO TROUBLE YOU LIKE THIS, BUT THANKS. I'LL WAIT OUTSIDE.
OKAY.

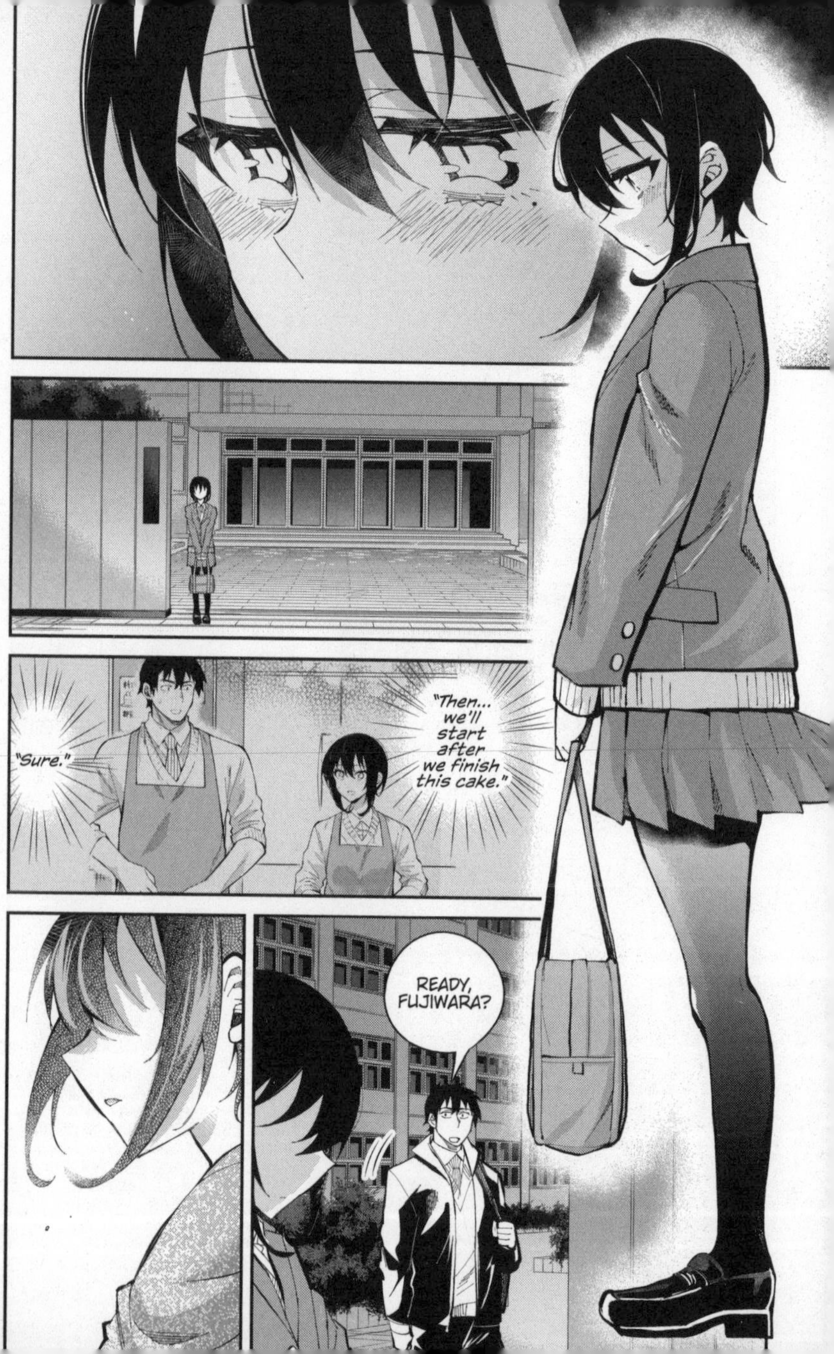

"Then... we'll start after we finish this cake."
"Sure."
READY, FUJIWARA?

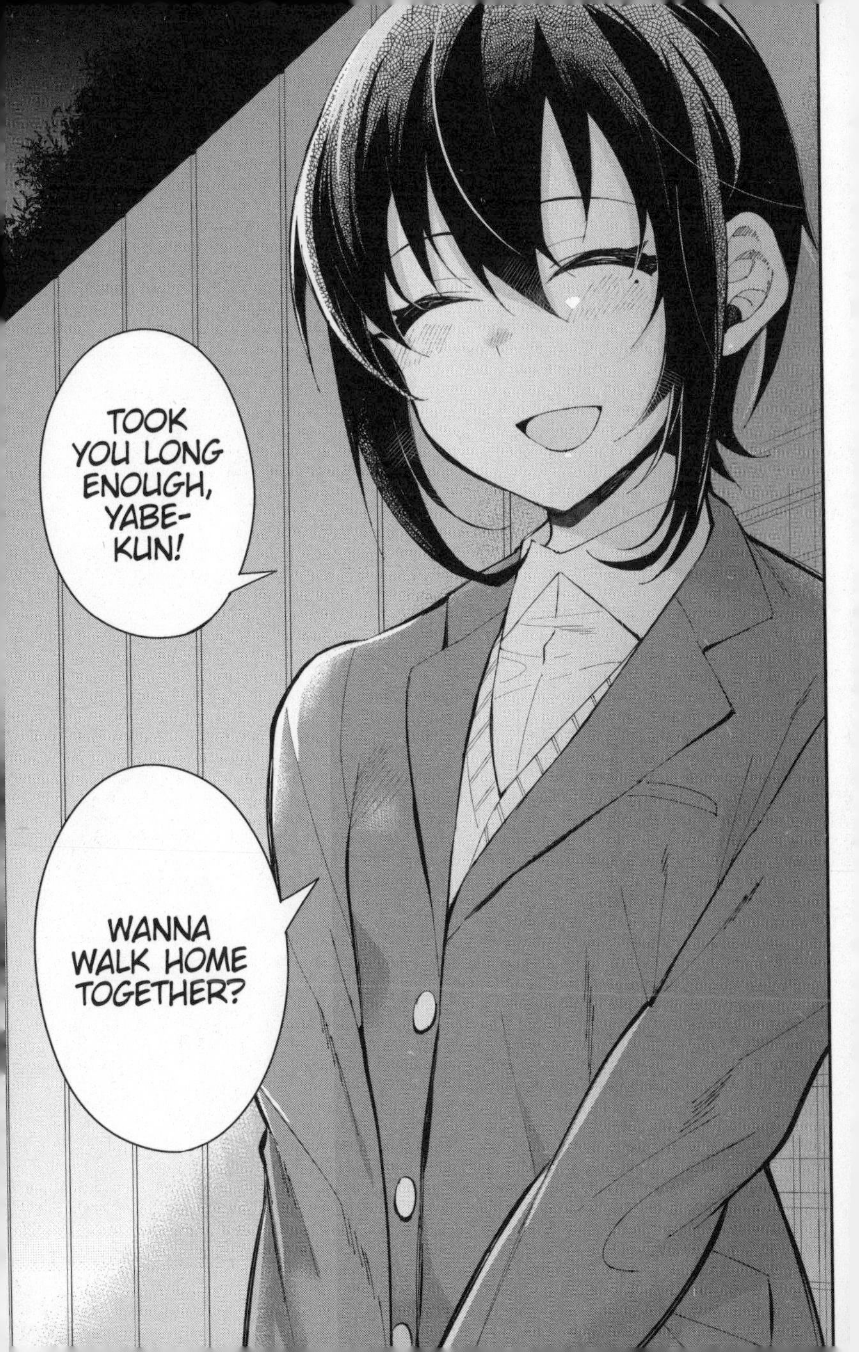
TOOK YOU LONG ENOUGH, YABE-KUN!
WANNA WALK HOME TOGETHER?

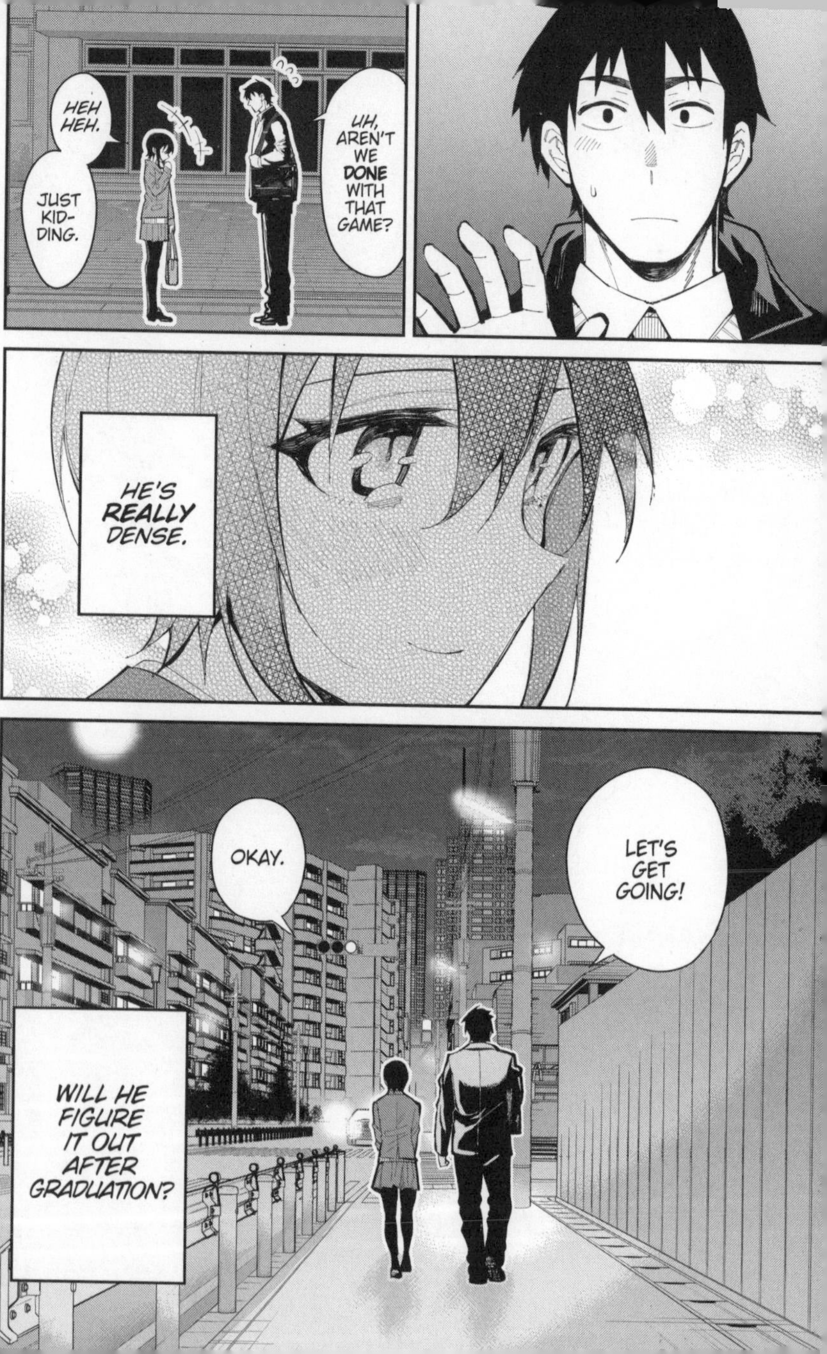
UH, AREN'T WE DONE WITH THAT GAME?
HEH HEH.
JUST KID-DING.
HE'S REALLY DENSE.
LET'S GET GOING!
OKAY.
WILL HE FIGURE IT OUT AFTER GRADUATION?

Gal
Gohan

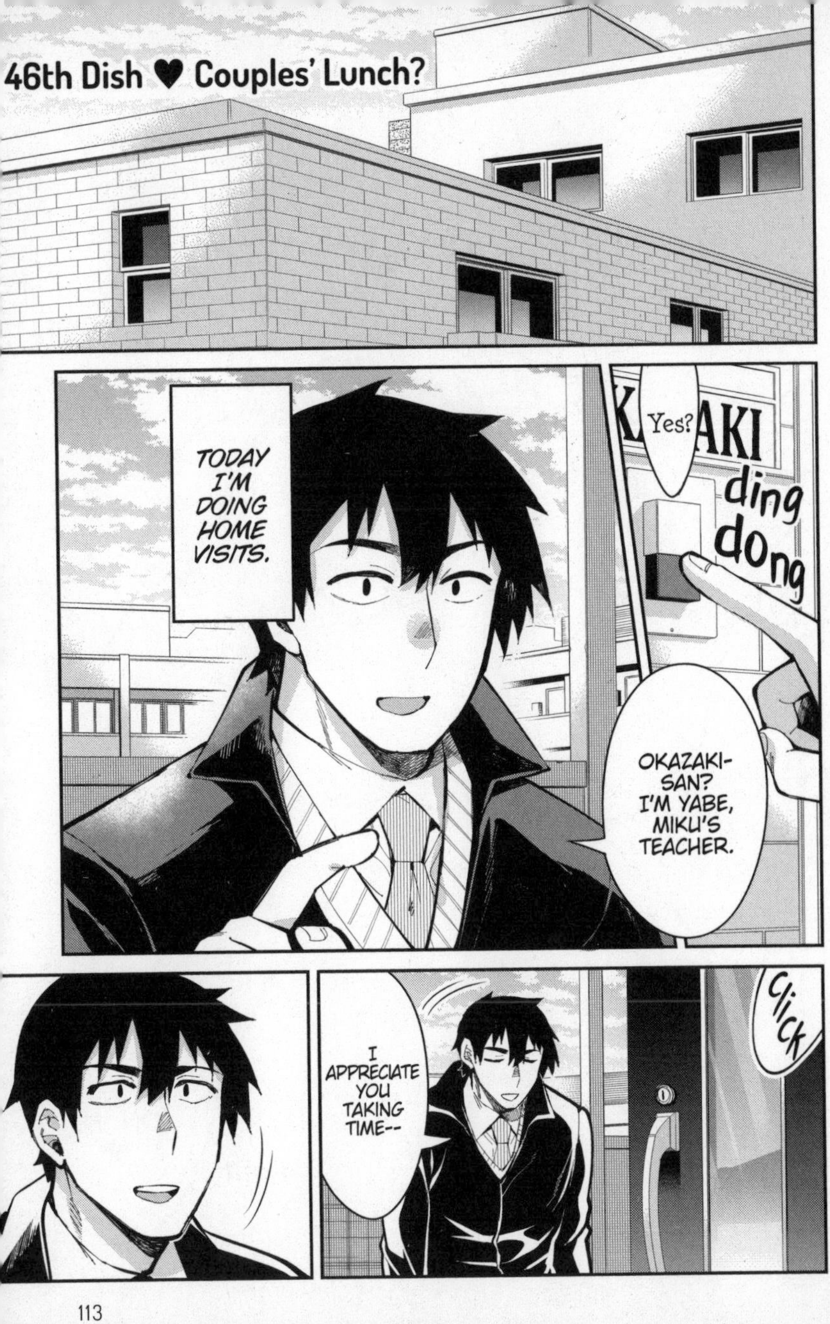
46th Dish ♥ Couples' Lunch?
Yes?
ding dong
OKAZAKI-SAN? I'M YABE, MIKU'S TEACHER.
TODAY I'M DOING HOME VISITS.
CLICK
I APPRECIATE YOU TAKING TIME--

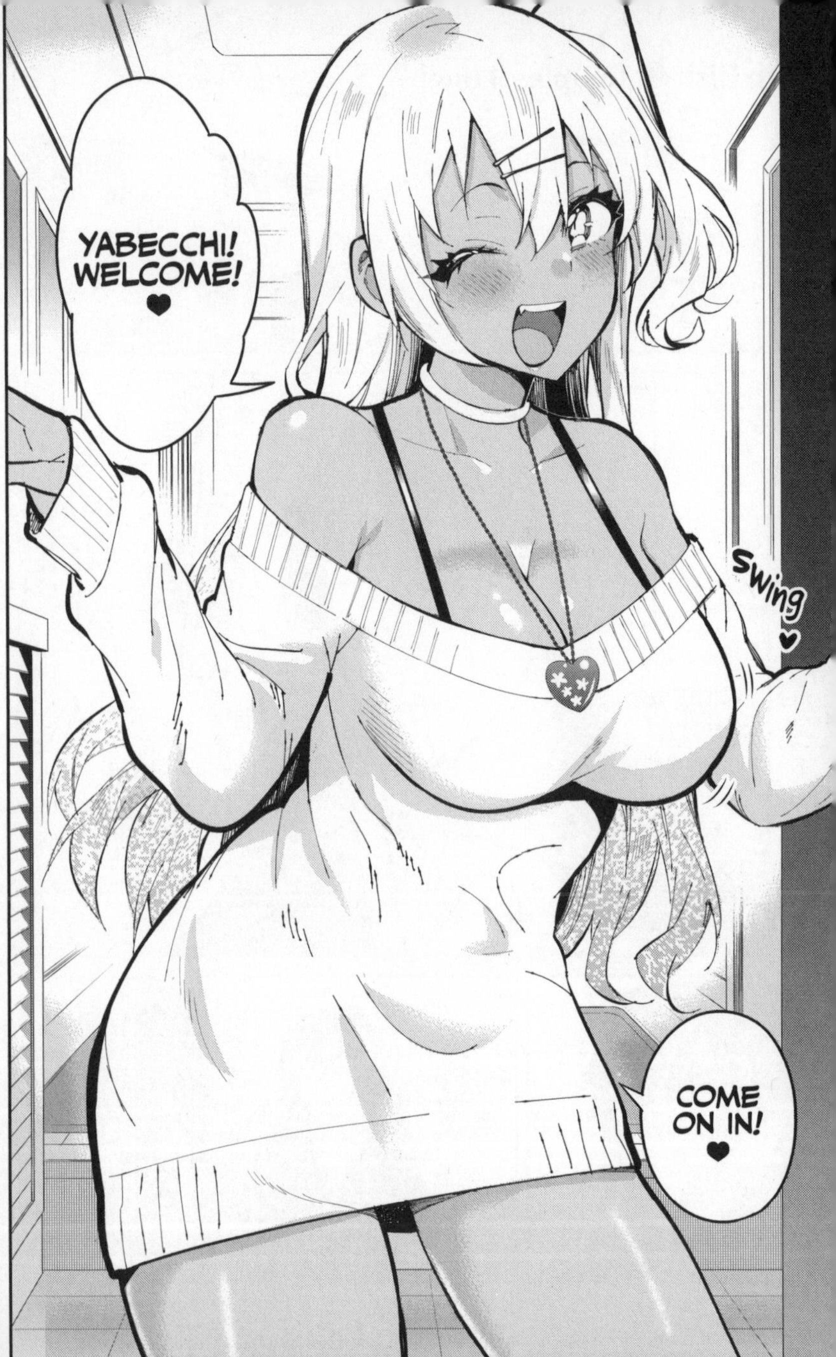
YABECCHI! WELCOME! ♥
Swing ♥
COME ON IN! ♥

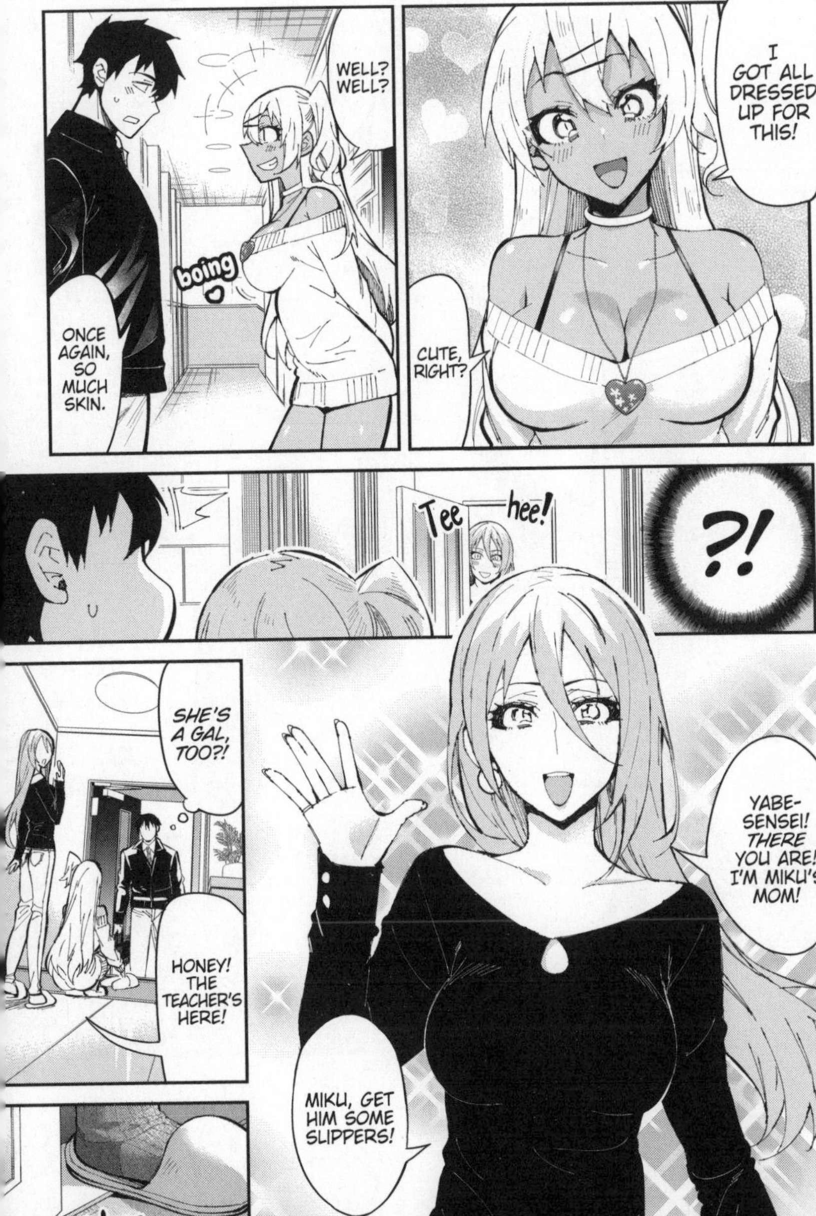
I GOT ALL DRESSED UP FOR THIS!
CUTE, RIGHT?
WELL? WELL?
boing
ONCE AGAIN, SO MUCH SKIN.
?!
Tee hee!
YABE-SENSEI! THERE YOU ARE! I'M MIKU'S MOM!
MIKU, GET HIM SOME SLIPPERS!
SHE'S A GAL, TOO?!
HONEY! THE TEACHER'S HERE!
Shff

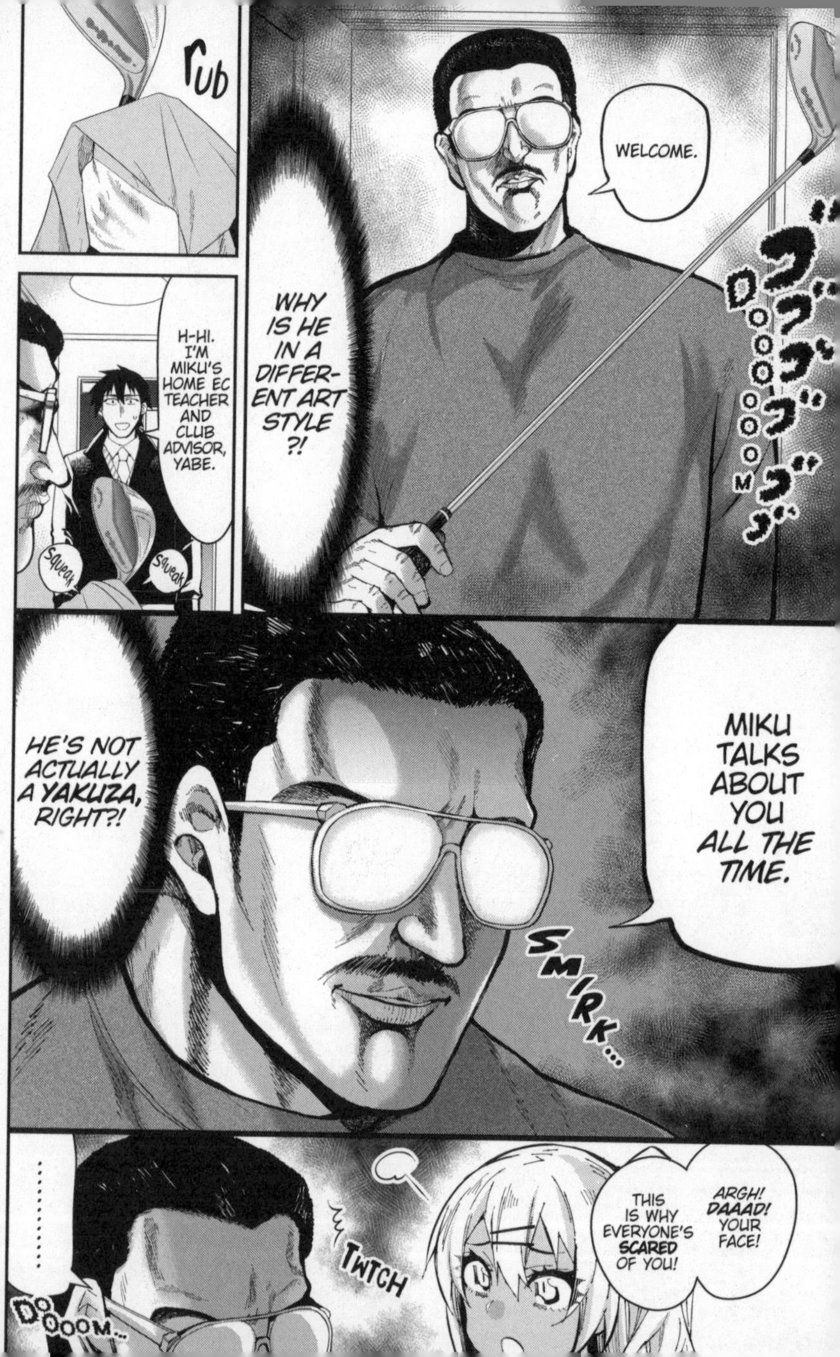
WELCOME.
DOOOOOOM
WHY IS HE IN A DIFFERENT ART STYLE ?!
rub
H-HI. I'M MIKU'S HOME EC TEACHER AND CLUB ADVISOR, YABE.
squeak
squeak
MIKU TALKS ABOUT YOU ALL THE TIME.
SMIRK...
HE'S NOT ACTUALLY A YAKUZA, RIGHT?!
ARGH! DAAAD! YOUR FACE!
THIS IS WHY EVERYONE'S SCARED OF YOU!
TWITCH
....
DOOOOM...

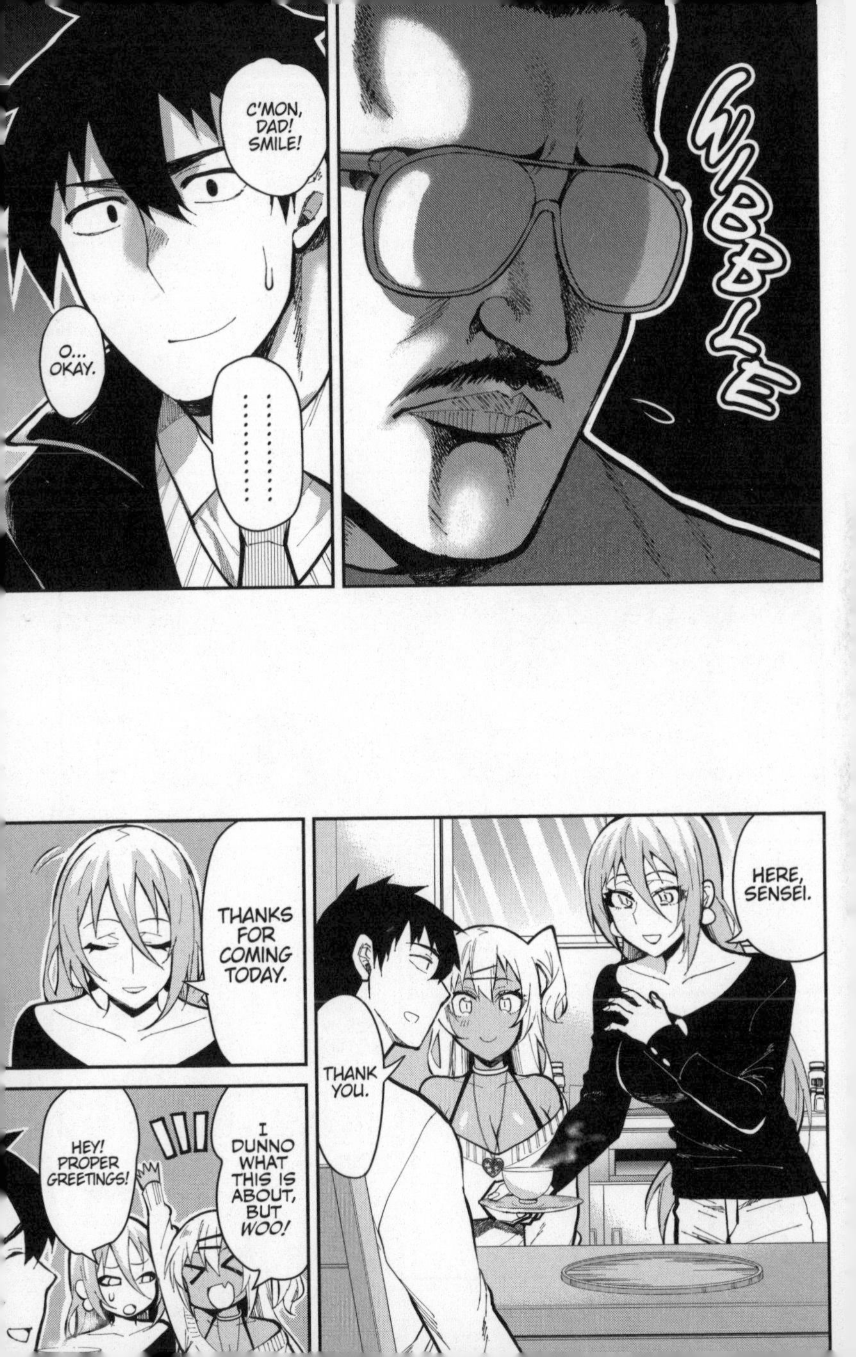
WIBBLE
C'MON, DAD! SMILE!
......
O... OKAY.
HERE, SENSEI.
THANK YOU.
THANKS FOR COMING TODAY.
I DUNNO WHAT THIS IS ABOUT, BUT WOO!
HEY! PROPER GREETINGS!

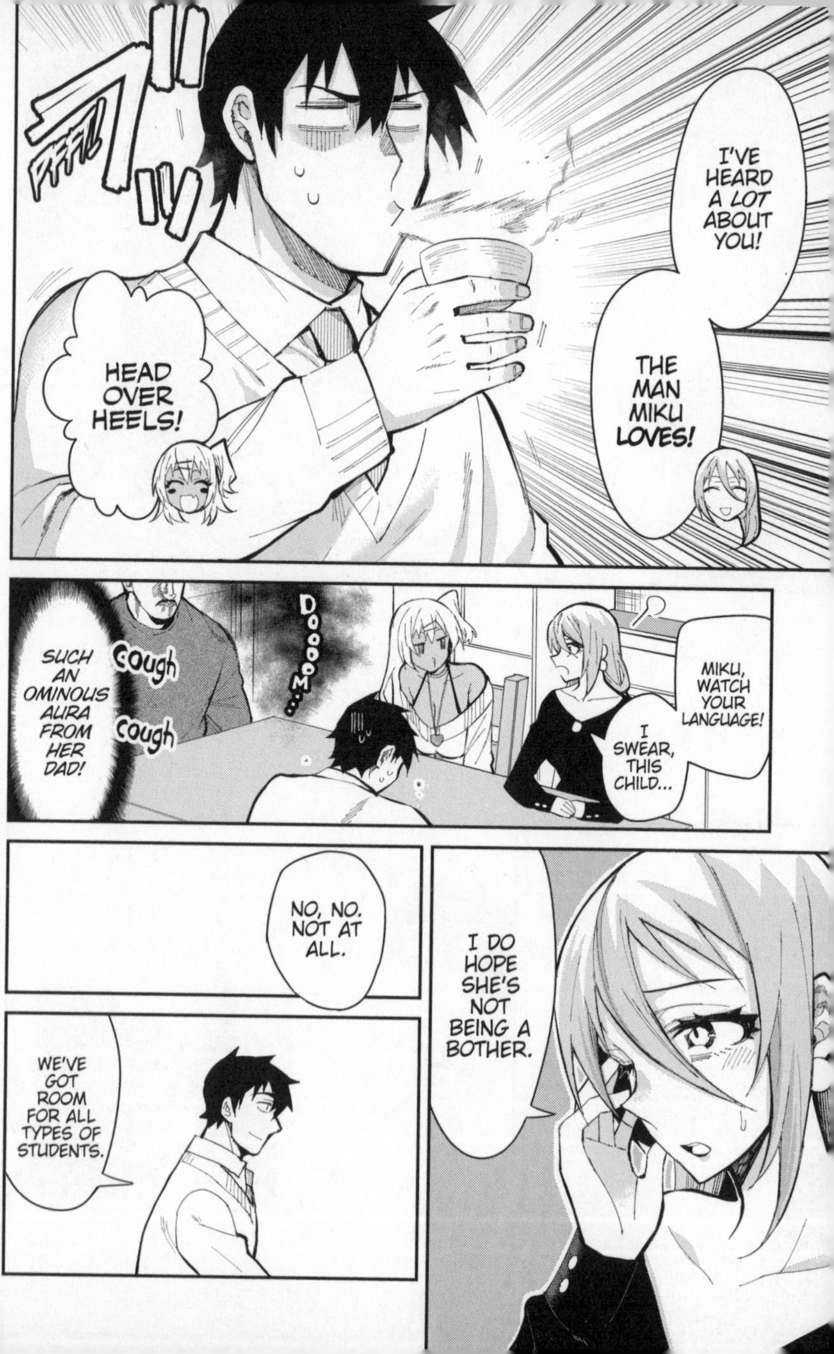

I'VE HEARD A LOT ABOUT YOU!
THE MAN MIKU LOVES!
HEAD OVER HEELS!
MIKU, WATCH YOUR LANGUAGE!
I SWEAR, THIS CHILD...
DOOOOOM...
Cough
Cough
SUCH AN OMINOUS AURA FROM HER DAD!
I DO HOPE SHE'S NOT BEING A BOTHER.
NO, NO. NOT AT ALL.
WE'VE GOT ROOM FOR ALL TYPES OF STUDENTS.

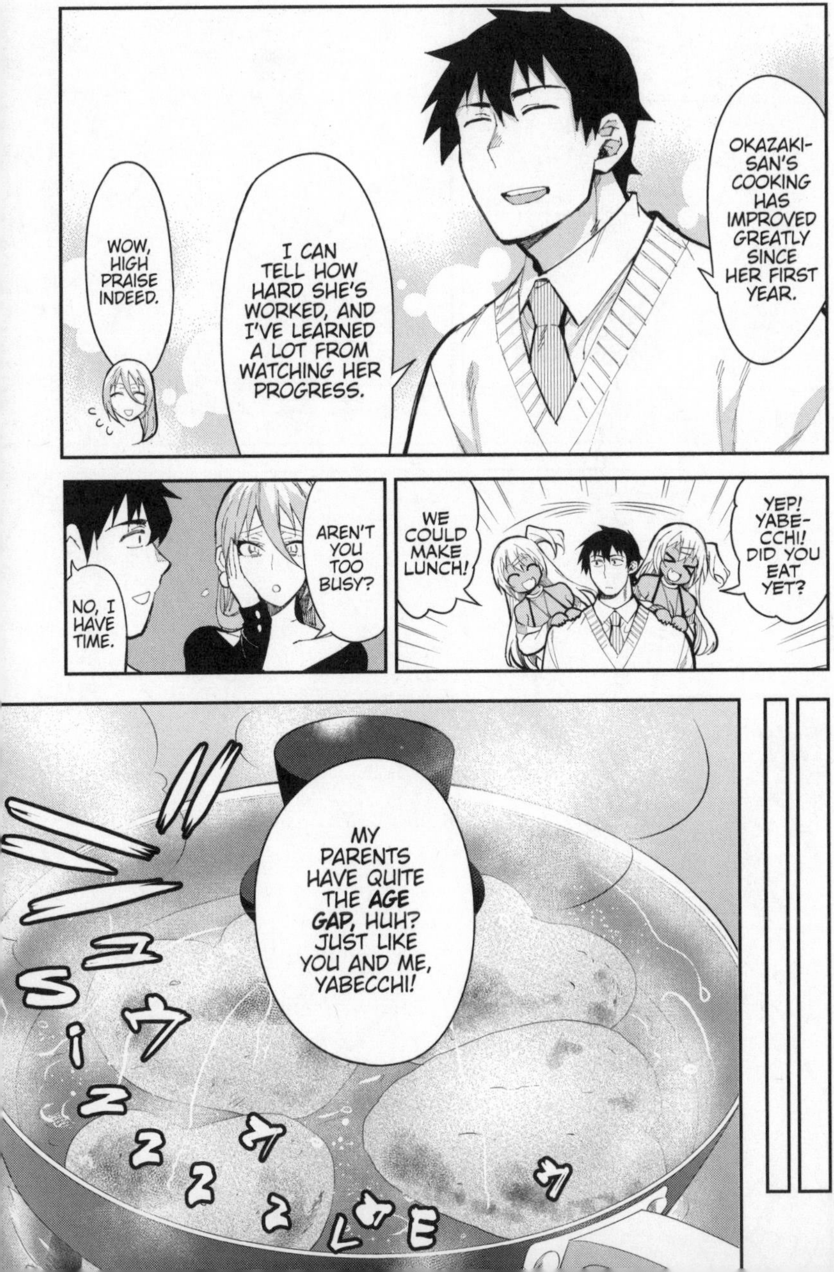
OKAZAKI-SAN'S COOKING HAS IMPROVED GREATLY SINCE HER FIRST YEAR.
I CAN TELL HOW HARD SHE'S WORKED, AND I'VE LEARNED A LOT FROM WATCHING HER PROGRESS.
WOW, HIGH PRAISE INDEED.
YEP! YABECCHI! DID YOU EAT YET?
WE COULD MAKE LUNCH!
AREN'T YOU TOO BUSY?
NO, I HAVE TIME.
MY PARENTS HAVE QUITE THE **AGE GAP**, HUH? JUST LIKE YOU AND ME, YABECCHI!

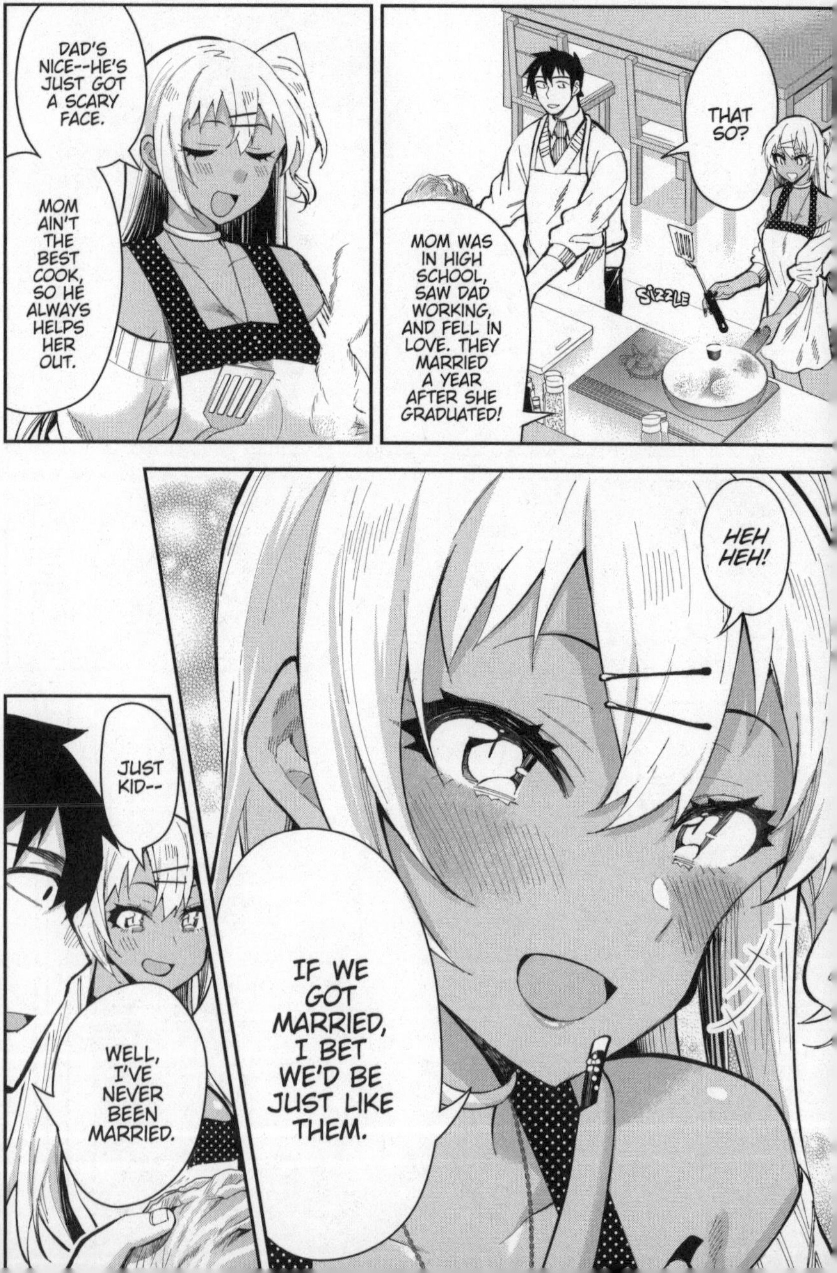
THAT SO?
MOM WAS IN HIGH SCHOOL, SAW DAD WORKING, AND FELL IN LOVE. THEY MARRIED A YEAR AFTER SHE GRADUATED!
SIZZLE
DAD'S NICE--HE'S JUST GOT A SCARY FACE.
MOM AIN'T THE BEST COOK, SO HE ALWAYS HELPS HER OUT.
HEH HEH!
IF WE GOT MARRIED, I BET WE'D BE JUST LIKE THEM.
JUST KID--
WELL, I'VE NEVER BEEN MARRIED.

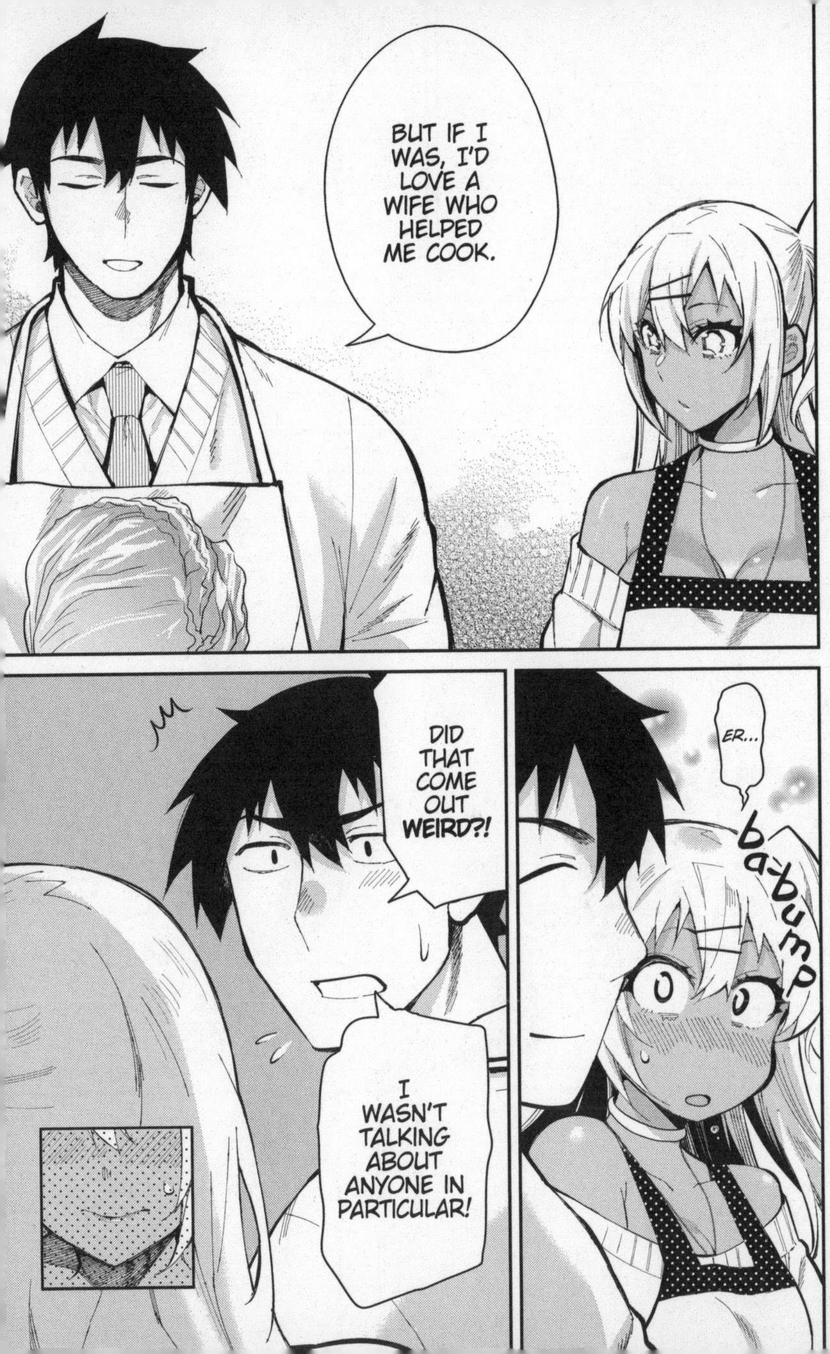
BUT IF I WAS, I'D LOVE A WIFE WHO HELPED ME COOK.
ER...
ba-bump
DID THAT COME OUT WEIRD?!
I WASN'T TALKING ABOUT ANYONE IN PARTICULAR!

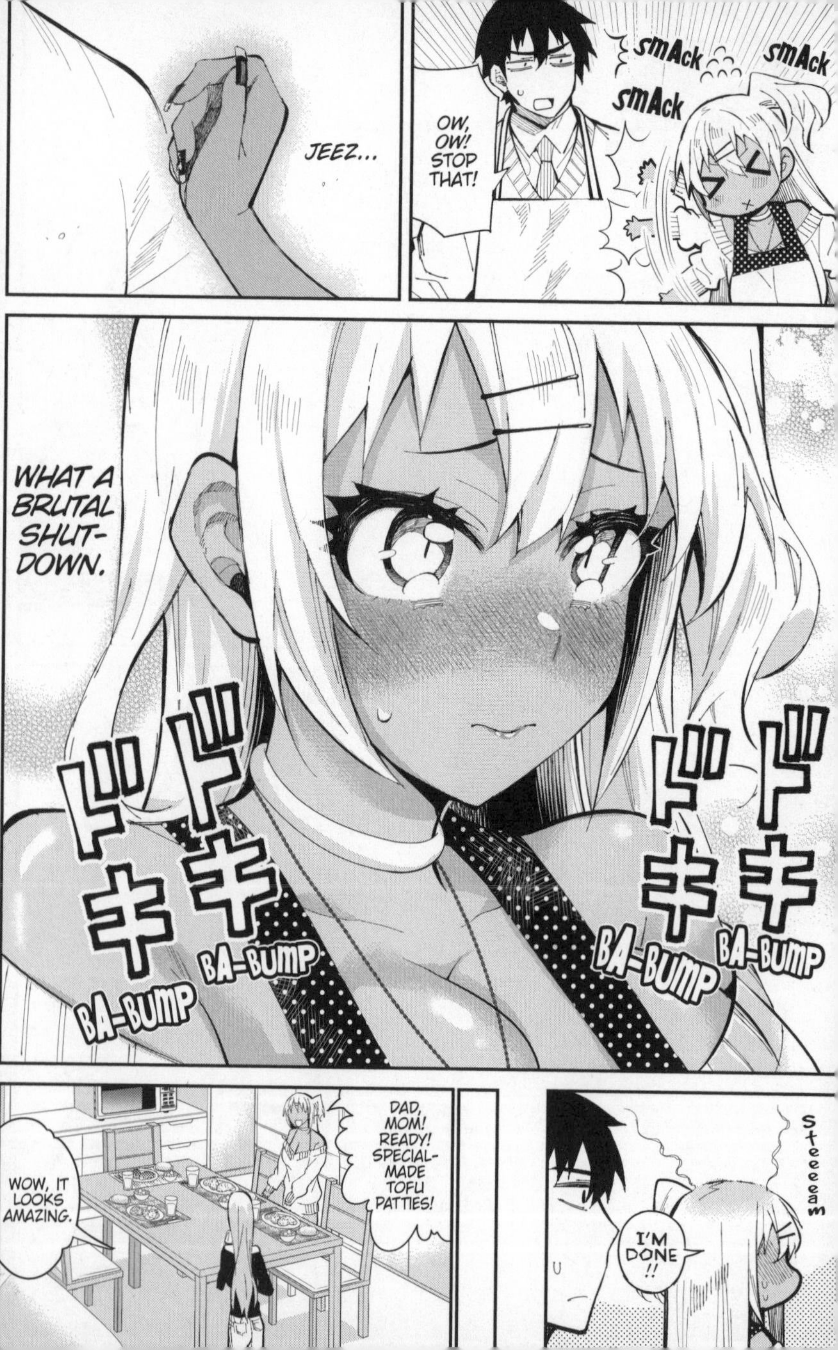
SMACK
SMACK
SMACK
OW, OW! STOP THAT!
JEEZ...
WHAT A BRUTAL SHUT-DOWN.
ドキドキ
BA-BUMP
BA-BUMP
ドキドキ
BA-BUMP
BA-BUMP
Steeeeam
I'M DONE!!
DAD, MOM! READY! SPECIAL-MADE TOFU PATTIES!
WOW, IT LOOKS AMAZING.

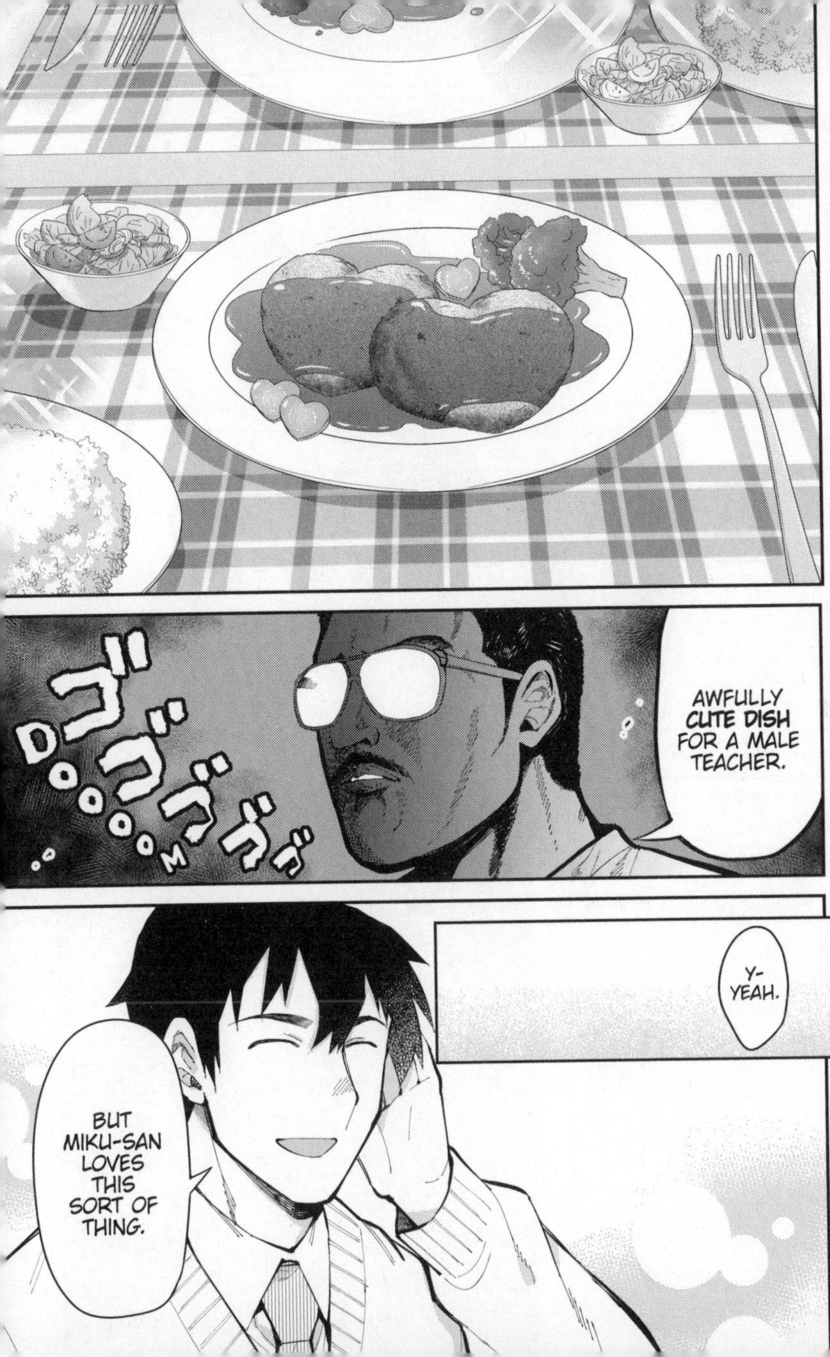

AWFULLY CUTE DISH FOR A MALE TEACHER.
ゴゴゴゴゴゴ
DOOOOOOM
Y-YEAH.
BUT MIKU-SAN LOVES THIS SORT OF THING.

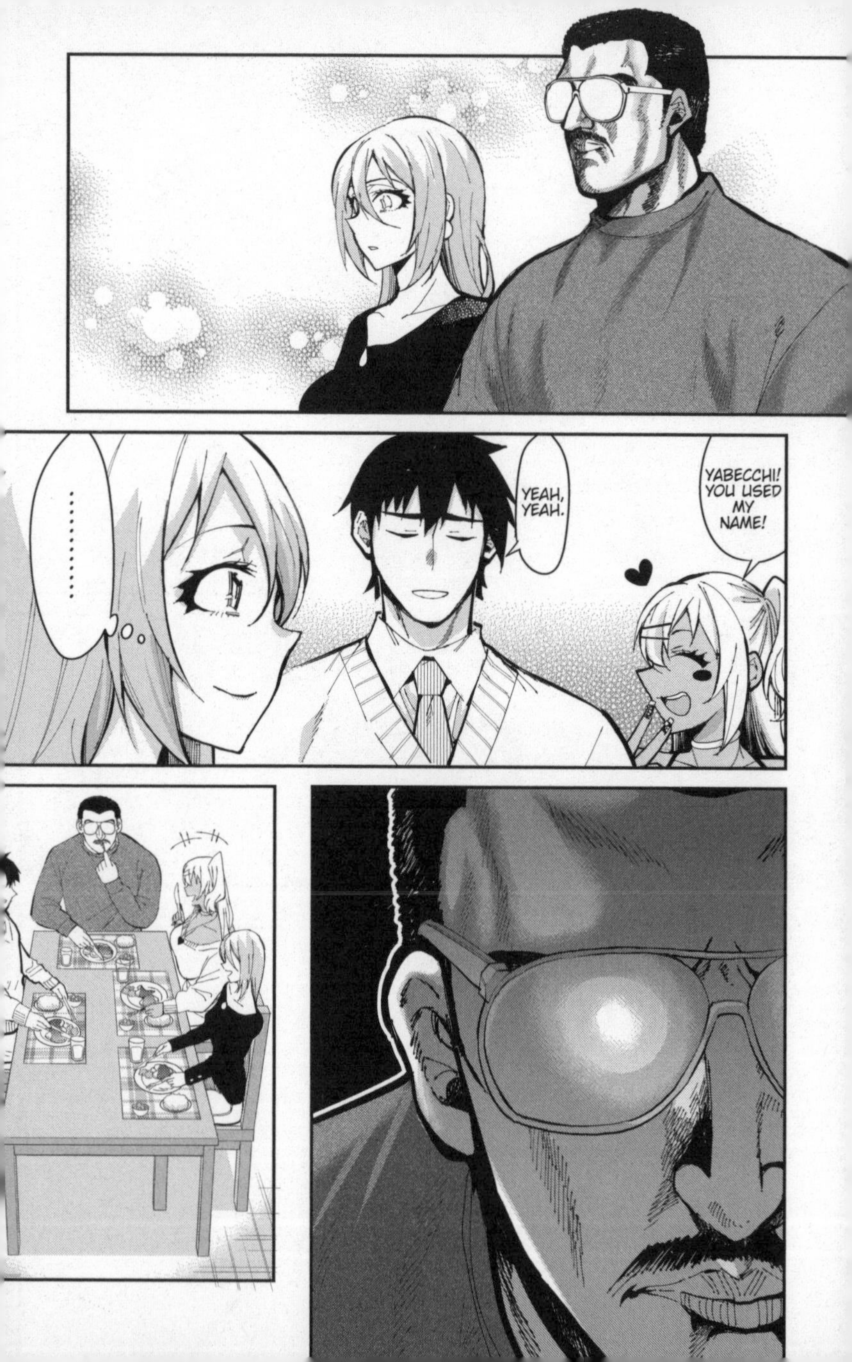
YABECCHI! YOU USED MY NAME!
YEAH, YEAH.
......

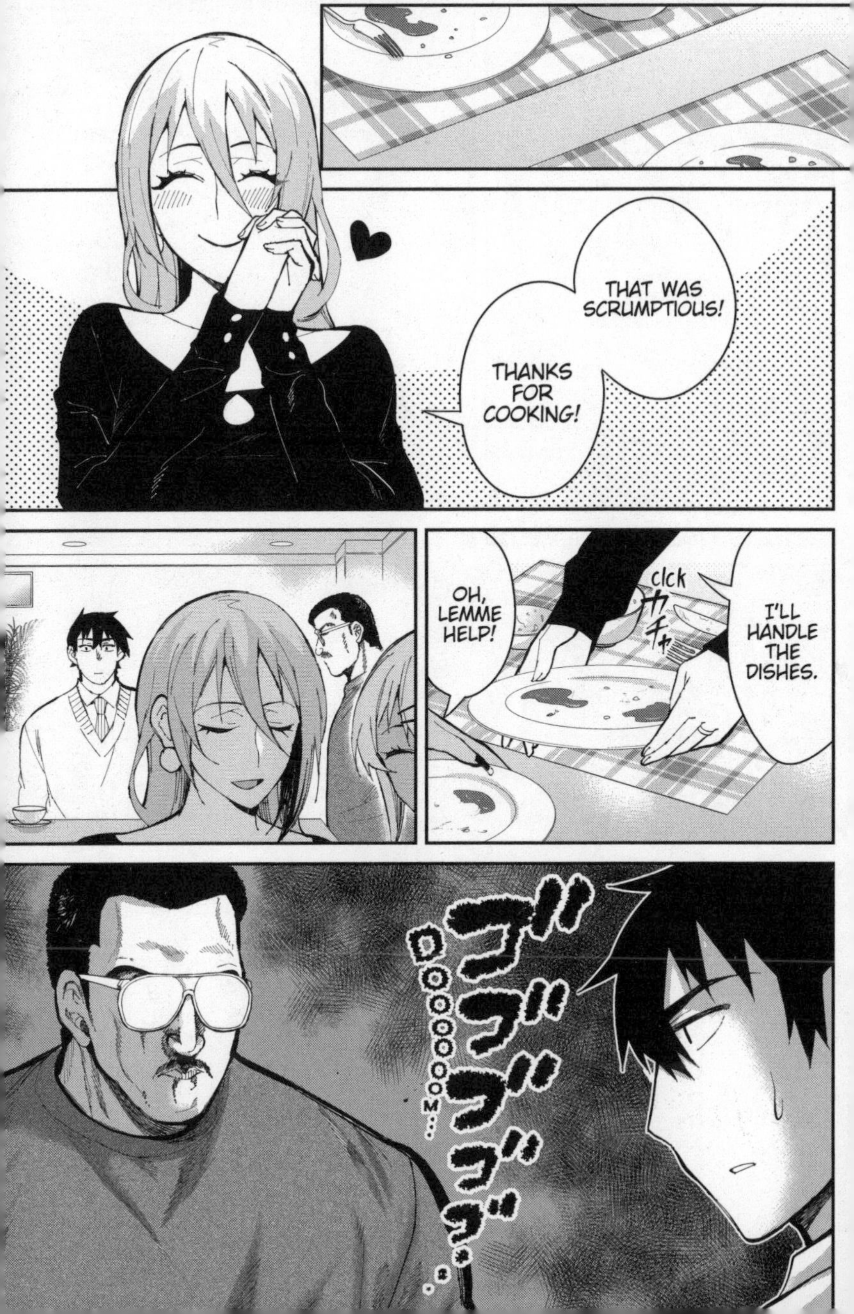
THAT WAS SCRUMPTIOUS!
THANKS FOR COOKING!
I'LL HANDLE THE DISHES.
clck
カチャ
OH, LEMME HELP!
ゴゴゴゴ
DOOOOOOOOM...

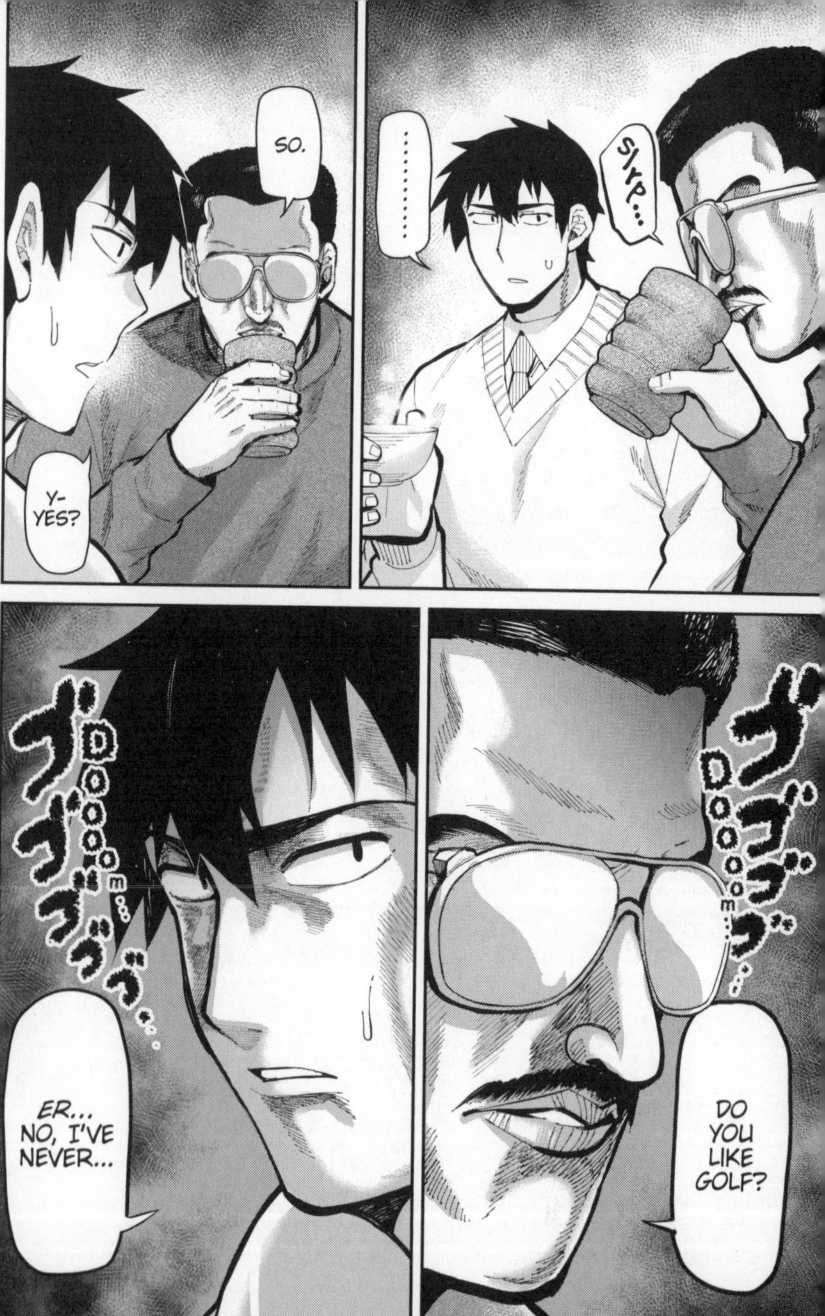
SIP...
......
SO.
Y-YES?
DOOOOm...
DO YOU LIKE GOLF?
DOOOOm...
ER... NO, I'VE NEVER...

THEN... DO YOU LIKE FLOWERS?

GOGOGO

DOOM...

I SEE.

....

I'M GONNA GO WITH YES.

THONK

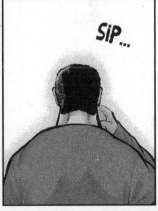

SIP...

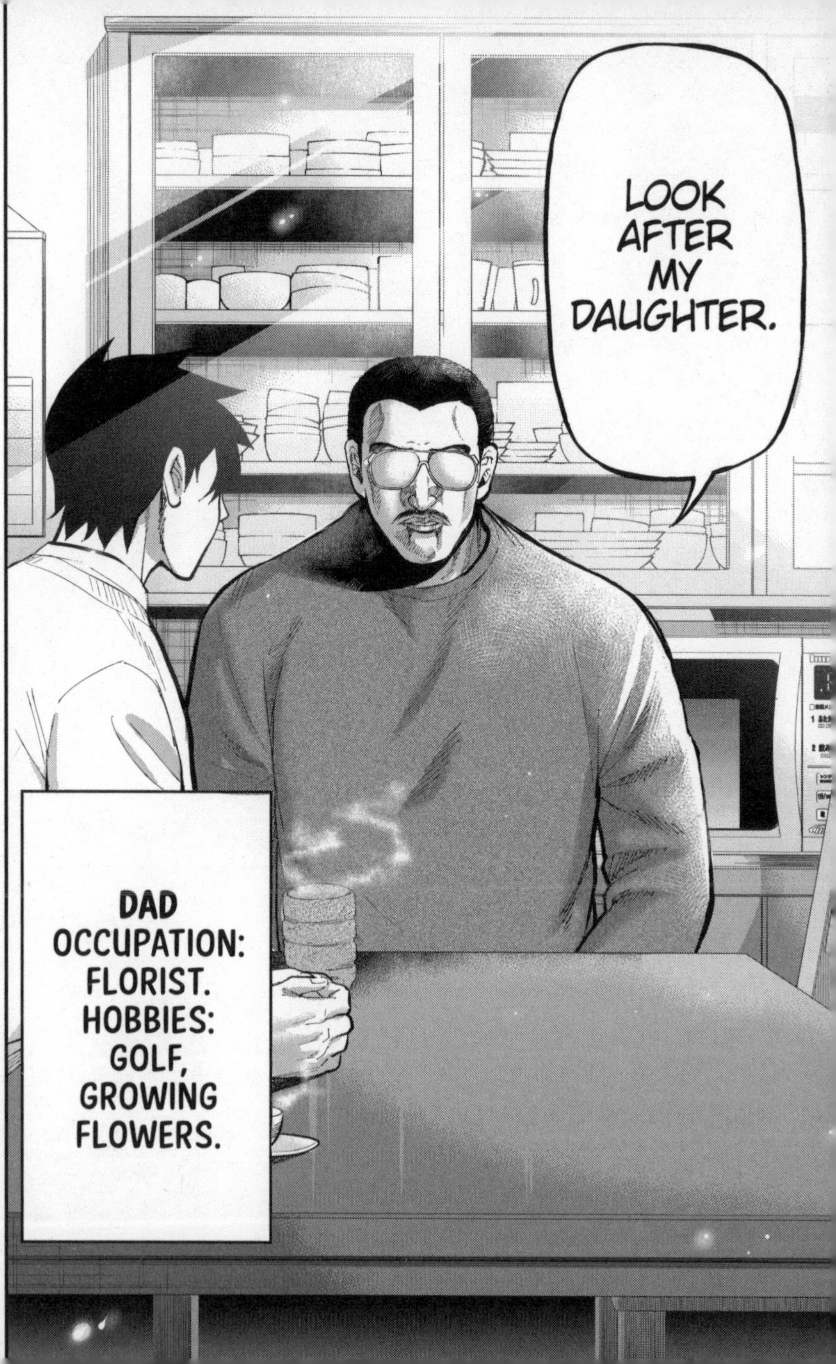
LOOK AFTER MY DAUGHTER.
DAD
OCCUPATION: FLORIST.
HOBBIES: GOLF, GROWING FLOWERS.

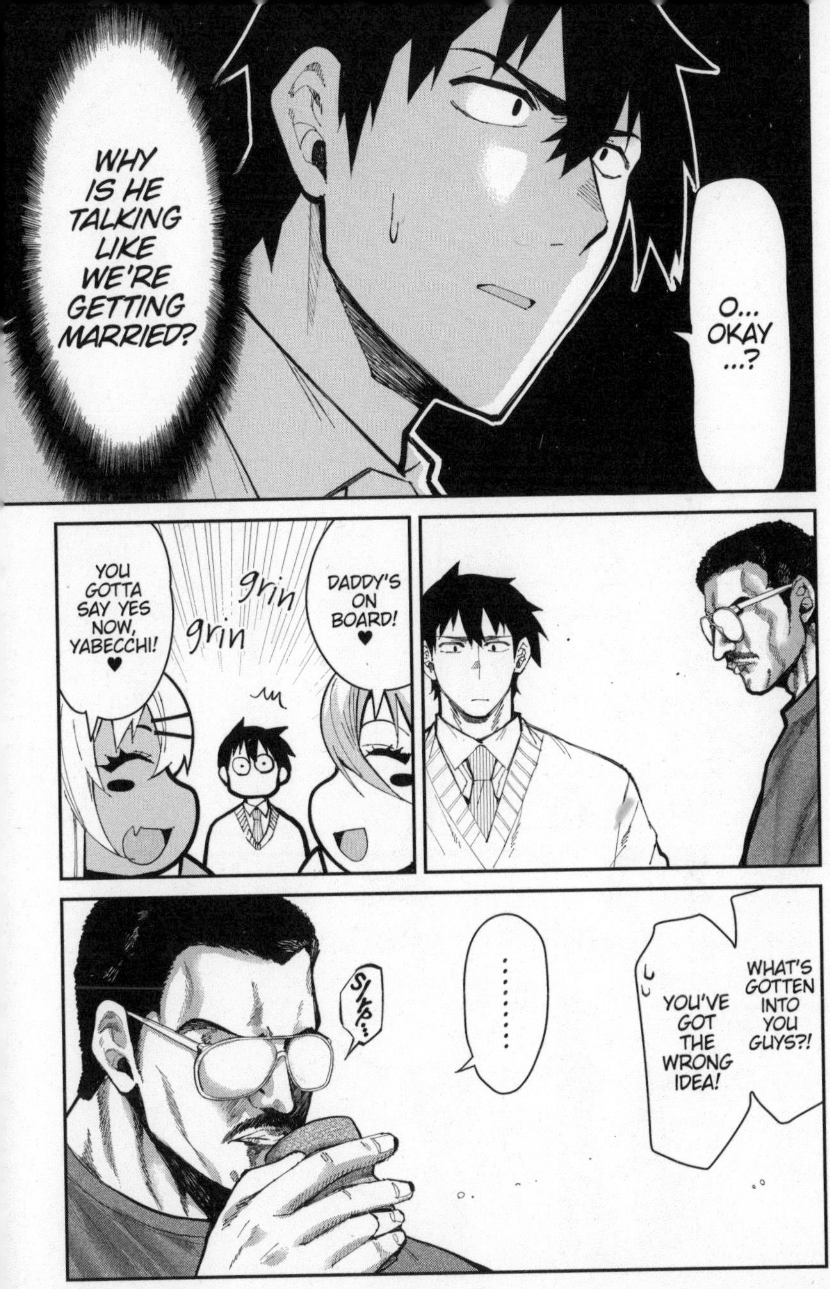
O... OKAY ...?
WHY IS HE TALKING LIKE WE'RE GETTING MARRIED?
DADDY'S ON BOARD! ♥
grin
grin
YOU GOTTA SAY YES NOW, YABECCHI! ♥
WHAT'S GOTTEN INTO YOU GUYS?!
YOU'VE GOT THE WRONG IDEA!
......
SIP...

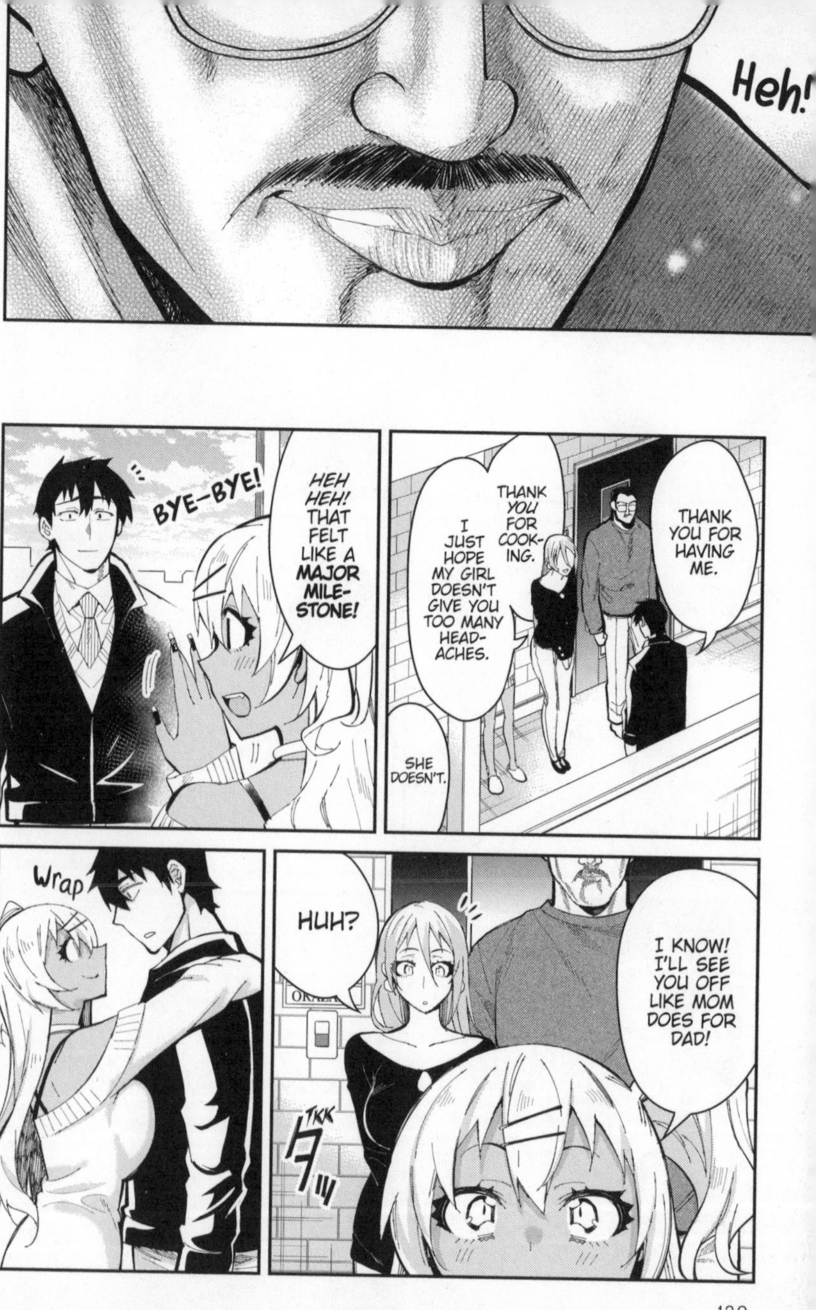

Heh!
THANK YOU FOR HAVING ME.
THANK YOU FOR COOKING.
I JUST HOPE MY GIRL DOESN'T GIVE YOU TOO MANY HEADACHES.
SHE DOESN'T.
HEH HEH! THAT FELT LIKE A MAJOR MILESTONE!
BYE-BYE!
I KNOW! I'LL SEE YOU OFF LIKE MOM DOES FOR DAD!
HUH?
TKK
Wrap

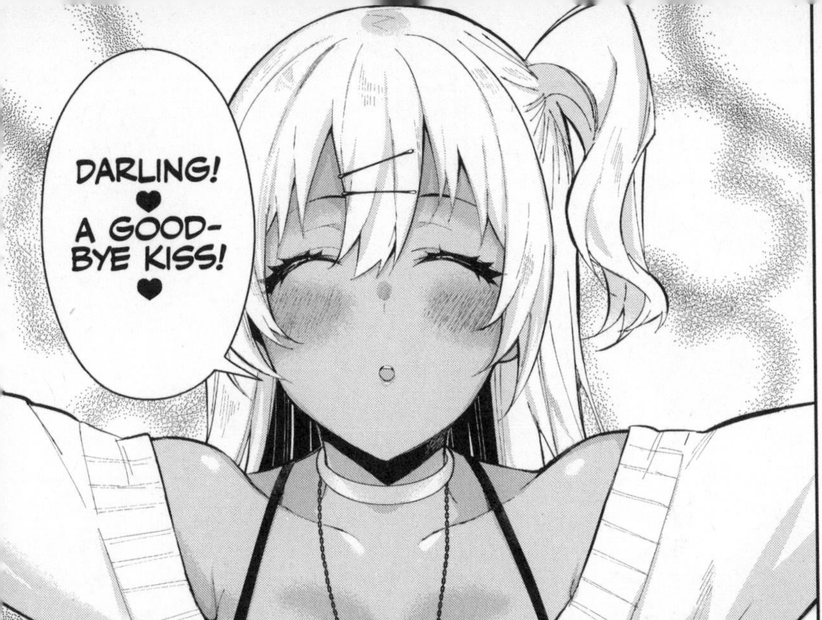
DARLING! ♥ A GOOD-BYE KISS! ♥
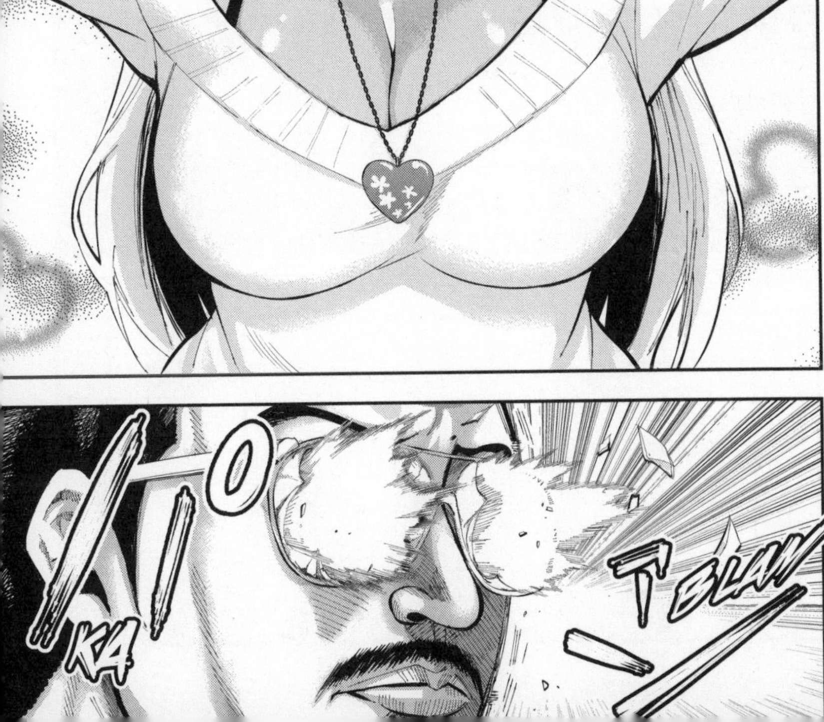
T BLAM
KA

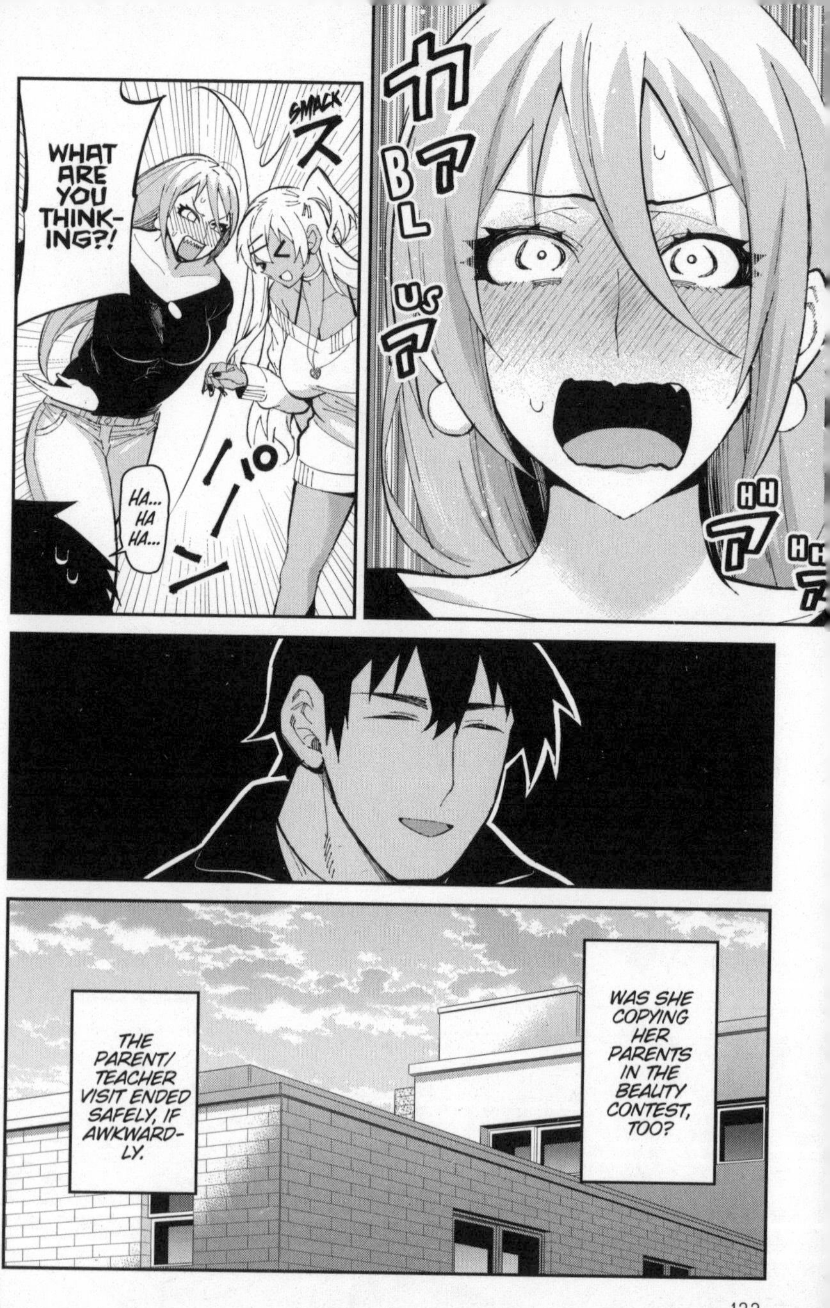
SMACK
WHAT ARE YOU THINKING?!
HA... HA HA...
WAS SHE COPYING HER PARENTS IN THE BEAUTY CONTEST, TOO?
THE PARENT/TEACHER VISIT ENDED SAFELY, IF AWKWARDLY.

Gal
Gohan

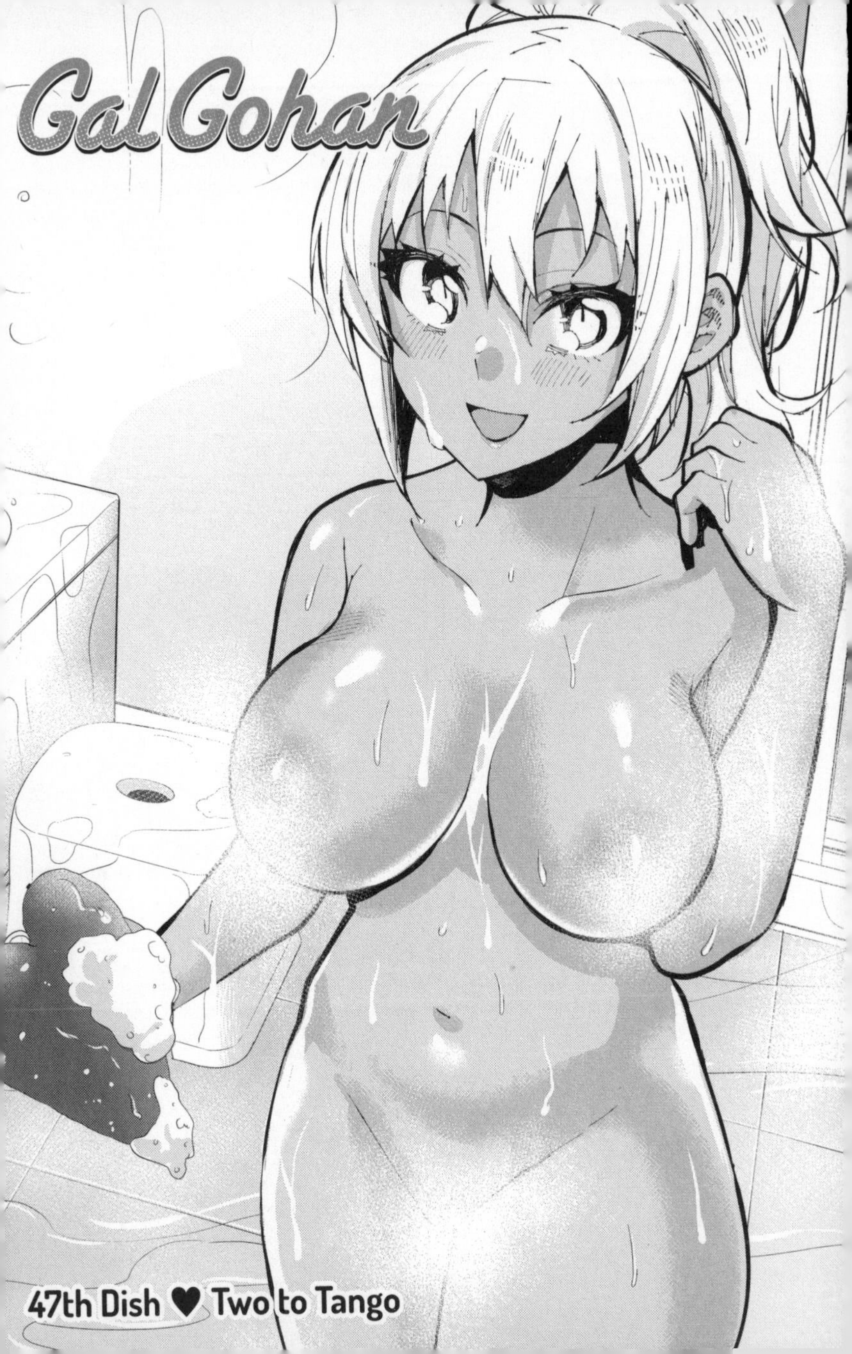
Gal Gohan
47th Dish ♥ Two to Tango

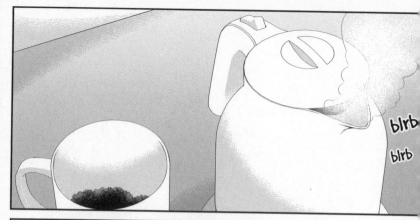
blrb

blrb

DECEMBER 25TH. CHRISTMAS.

GLUG GLUG...

clk

CLCk

THAT'S NOT A GOOD SIGN.

DING DONG

DING DONG

DING DONG

DING DONG

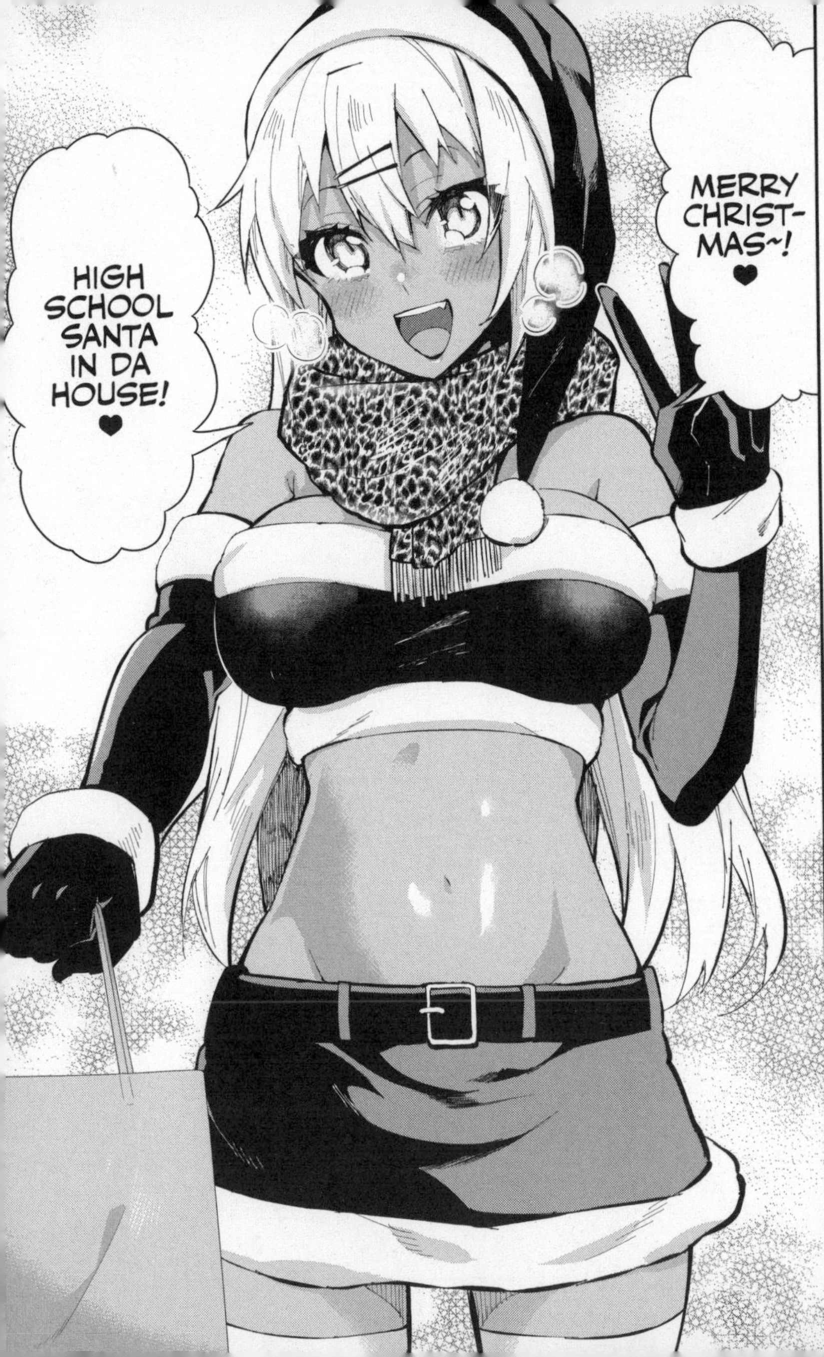
MERRY CHRIST-MAS~! ♥
HIGH SCHOOL SANTA IN DA HOUSE! ♥

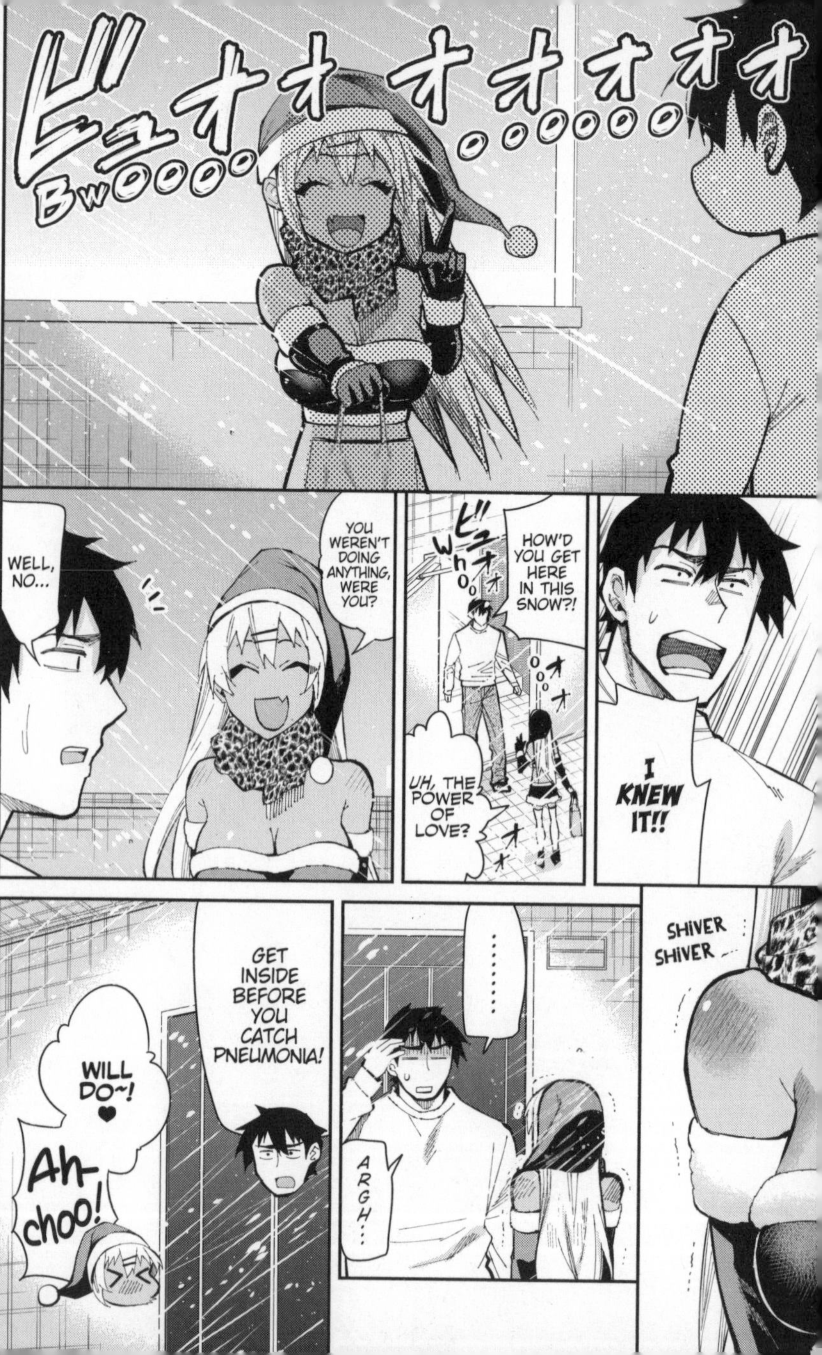
ビュオオ オオオオオオ
BwOOOO
OOOOOO
I KNEW IT!!
HOW'D YOU GET HERE IN THIS SNOW?!
ビュ
Whoo
オオ
UH, THE POWER OF LOVE?
YOU WEREN'T DOING ANYTHING, WERE YOU?
WELL, NO...
SHIVER SHIVER
......
ARGH...
GET INSIDE BEFORE YOU CATCH PNEUMONIA!
WILL DO~! ♥
Ah-choo!

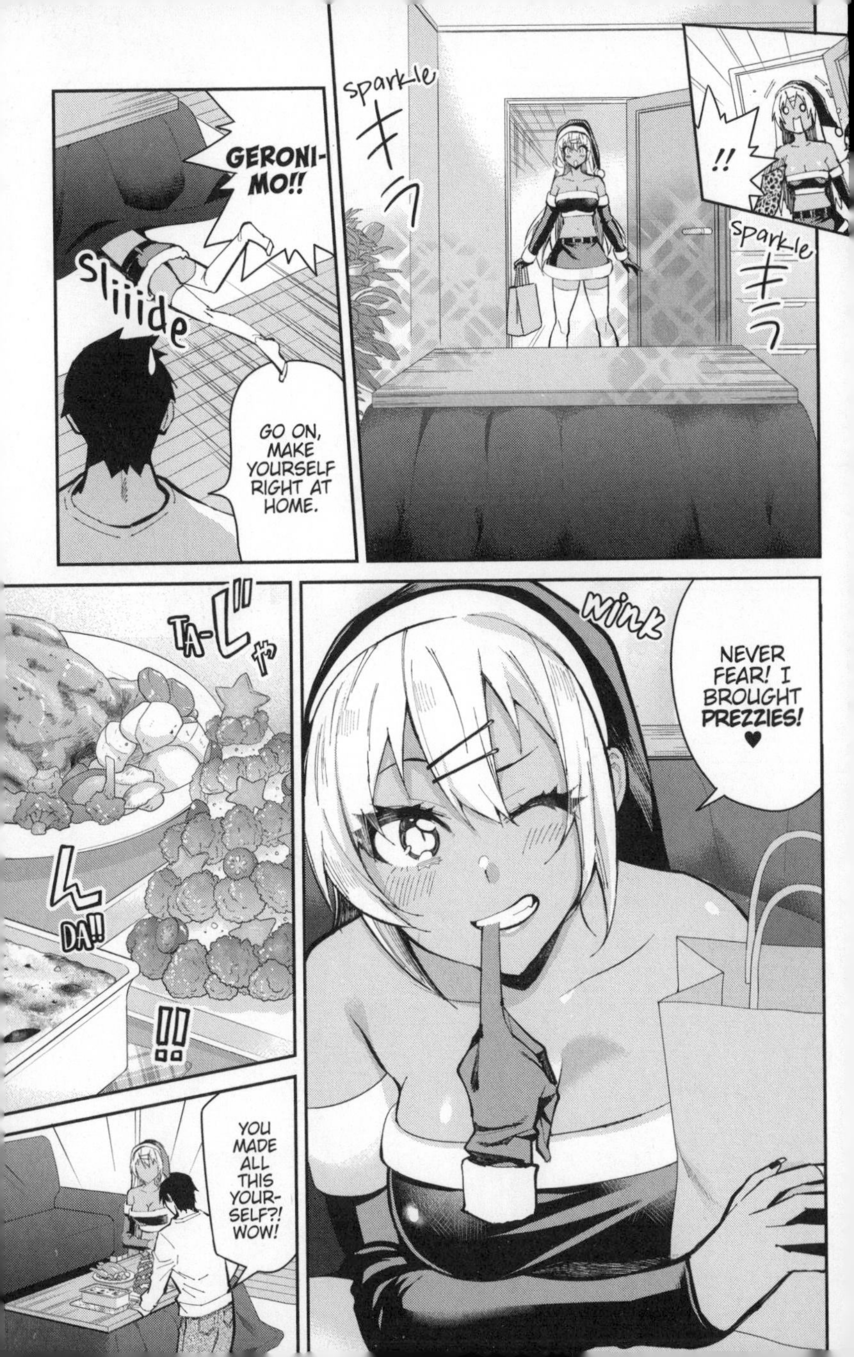

!!
sparkle
キラ
sparkle
キラ
GERONI-MO!!
Sliiiide
GO ON, MAKE YOURSELF RIGHT AT HOME.
wink
NEVER FEAR! I BROUGHT PREZZIES! ♥
TA-じゃ
ん
DA!!
!!
YOU MADE ALL THIS YOURSELF?! WOW!

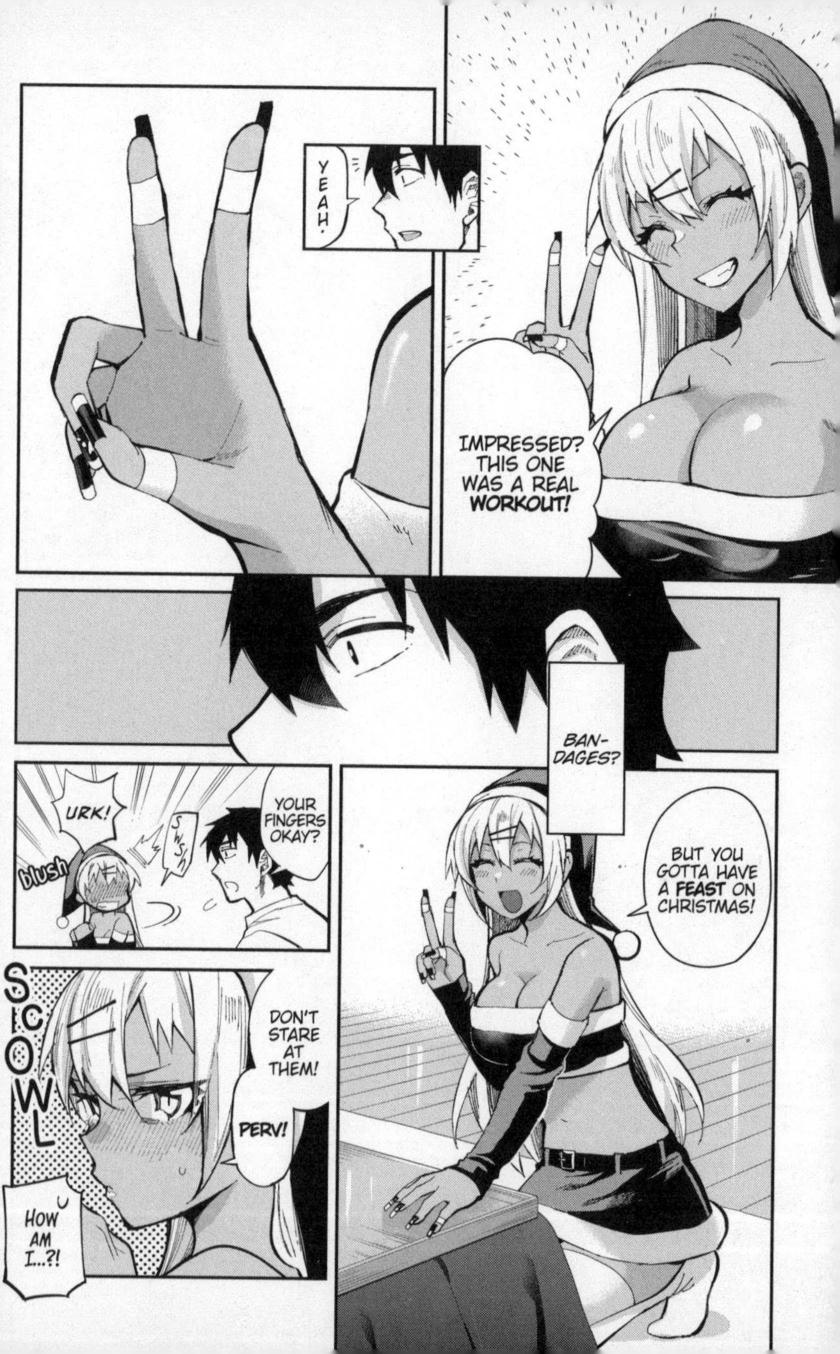
IMPRESSED? THIS ONE WAS A REAL WORKOUT!
YEAH.
BAN-DAGES?
BUT YOU GOTTA HAVE A FEAST ON CHRISTMAS!
YOUR FINGERS OKAY?
SWSH
URK!
blush
SCOWL
DON'T STARE AT THEM!
PERV!
HOW AM I...?!

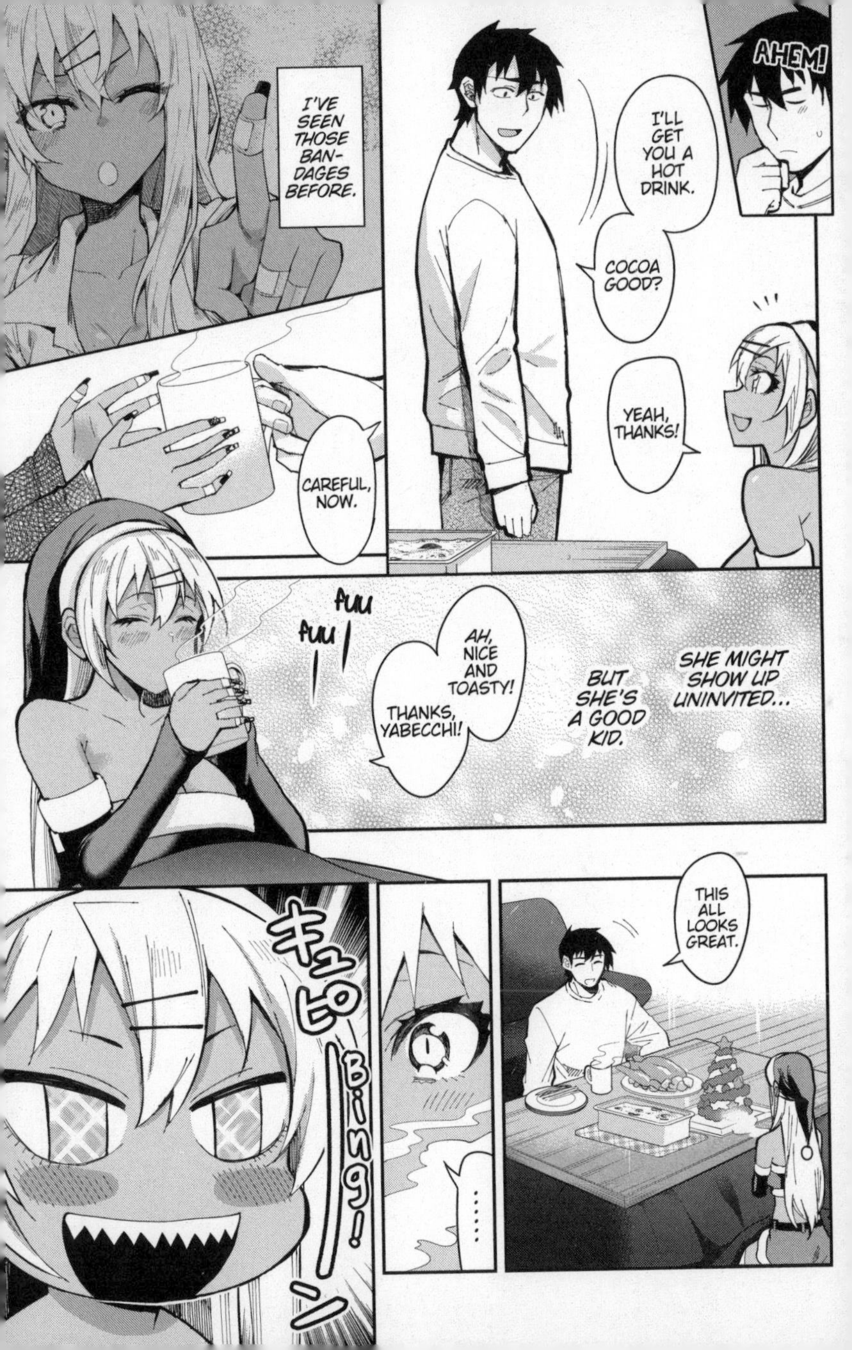
AHEM!
I'LL GET YOU A HOT DRINK.
COCOA GOOD?
YEAH, THANKS!
I'VE SEEN THOSE BANDAGES BEFORE.
CAREFUL, NOW.
SHE MIGHT SHOW UP UNINVITED...
BUT SHE'S A GOOD KID.
AH, NICE AND TOASTY!
THANKS, YABECCHI!
fuu
fuu
THIS ALL LOOKS GREAT.
......
キュピーン
Bing!

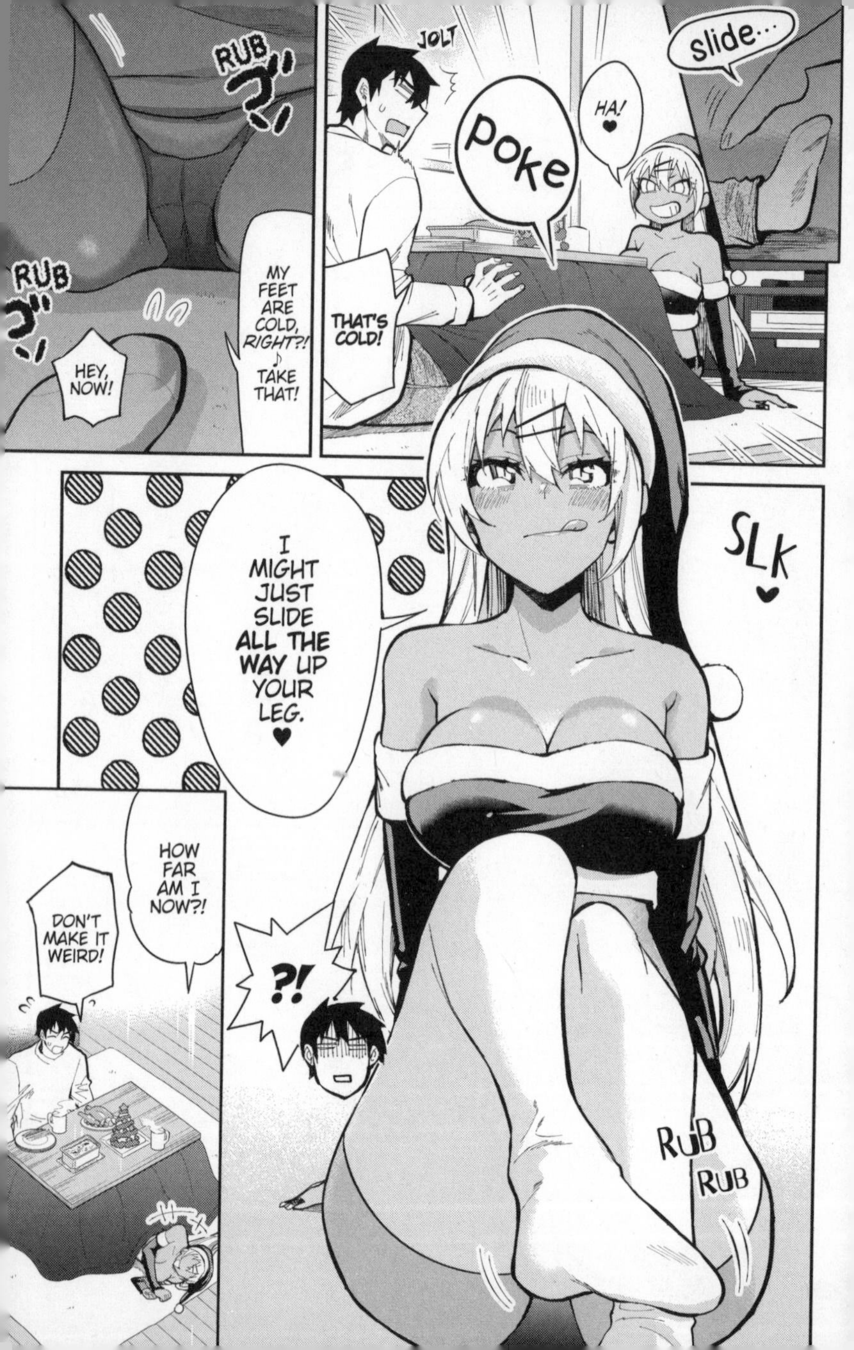
slide...
HA! ♥
poke
JOLT
THAT'S COLD!
RUB
MY FEET ARE COLD, RIGHT?! ♪ TAKE THAT!
RUB
HEY, NOW!
SLK ♥
I MIGHT JUST SLIDE ALL THE WAY UP YOUR LEG. ♥
?!
RUB
RUB
HOW FAR AM I NOW?!
DON'T MAKE IT WEIRD!

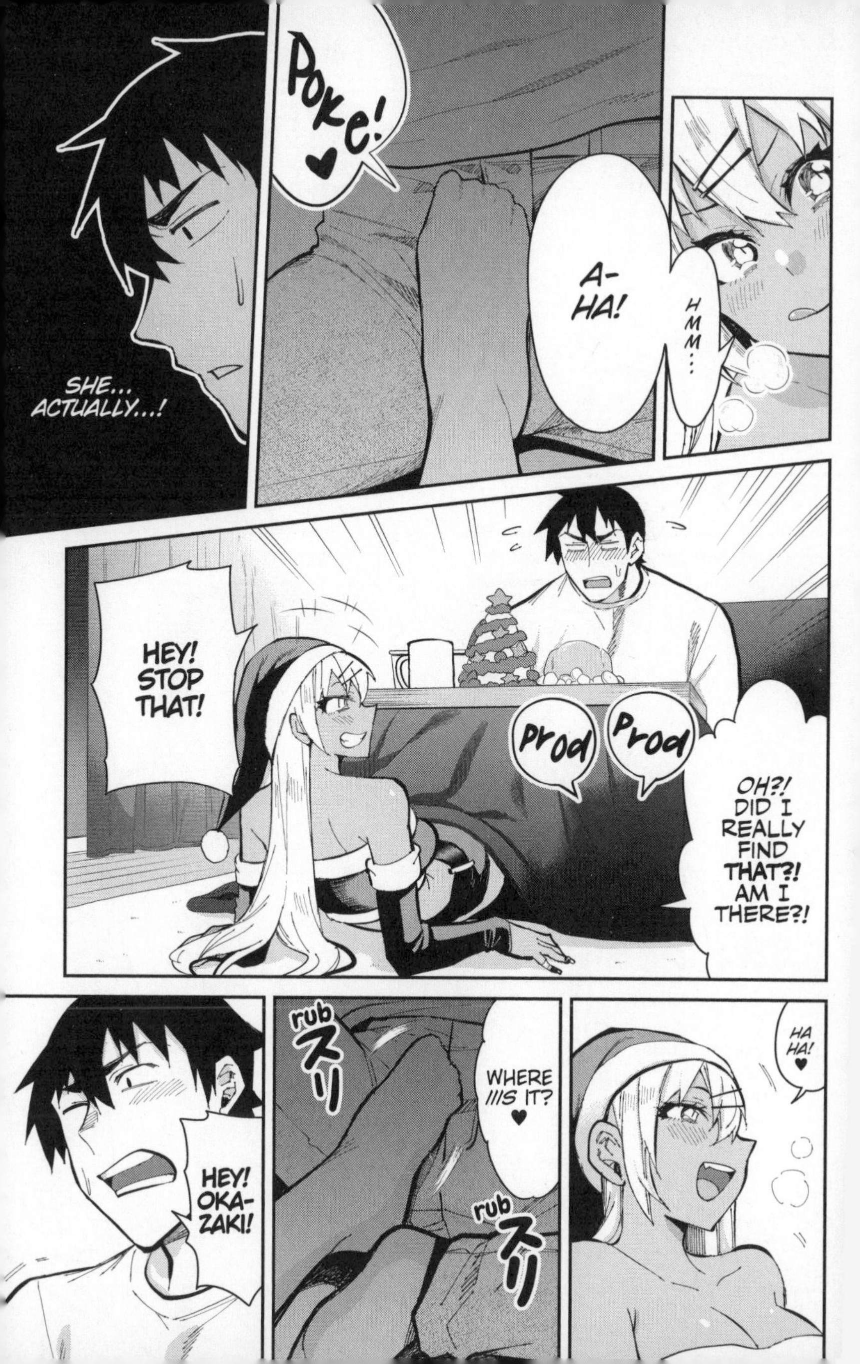
HMM...
A-HA!
Poke! ♥
SHE... ACTUALLY...!
OH?! DID I REALLY FIND THAT?! AM I THERE?!
Prod
Prod
HEY! STOP THAT!
HA HA! ♥
WHERE IIIS IT? ♥
rub スリ
rub スリ
HEY! OKA-ZAKI!

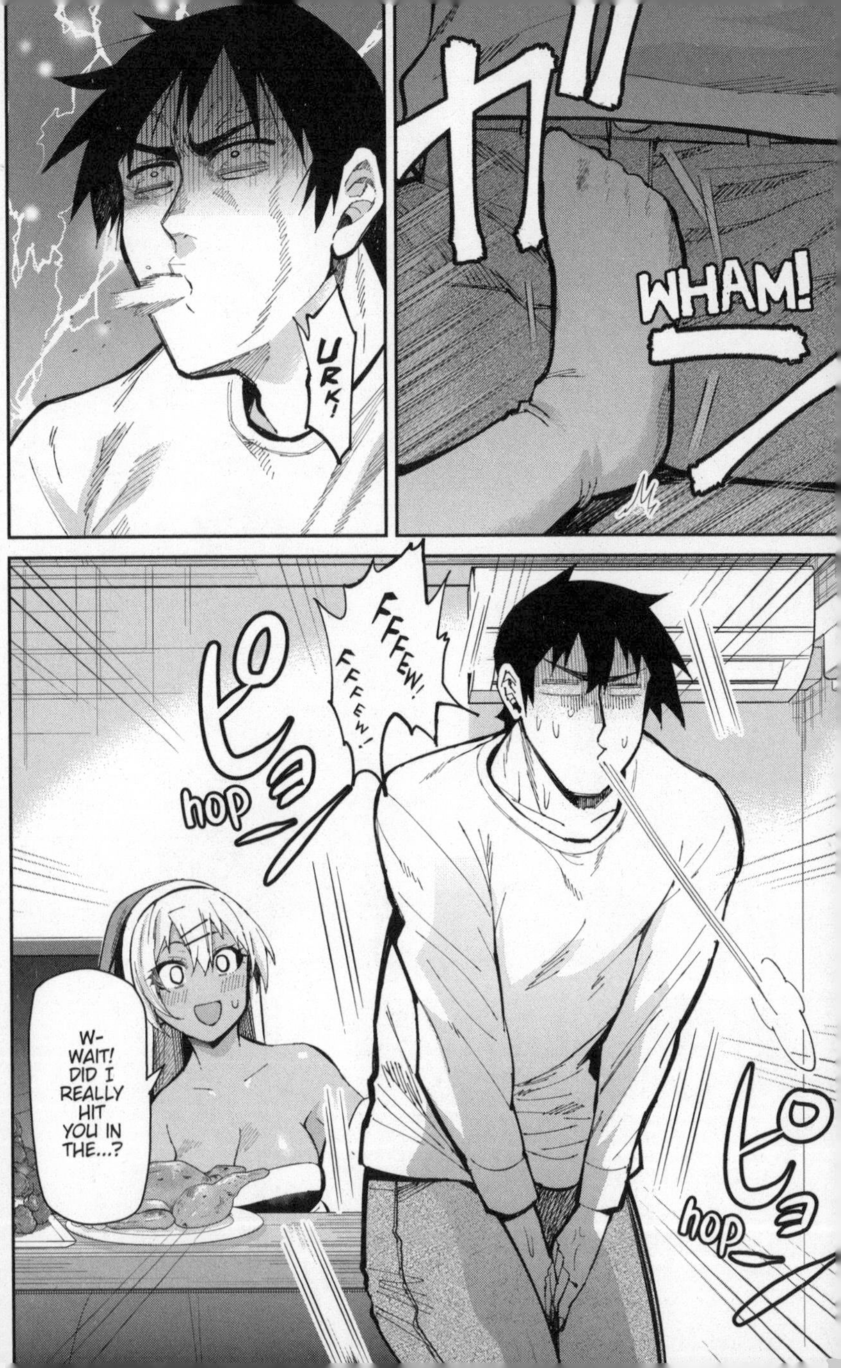
WHAM!
URK!
FFFEW!
FFFEW!
ピョ
hop
ピョ
hop
W-WAIT! DID I REALLY HIT YOU IN THE...?

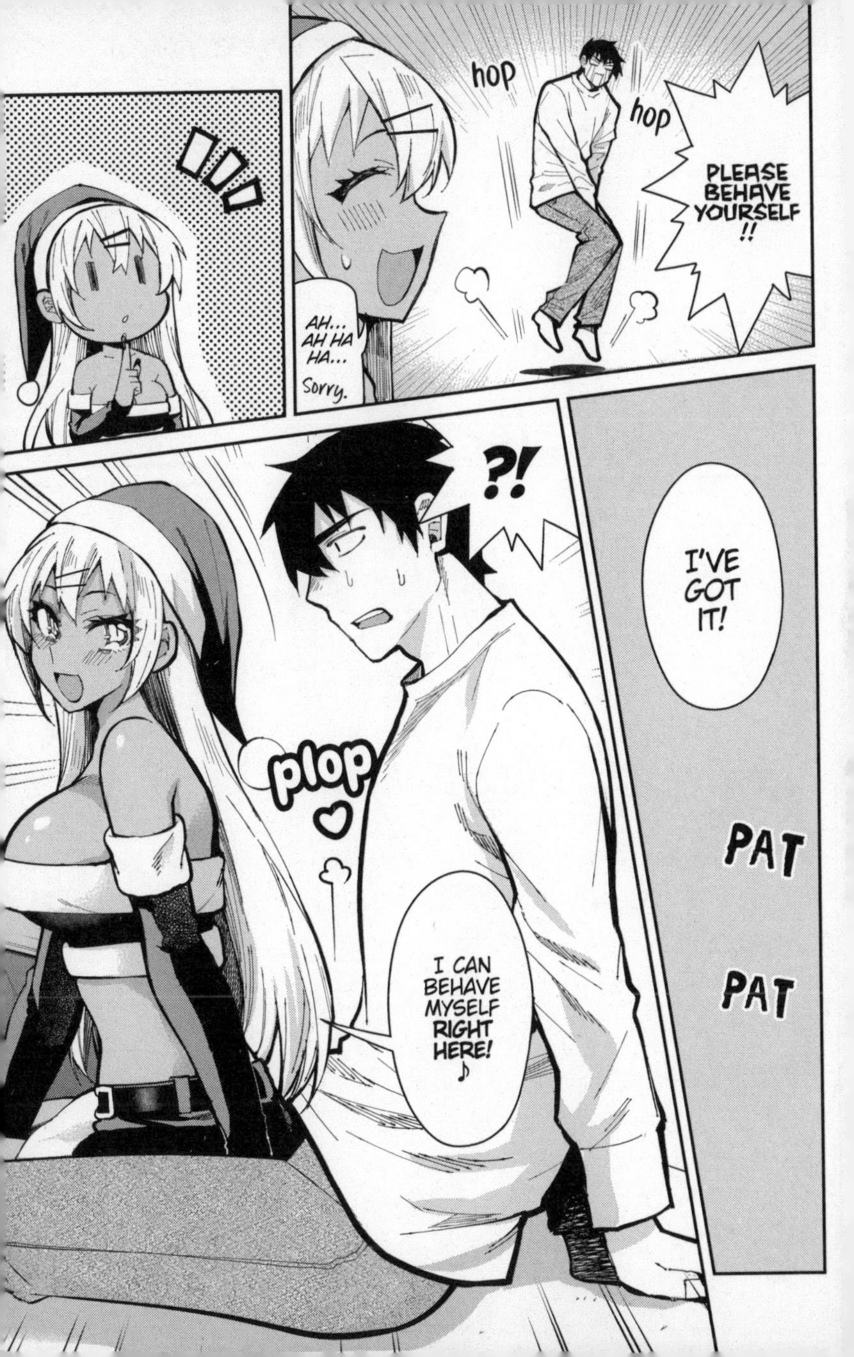
hop
hop
PLEASE BEHAVE YOURSELF !!
AH... AH HA HA...
Sorry.
I'VE GOT IT!
PAT
PAT
?!
plop ♥
I CAN BEHAVE MYSELF RIGHT HERE! ♪

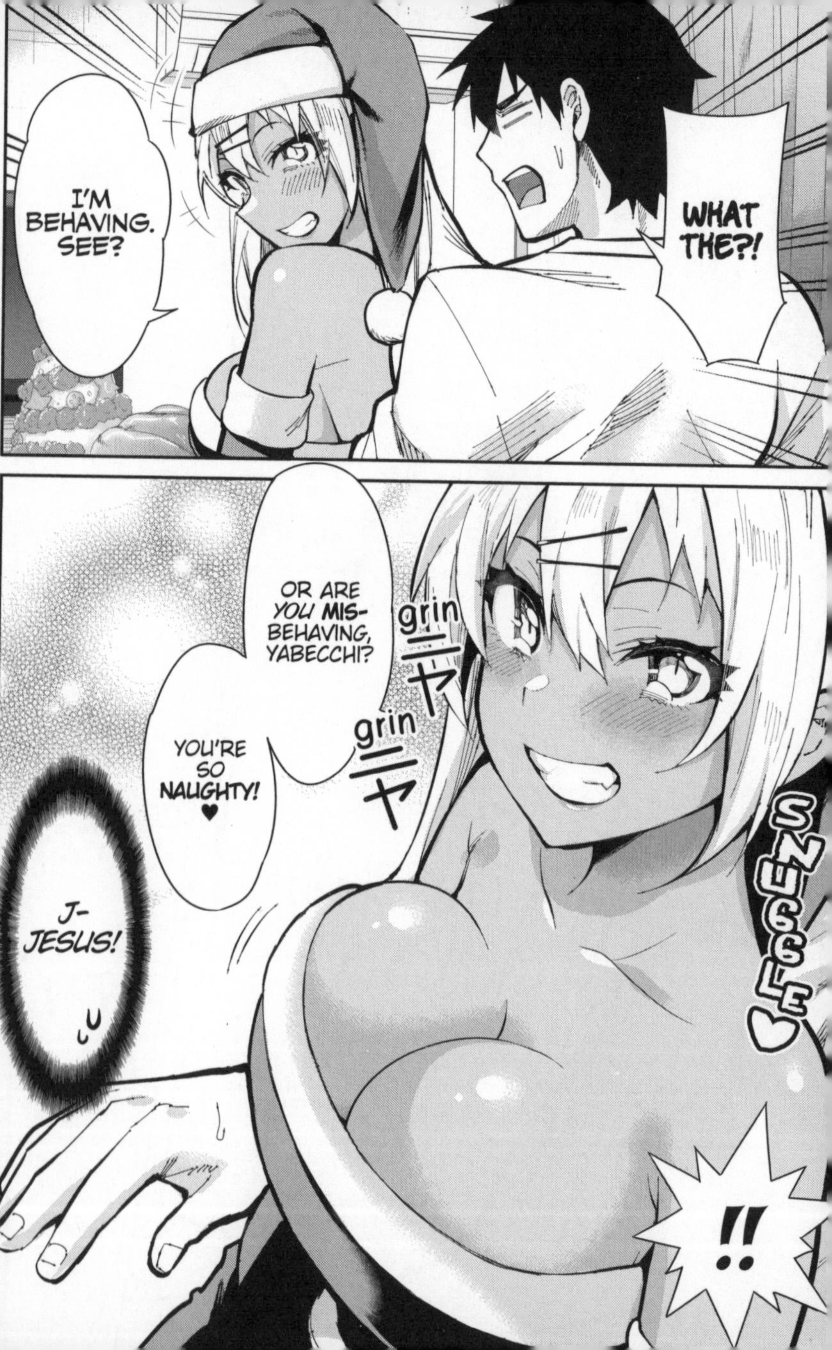

WHAT THE?!
I'M BEHAVING. SEE?
grin ニヤ
OR ARE YOU MIS-BEHAVING, YABECCHI?
grin ニヤ
YOU'RE SO NAUGHTY! ♥
SNUGGLE ♥
J-JESUS!
!!

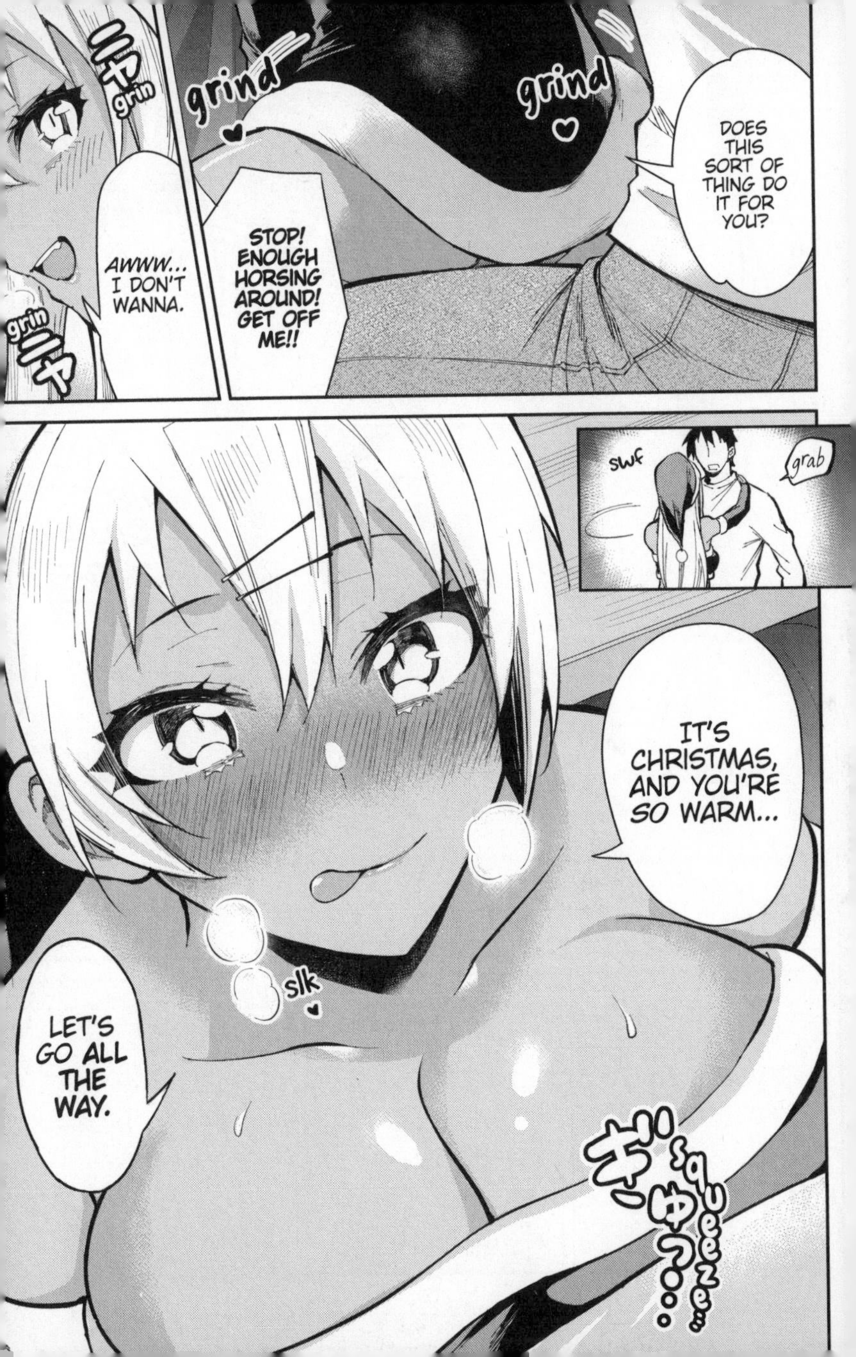
grind
grind
DOES THIS SORT OF THING DO IT FOR YOU?
STOP! ENOUGH HORSING AROUND! GET OFF ME!!
ニヤ grin
AWWW... I DON'T WANNA.
ニヤ grin
grab
swf
IT'S CHRISTMAS, AND YOU'RE SO WARM...
slk
LET'S GO ALL THE WAY.
ぎゅっ… squeeze...

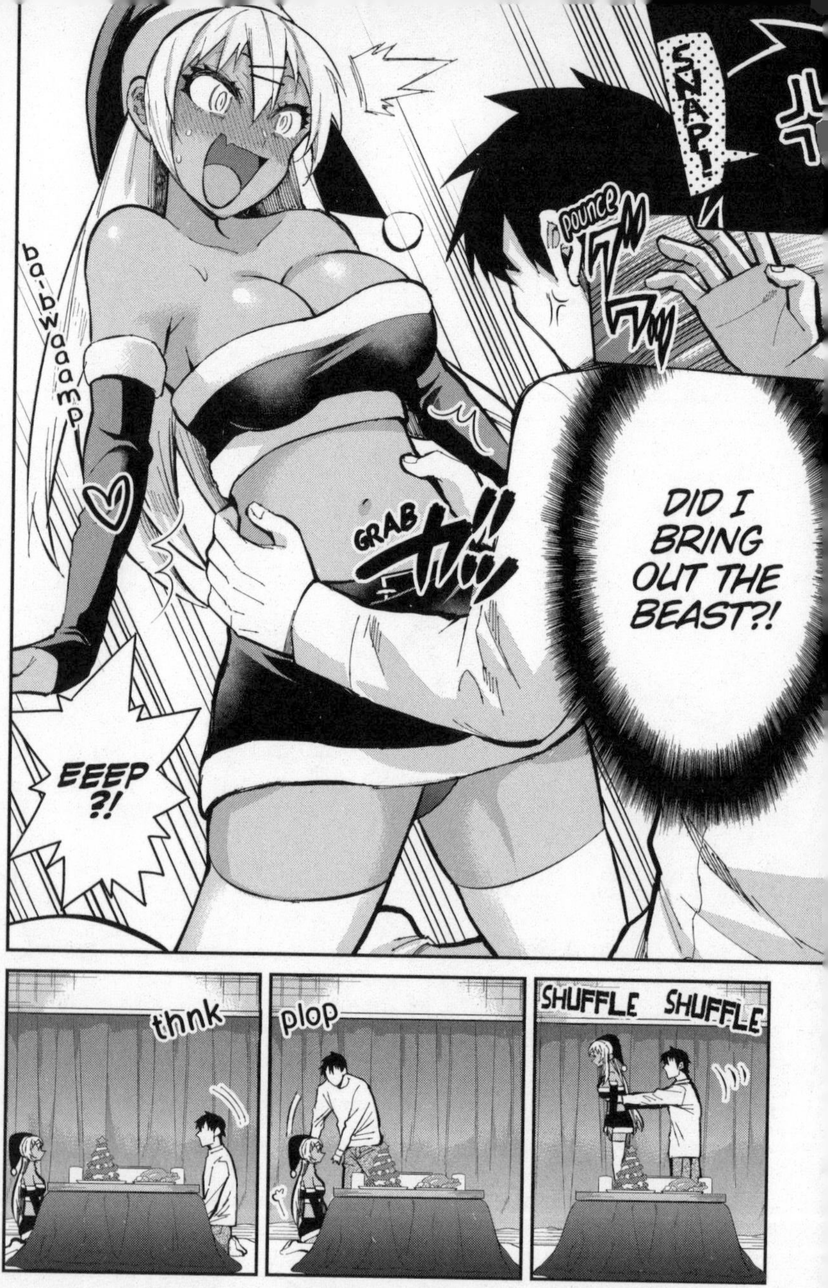
SNAP!
pounce
DID I BRING OUT THE BEAST?!
GRAB
baibwaaaamp
EEEP ?!
SHUFFLE SHUFFLE
plop
thnk

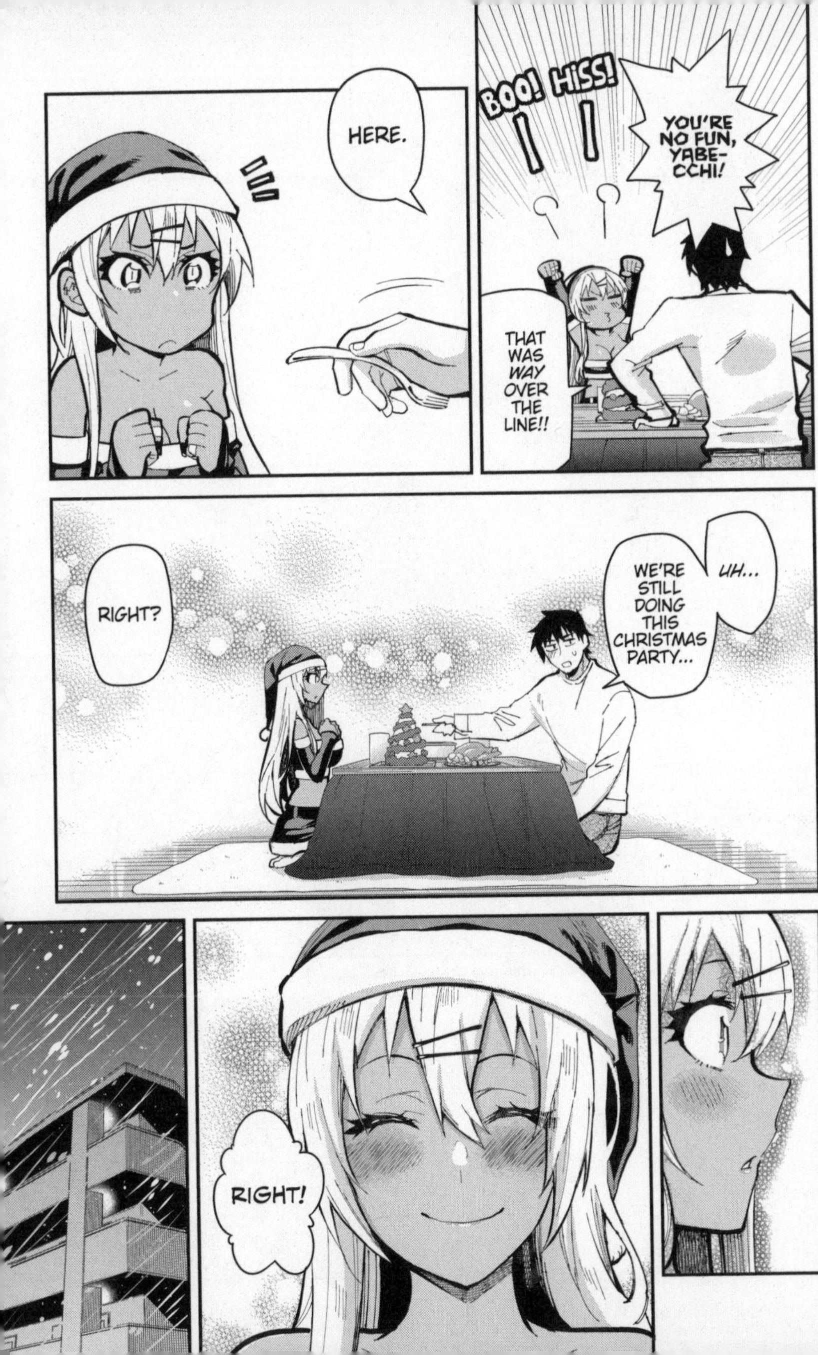
BOO! HISS!
YOU'RE NO FUN, YABE-CCHI!
THAT WAS WAY OVER THE LINE!!
HERE.
UH...
WE'RE STILL DOING THIS CHRISTMAS PARTY...
RIGHT?
RIGHT!

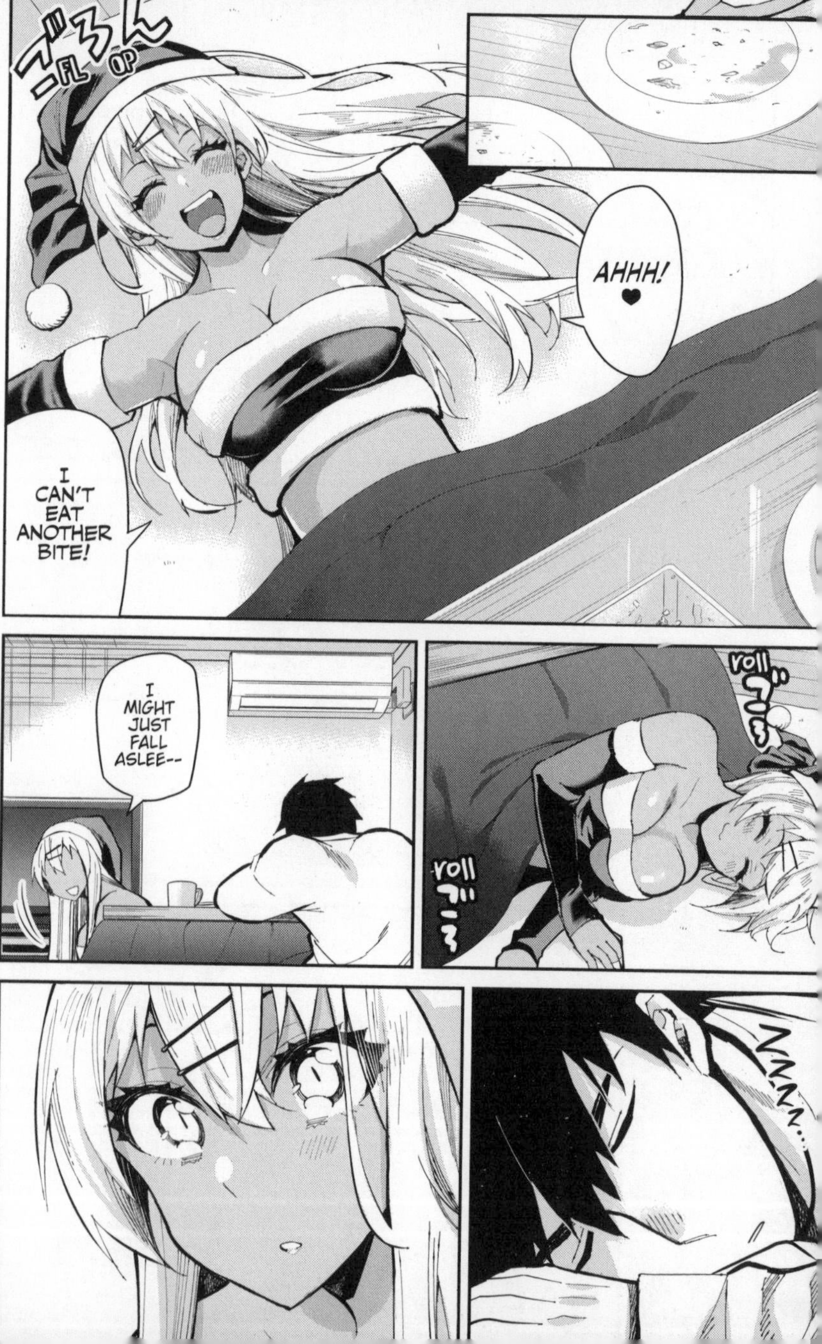
AHHH! ❤
ごろん FLOP
I CAN'T EAT ANOTHER BITE!
roll ゴロ
roll ゴロ
I MIGHT JUST FALL ASLEE--
ZZZZZ...

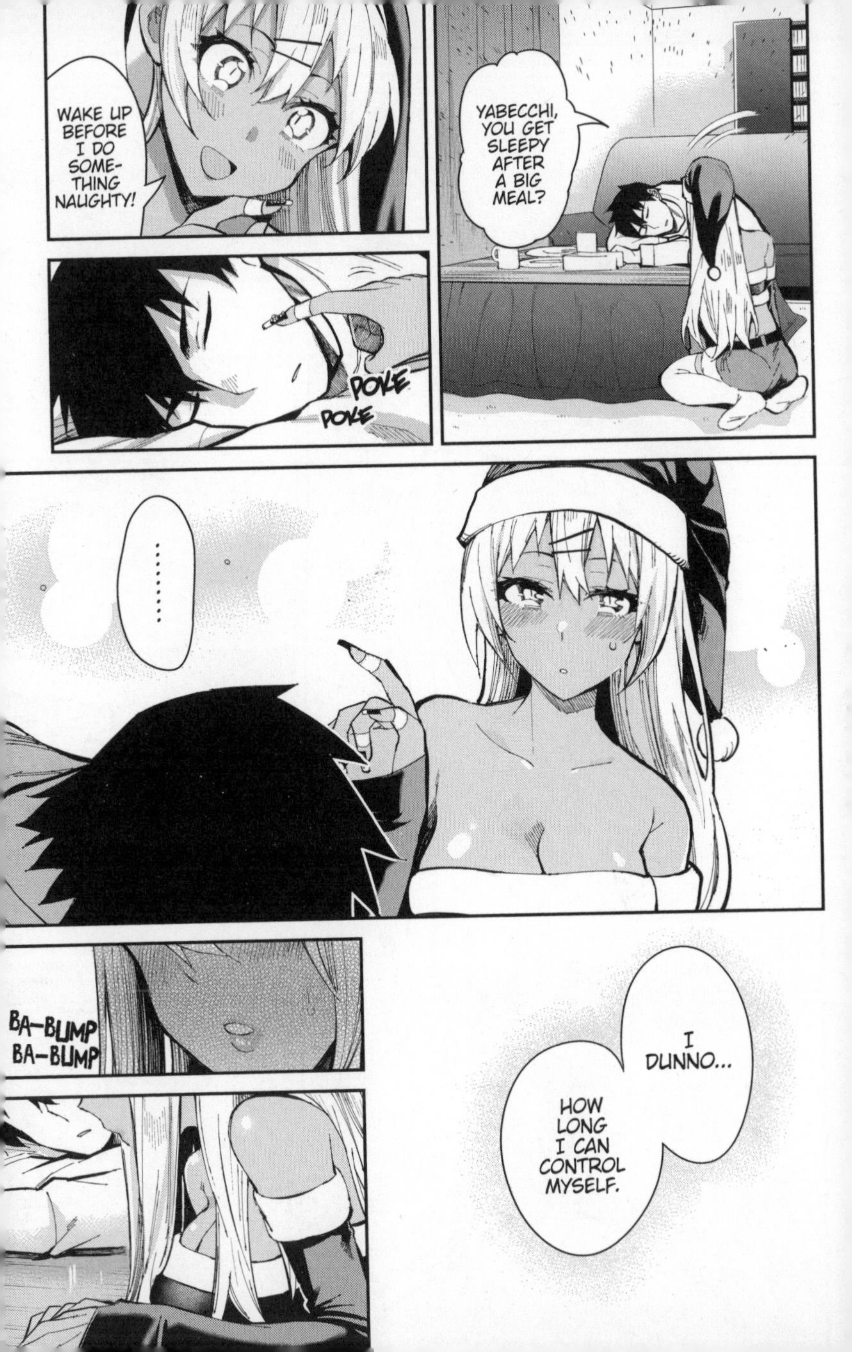
YABECCHI, YOU GET SLEEPY AFTER A BIG MEAL?
WAKE UP BEFORE I DO SOME-THING NAUGHTY!
POKE
POKE
....
I DUNNO...
HOW LONG I CAN CONTROL MYSELF.
BA-BUMP BA-BUMP

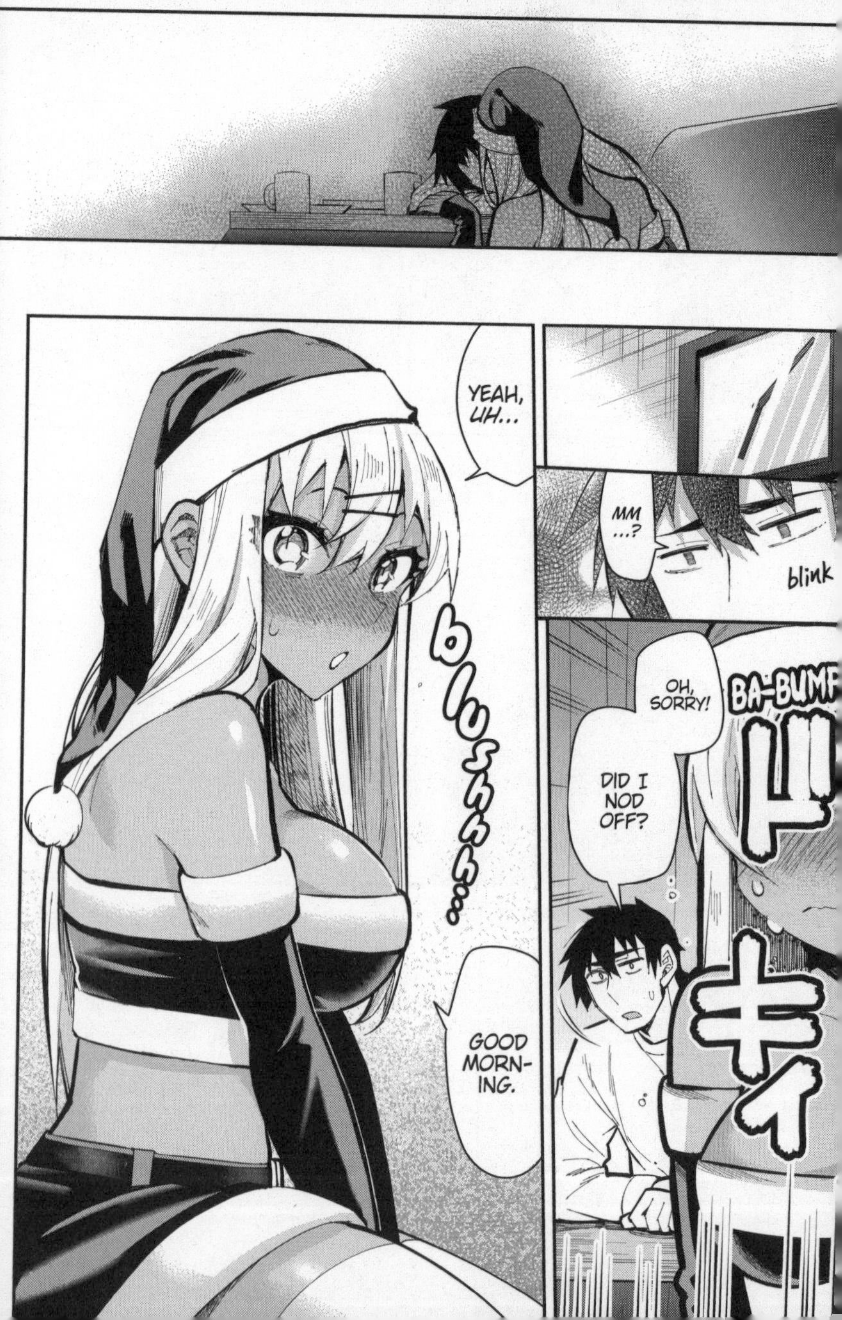
MM ...?
blink
OH, SORRY!
DID I NOD OFF?
BA-BUMP
ドキイ
YEAH, UH...
blushhh...
GOOD MORN-ING.

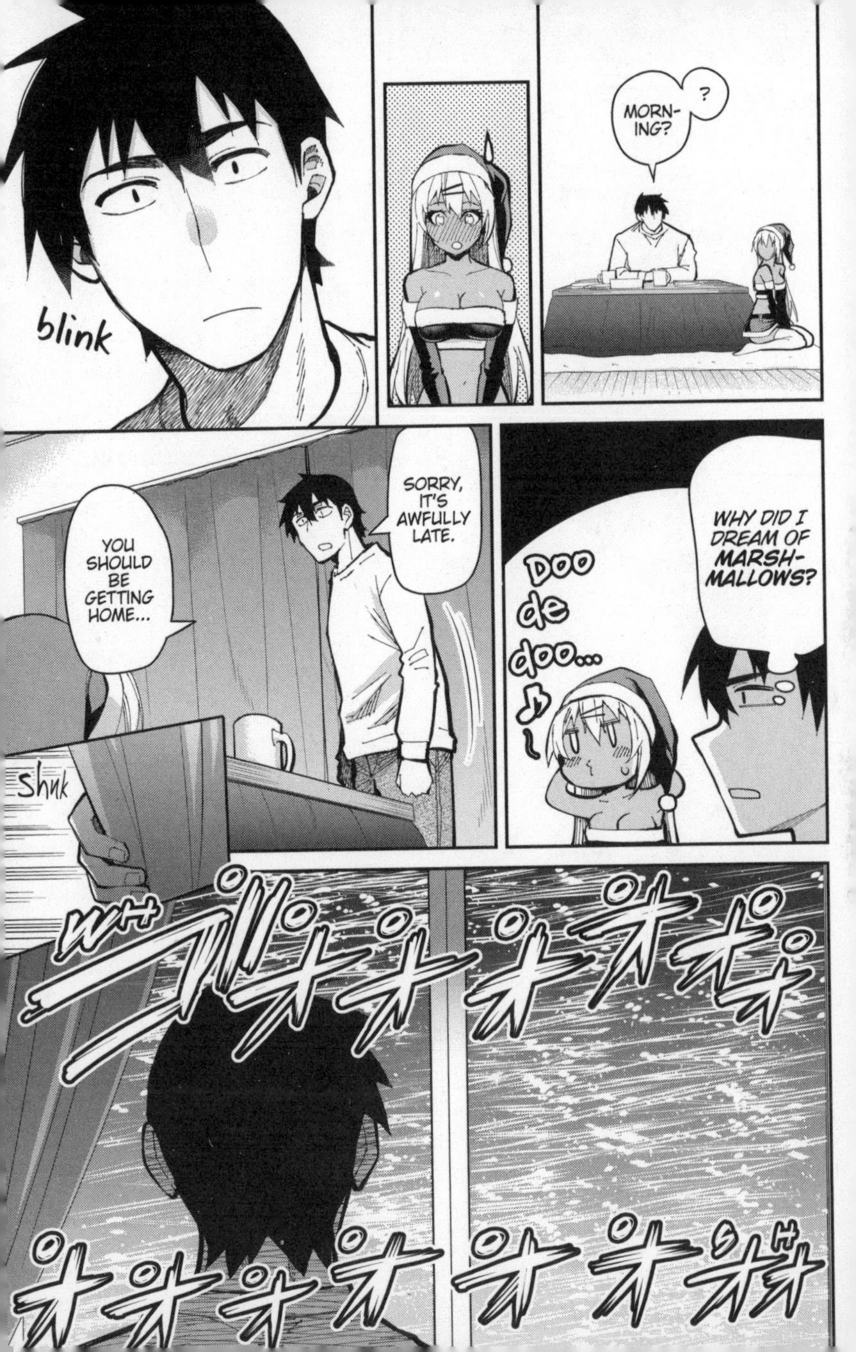
MORN-ING?
?
blink
WHY DID I DREAM OF MARSH-MALLOWS?
Doo de doo... ♪ ~
SORRY, IT'S AWFULLY LATE.
YOU SHOULD BE GETTING HOME...
Shuk
Wh
SH

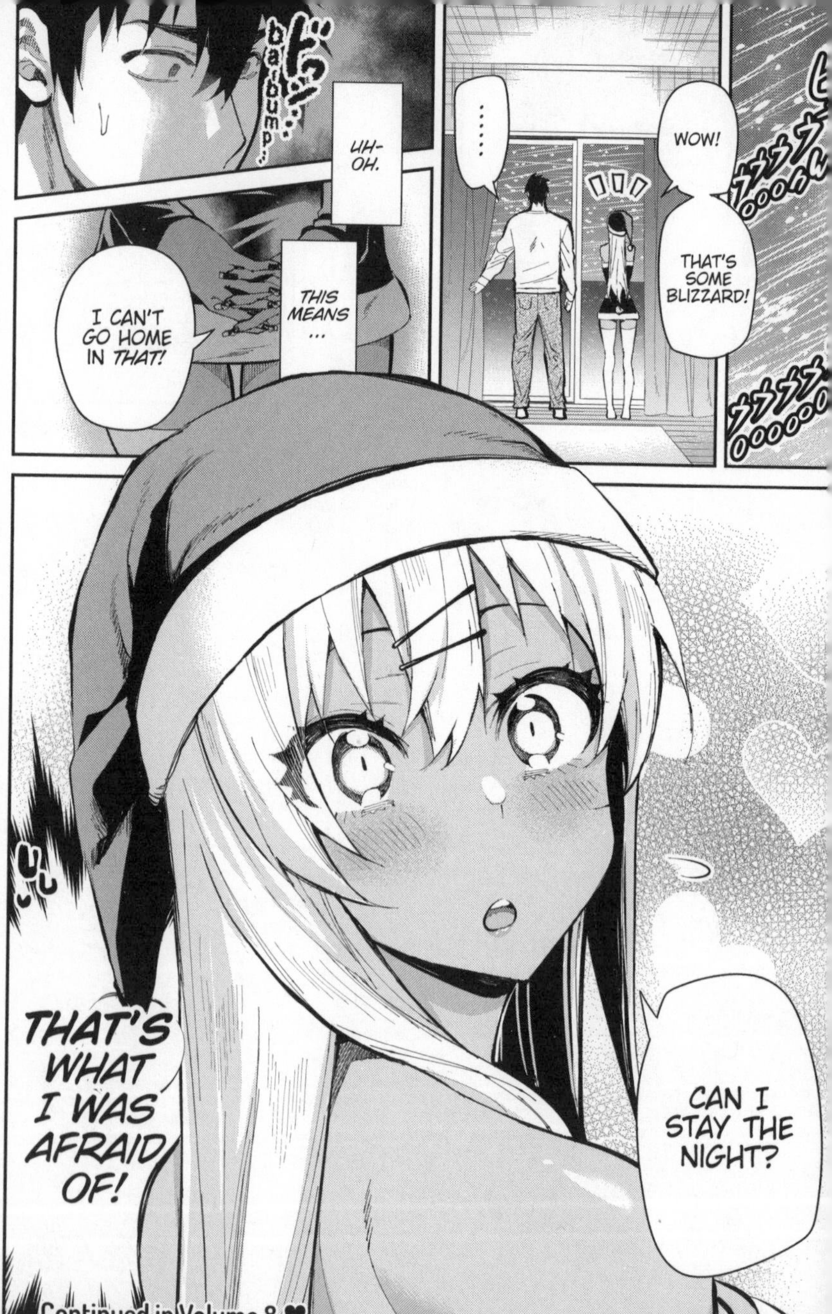
WOW!
THAT'S SOME BLIZZARD!
......
ba-bump..
UH-OH.
THIS MEANS ...
I CAN'T GO HOME IN THAT!
CAN I STAY THE NIGHT?
THAT'S WHAT I WAS AFRAID OF!

Continued in Volume 8 ♥

Gal Gohan

The afterword.
Thank you for reading and buying!

Looking back on it, both Miku-chan
and Fujiwara-chan make up their
minds in this volume.

Putting their fears aside and making
real progress--look forward to seeing
where love takes them!

Let's meet again
in Volume 8!

Narii Taiyou

THANKS!

TO
EVERYONE!

WHO
READS!!!

I'M
GLAD
WE
MET!

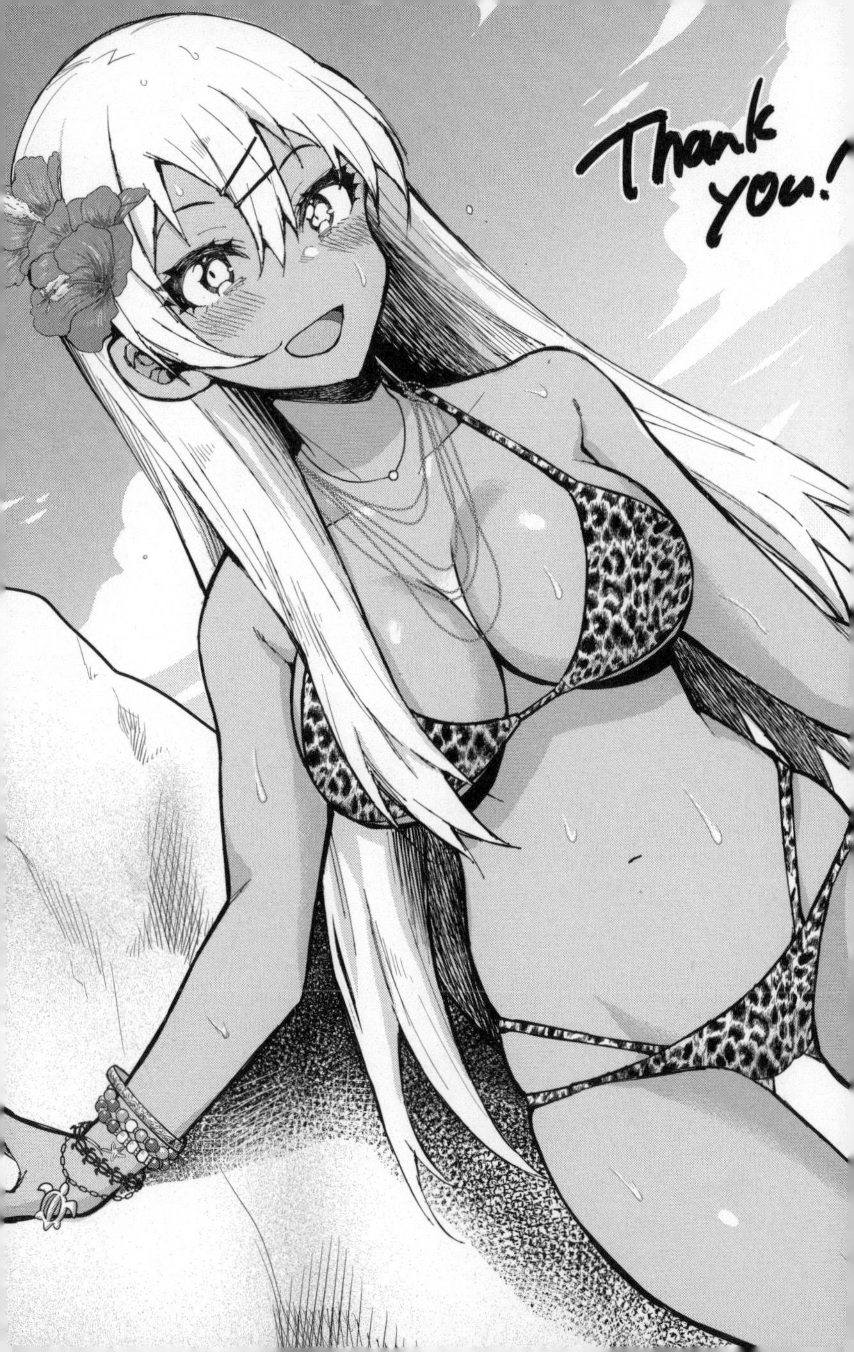
Thank you!

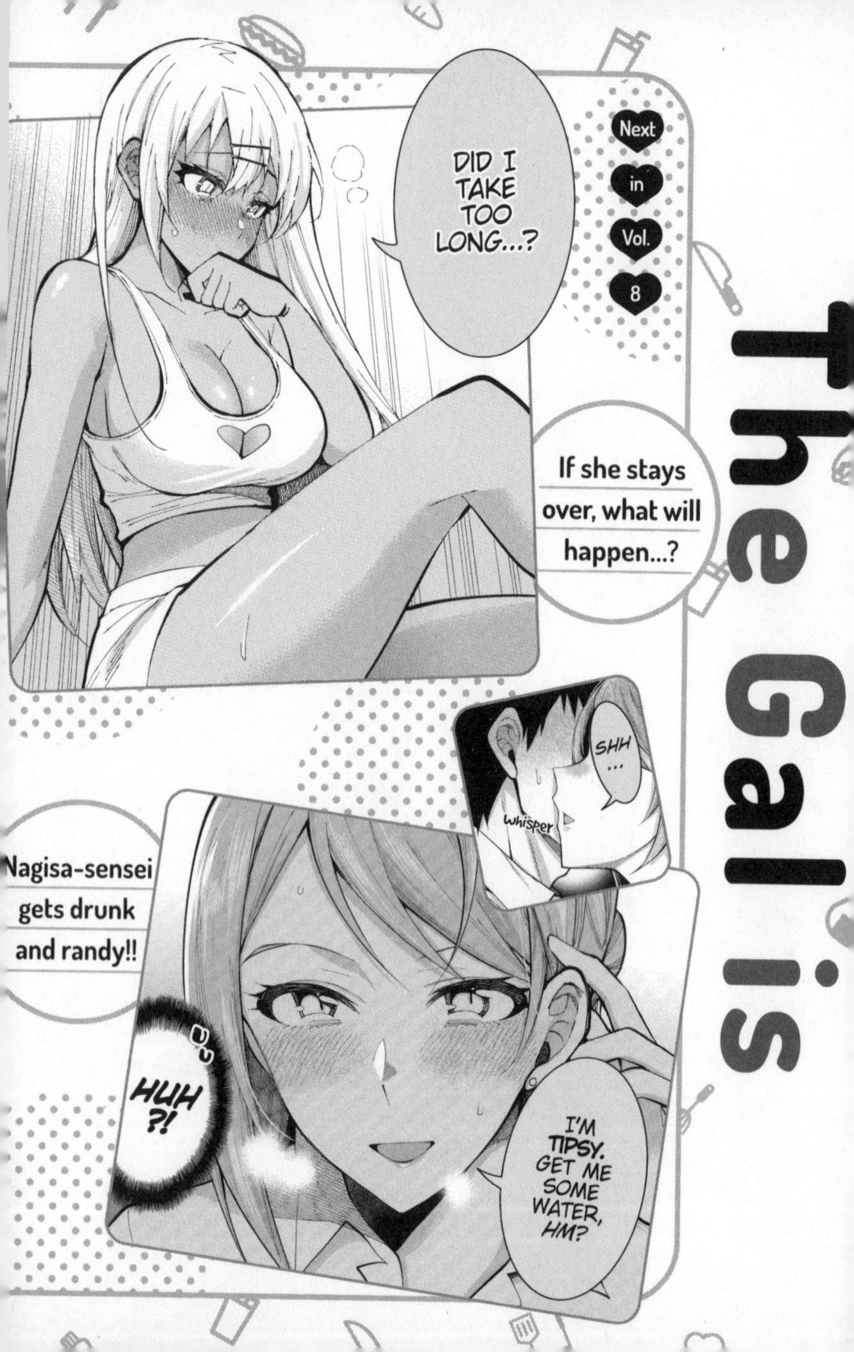
The Gal is
Next in Vol. 8
DID I TAKE TOO LONG...?
If she stays over, what will happen...?
SHH ...
whisper
I'M TIPSY. GET ME SOME WATER, HM?
HUH?!
Nagisa-sensei gets drunk and randy!!

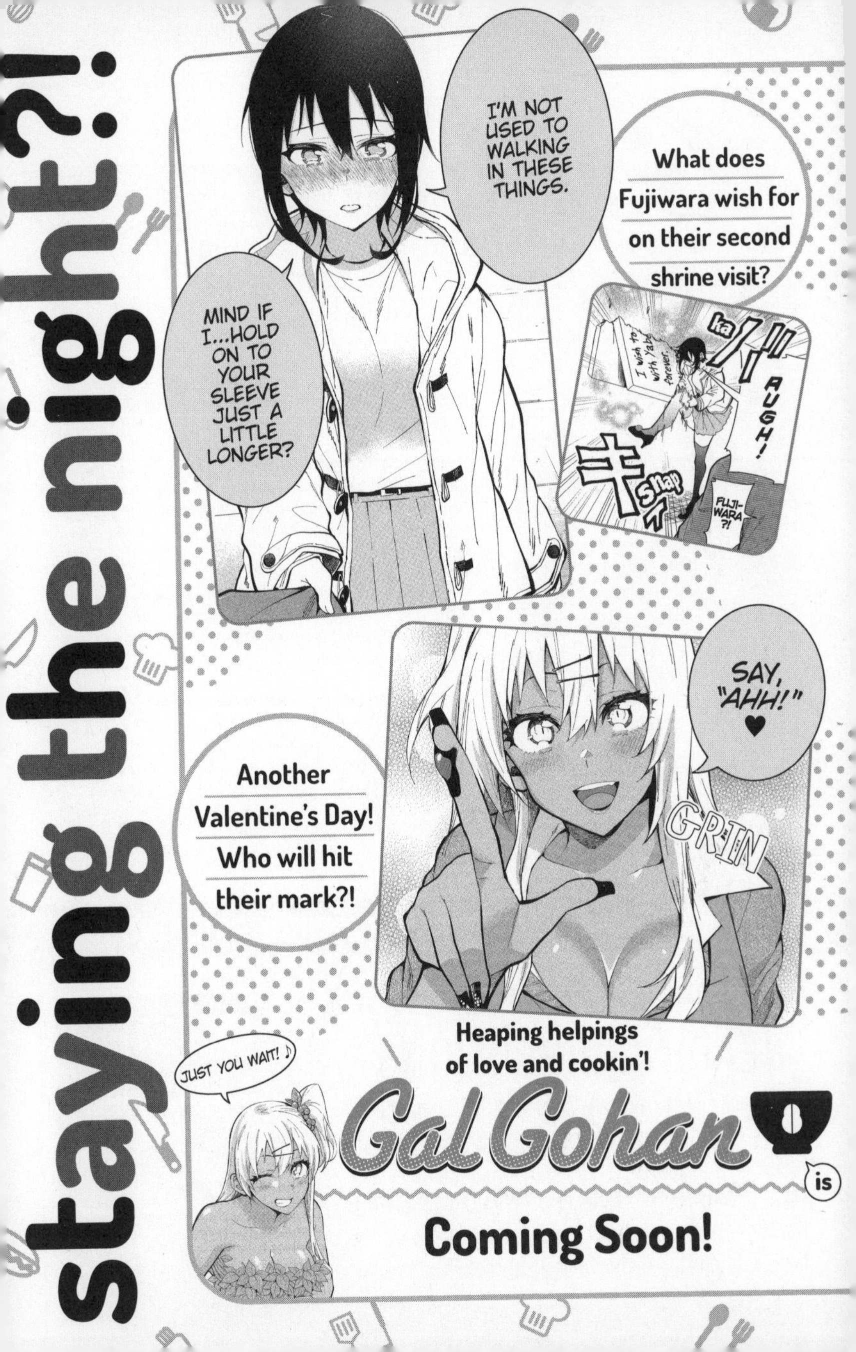
staying the night?!
What does Fujiwara wish for on their second shrine visit?
I wish to... with Yabe forever.
ka
AUGH!
snap
FUJI-WARA?!
I'M NOT USED TO WALKING IN THESE THINGS.
MIND IF I...HOLD ON TO YOUR SLEEVE JUST A LITTLE LONGER?
SAY, "AHH!" ♥
GRIN
Another Valentine's Day! Who will hit their mark?!
Heaping helpings of love and cookin'!
JUST YOU WAIT! ♪
Gal Gohan
is
Coming Soon!

SEVEN SEAS ENTERTAINMENT PRESENTS

Gal Gohan

story and art by **MARII TAIYOU**

VOLUME 7

TRANSLATION
Andrew Cunningham

ADAPTATION
Bambi Eloriaga-Amago

LETTERING
Carolina Hernández Mendoza

COVER DESIGN
Kris Aubin

PROOFREADER
Dawn Davis
Brett Hallahan

EDITOR
Shanti Whitesides

PREPRESS TECHNICIAN
Rhiannon Rasmussen-Silverstein

PRODUCTION MANAGER
Lissa Pattillo

MANAGING EDITOR
Julie Davis

ASSOCIATE PUBLISHER
Adam Arnold

PUBLISHER
Jason DeAngelis

GAL GOHAN by Marii Taiyou

First published in Japan in 2019 by HAKUSENSHA, INC., Tokyo.
English language translation rights in U.S.A. arranged with HAKUSENSHA, INC., Tokyo through TOHAN CORPORATION, Tokyo.

Seven Seas press and purchase enquiries can be sent to Marketing Manager Lianne Sentar at press@gomanga.com. Information regarding the distribution and purchase of digital editions is available from Digital Manager CK Russell at digital@gomanga.com.

ISBN: 978-1-64827-096-3

Printed in Canada

First Printing: April 2021

10 9 8 7 6 5 4 3 2 1

FOLLOW US ONLINE: ***www.sevenseasentertainment.com***

READING DIRECTIONS

This book reads from ***right to left***, Japanese style. If this is your first time reading manga, you start reading from the top right panel on each page and take it from there. If you get lost, just follow the numbered diagram here. It may seem backwards at first, but you'll get the hang of it! Have fun!!

1
2
3
4
5
6
7
8
9

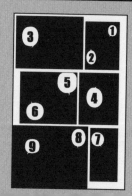